Green Cities, Governance and the Law

This book focusses on the developing role that the city currently plays in dealing with the effects of climate change and the instruments that can be utilised to make them truly green. Cities are at the centre of European directives aimed at tackling climate change, representing a key part of the European Green Deal and the National Recovery and Resilience Plans. As such, they provide valuable case studies for other countries grappling with how to address sustainability issues. This book is divided into three parts, with the first analysing Green urban planning and local governments in the European framework. The second examines various thematic aspects relating to this intersection, looking at the National Recovery and Resilience Plans, the right of the city and environmental issues. The third and final part presents case studies from four European cities showing how they are facing this transformation. These include Bologna, Paris, Barcelona and Valencia, each chosen by the Mission climate-neutral and smart cities by 2030. Bringing together leading experts, some of whom have been directly involved in developments, the book presents invaluable comparisons that will be of interest to a wider international readership. The book will be of interest to academics, researchers and policymakers working in the areas of Public Law, Environmental Law, Urban Law and Governance.

Andrés Boix Palop is Professor of Administrative Law at the University of Valencia, Spain.

Giorgia Pavani is Professor of Comparative Public Law at the University of Bologna, Italy.

Green Cities, Governance and the Law

Impact of the European Green Deal and the Next Generation EU

Edited by Andrés Boix Palop and Giorgia Pavani

Routledge
Taylor & Francis Group
LONDON AND NEW YORK

First published 2025
by Routledge
4 Park Square, Milton Park, Abingdon, Oxon OX14 4RN

and by Routledge
605 Third Avenue, New York, NY 10158

Routledge is an imprint of the Taylor & Francis Group, an informa business

British Library Cataloguing-in-Publication Data
A catalogue record for this book is available from the British Library

Library of Congress Cataloging-in-Publication Data
Names: Boix Palop, Andrés, editor. | Pavani, Giorgia, 1975- editor.
Title: Green cities, governance, and the law: impact of the European green deal and the next generation EU / edited by Andrés Boix Palop and Giorgia Pavani.
Description: Abingdon, Oxon [UK]; New York, NY: Routledge, 2025. | Includes bibliographical references and index.
Identifiers: LCCN 2024025415 (print) | LCCN 2024025416 (ebook) | ISBN 9781032650265 (hardback) | ISBN 9781032665160 (paperback) | ISBN 9781032665184 (ebook)
Subjects: LCSH: City planning and redevelopment law–European Union countries. | Environmental impact analysis–Law and legislation–European Union countries. | Climatic changes–Law and legislation–European Union countries. | Environmental policy–European Union countries. | Sustainable development–Law and legislation–European Union countries. | Sustainability–Government policy–European Union countries. | Green New Deal–European Union countries. | International and municipal law–European Union countries.
Classification: LCC KJE6140 .G74 2025 (print) | LCC KJE6140 (ebook) | DDC 346.404/5–dc23/eng/20240612
LC record available at https://lccn.loc.gov/2024025415
LC ebook record available at https://lccn.loc.gov/2024025416

ISBN: 978-1-032-65026-5 (hbk)
ISBN: 978-1-032-66516-0 (pbk)
ISBN: 978-1-032-66518-4 (ebk)

DOI: 10.4324/9781032665184

Typeset in Galliard
by Deanta Global Publishing Services, Chennai, India

Contents

Contributors

Jean-Bernard Auby
Emeritus Public Law Professor of Sciences Po-Paris, France

Giacomo Bergamini
Alma Mater Studiorum – University of Bologna, Italy
https://orcid.org/0000-0002-2135-4073

Andrés Boix Palop
University of Valencia, Spain
https://orcid.org/0000-0002-8324-7492

Marzia De Donno
University of Ferrara, Italy
https://orcid.org/0000-0001-9944-2404

Tomàs Font i Llovet
University of Barcelona, Spain
https://orcid.org/0000-0003-1842-0946

Giuseppe Franco Ferrari
Emeritus University of Bocconi Milan, Italy
https://orcid.org/0000-0001-7467-0443

Clàudia Gimeno Fernández
University of Valencia, Spain
https://orcid.org/0009-0007-9922-9946

Camille Mialot
Maître de Conférence à l'école de Droit de SciencesPo Paris, France
https://orcid.org/0000-0002-5009-8101

Gian Luca Morini
Alma Mater Studiorum – University of Bologna, Italy
https://orcid.org/0000-0002-4881-4623

Giorgia Pavani
Alma Mater Studiorum – University of Bologna, Italy
https://orcid.org/0000-0002-6150-9615

Angela Santangelo
Alma Mater Studiorum – University of Bologna, Italy
https://orcid.org/0000-0002-6488-3872

Simona Tondelli
Alma Mater Studiorum – University of Bologna, Italy
https://orcid.org/0000-0003-0891-7852

Claudia Tubertini
Alma Mater Studiorum – University of Bologna, Italy
https://orcid.org/0000-0002-8988-5823

Marc Vilalta Reixach
University of Barcelona, Spain
https://orcid.org/0000-0002-2387-7900

Introduction

Giorgia Pavani and Andrés Boix Palop

The book you have in your hands is the result of a collaborative effort made by a group of authors from various European universities with a long history of studying the legal framework and the political, social, and economic implications of decisions made at the local level.

An early version of some of the essays that appear in the book was discussed during an event organized in Bologna as part of the Jean Monnet Network "Sharing economy and Inequalities across Europe (SHINE)", and the Jean Monnet Chair "A new paradigm of solidarity and sustainable cities in the European framework (SO_CITIES)".

The book aims to analyze the growing and increasingly significant impact of the environmental dimension on the design and implementation of local public policies. This is particularly relevant following the approval of European recovery and resilience plans launched by the European Union after the COVID-19 pandemic. The analysis of the development and characteristics of green cities in light of National Recovery and Resilience Plans (NRRPs), as well as Next Generation EU (NGEU) and European Green Deal implementation, has to take into account that they were conceived not only to assist in economic and social recovery after the crisis induced by the pandemic and the measures taken to contain it but also to guide these public policies and local planning at all levels toward increasingly demanding environmental goals. Thus, through various analytical perspectives provided by each author, we offer an attempt to thoroughly and meticulously analyze the impact of these measures. The final result is particularly focused on the countries of Mediterranean Europe, which have also been the most affected by the successive crises of recent years.

Chapter 1, Part I by Giorgia Pavani, reflects on the role cities play in the European context, after almost two decades of reforms targeting local government functions and structures as well as public administration in general. The comparative picture that emerges from this period following the 2008 economic and financial crisis allows us to understand how, and with what instruments, local authorities responded to the pandemic and, above all, how they may interpret their role as privileged actors in post-pandemic European policies.

DOI: 10.4324/9781032665184-1

After that, completing the first part of the book, Andrés Boix Palop and Clàudia Gimeno Fernández deal with the legal framework of green urban planning across Europe, not only from a legal perspective (legal instruments), but also an analytical one (focusing on which are the goals settled and how the implementation throughout the NRRPs is being made). As a result, Chapter 2 of Part I shows how the process undertaken by European cities to move towards the goal of becoming truly green cities using the NRRPs requires coordinated efforts at many levels (mobility, public space, energy, emotional, demographic dynamics, productive structure, economic effects, reform of the legal framework, application of technology, consumption, circular economy, etc.) which oblige local public authorities to act in all these areas in a coherent manner. This is being achieved, with the incentive of European funds, through a wide range of urban planning models that already allow a series of guidelines to be established at the European level.

The second part of the work is dedicated to, following the example set in some countries, understanding how some essential elements of the right to the city align with traditional European local law, recovery and resilience plans, and the need for new and more ambitious environmental policies. These chapters, written by professors from various universities and European countries, address diverse issues such as inclusivity, solidarity, social justice, or participation, as well as local government law, in relation to the "right to the city" and its connection with this new model of environmentally responsible and sustainable urban policies.

The first chapter of this second part, by Jean-Bernard Auby and Camille Mialot, explains the crucial interaction between inclusivity and environmental sustainability, taking as a starting point the example of France, where its NRRP is not especially city-oriented. In this respect, in the absence of clear decisions at the state level, we can see, after the French instance, how cities are both "on the front line" and "at the end of the line" in imagining lifestyles that are compatible with the limits of the earth and the climate, and sometimes in making the final (and hard) choices that have to unite different goals.

Continuing along this line of thought, Tomàs Font i Llovet takes the lead and devotes a comprehensive chapter to reviewing the complicated relationship between city law, solidarity, and sustainability, taking the Spanish case, and how Spanish city law has dealt with this issue, as an example. Chapter 2 of Part II explains the new role that European cities develop at present as an institutional subject of political representation but also as a powerful institutional tool for administrative action, this chapter analyzes how Spanish cities and NRRP are in charge of the execution of some of the European Next Generation Funds, as well as its impact on administrative regulation of a general nature, is carried out where most of these conflicts appear. In particular, the analysis focuses on how energy and climate change regulations related to mobility or air pollution have to be completed through shared administration of common goods because of solidarity and sustainability concerns.

Chapter 3, Part II by Claudia Tubertini takes an Italian perspective, dealing also with the relationship between city law, the so-called "right to the city" and how NRRPs have been developed and executed at the local level in Italy, after a complex decision-making system regarding the allocation of funds and final decisions on which aims and projects should be considered. Those conflicts, in the absence of a city law perspective, risk being solved without due consideration of local needs and the rights of its inhabitants.

Finally, Chapter 4, the final chapter of this second part of the book, authored by Marzia De Donno, relates to the connection between the law of the city, spatial justice, and participatory democracy, thus focusing on the new forms of civic participation recently developed in the government of Italian cities, with very interesting examples such as the so-called citizens' assemblies and other mechanisms of public decision-making. The chapter dedicates special attention to the role played by these participative tools in order to try to make cities comply with the justice paradigm so as to fight a negative and hostile – particularly focusing on the more vulnerable segments of the population – model of city, a consideration that is crucial to take into account when developing local policies derived from the NRRPs.

The last part of the book (Part III) deals with particular cases in point across Europe that we have considered interesting because of the (relative) success of the experiences and the course of action on those mostly Mediterranean cities, which have been selected by the European Union to be climate-neutral and smart cities by 2030. It is therefore useful to analyze some of the strategies they are using to comply with these goals.

Chapter 1 of Part III covers the very interesting and successful role of the University of Bologna in contributing to the Climate City Contract process in the city of Bologna (Italy), written by Angelo Santangelo, Simona Tondelli, Gian Luca Morini, and Giacomo Bergamini. Bologna was selected in 2022 by the European Commission as one of the 100 European climate-neutral cities, and its local government has taken advantage in order to progress to that goal of the unique long-lasting city-university partnerships that characterize Bologna. This chapter describes the collaborative process behind the expression of interest of the Municipality of Bologna in the Cities Mission, and the contribution the University of Bologna is committed to giving to the climate-neutral goal in what we consider a very interesting case in point of how public bodies and different institutions should undertake successful collaboration.

The second actual experience explained in this part of the book is the case of Paris in Chapter 2 of Part III by Camille Mialot which explores how this city works on climate governance and climate planning. The chapter describes how strategies and climate plans have been traditionally developed without real coordination between the different levels of administration and without taking into account the need to coordinate adaptation and mitigation approaches, but it emphasizes how in more recent times Paris is showing some innovations in terms of governance and the use of public spaces, which may be really interesting and useful examples for other cities and local strategies.

The third chapter of Part III, crafted by Marc Vilalta Reixach, explains the approach used by Barcelona, with particular attention to the "Superblock" program launched by the city authorities while trying to develop a new model of city and urban planning. Actions regarding urban transformations using superblocks are not the only ones: from public-private financial instruments for the installation of photovoltaic panels to make buildings more energy-efficient, to the promotion of energy communities, passing also through other urban regeneration measures, initiatives to make Barcelona a climate-neutral city by 2030 are on the way. But the Superblock Program is particularly interesting because of its capacity to recover part of the space currently occupied by private vehicles for citizens and its systemic implications for a new urban model that favors sustainability, low-emission mobility, and fairer use of public spaces.

Lastly, Clàudia Gimeno Fernández explains in Chapter 4 the work done by the city of València, selected as European Green City 2024, another of the 100 European climate-neutral cities by 2030, with the aim of achieving European goals in terms of emissions, urban equality, and sustainability. Some of the administrative and institutional tools used by the city, as well as an ambitious green urban planning that tries to take advantage of some of the funding provided by the Spanish NRRP, may be a really promising example for other cities.

To conclude, the book tries to wrap up most of all the explained ideas and solutions with a brilliant recapitulation written by Giuseppe Franco Ferrari in Chapter 5, in which he explains different ranking methods to assess the process of uniting smart cities, landscapes, and urban regeneration.

As editors of this work, not only are we convinced of the quality of the contributions it contains, but also of its practical interest and importance. We trust that readers will find it valuable, and above all, that it can contribute to the improvement and development of the performance of local authorities in making our cities more livable, sustainable, and ultimately, better.

Andrés Boix Palop
Giorgia Pavani

Part I

Cities and the European Union

1 Green cities and local governments in the European framework

Giorgia Pavani

1.1 Introduction

Analysing the development and characteristics of green cities in light of National Recovery and Resilience Plans (NRRPs), as well as Next Generation EU (NGEU) and European Green Deal implementation, requires some preliminary reflections on the role cities play in the European context. The recent crises deeply affecting local governments across Europe also make this important. The 2008 economic and financial crisis began with the emblematic event of the Lehman Brothers default, announced on 15 September of that year. Indeed, there was only a brief period of time between then and the post COVID-19 period, marking when the NRRPs began to take effect rather than the end of the emergency. Over that period, European states adopted reforms targeting local government functions and structures as well as public administration in general. The comparative picture that emerges from this period following the 2008 economic and financial crisis allows us to understand how, and with what instruments, local authorities responded to the pandemic and, above all, how they may interpret their role as privileged actors in post-pandemic European policies. This chapter will analyse the main factors that have influenced the new territorial arrangements made by some European states and the increasing relevance of cities within the European legal framework.

1.2 Behind the (green) cities of the future are the local governments of the past

Local authorities – and cities – are increasingly at the centre of European policies on climate, anti-poverty, and inclusion efforts (the need for all these was accentuated during the pandemic and they are currently included in Next Generation EU objectives). Due to both the general measures adopted by the European institutions, as well as specific ones for some states in difficulty, the 2008 economic and financial crisis left its mark on the configuration of power at the local level as well as the way in which responsibility is allocated between authorities. This, in turn, has exacerbated a tendency towards centralisation which had been already widespread for some years. Indeed, the "golden"

DOI: 10.4324/9781032665184-3

period of local government studies, which began in the 1970s, was already in decline by the beginning of the new millennium due to both endogenous and exogenous causes (e.g. the natural exhaustion of local governments' capacity to respond to problems and the global crisis, respectively).

The pendulum, in terms of centre-periphery relations, has begun to swing more towards the centre; this has been the case in states characterised by more or less intense political decentralisation (federal states and regional states) as well as those characterised by only bureaucratic-administrative decentralisation (such as in France).[1] The image of a swinging pendulum cyclically changing its movement evokes the pattern of recentralising tendencies observed in terms of power in recent years. These tendencies have been confirmed and accentuated by new public administration and local-government reforms which have been adopted at a time experts have considered as unfavourable for passing reforms[2] (and some scholars have noted the "increasing neo-centralism of crisis legislation"[3]). It cannot be said with certainty that all the legislative reforms affecting local systems in various European states were adopted in response to crisis-imposed economic and financial rationalisation. However, it can certainly be asserted that all these reforms were enacted during the crisis period. Furthermore, many are linked to exceptional measures the European institutions adopted outside the normal *European method*.

With the signing of the *Memoranda of Understanding*, some states, such as Greece, Spain, and Portugal, committed to structurally reforming local and state administrative organisation along with economic reform since public administrations were often seen as one of the factors contributing to increased public spending in the context of the 2008 economic and financial crisis. Taken in isolation, these administrative reforms offer a schizophrenic panorama. But, if one compares them in terms of the conceptual frameworks or models of local government organisation, it is possible to identify some common structural and functional trends. The first trend that emerges is the concurrent strengthening of two levels of government: the intermediate (regional) level, regardless of the legislative or merely administrative functions attributed to territorial entities in the various European states, and the lower (municipal)

1 Silvia Bolgherini, *Navigando a vista. Governi locali in Europa tra crisi e riforme* (il Mulino 2015) 12–13. The image of a swinging pendulum has been used by political scientists and administrative science scholars going back to Karl Polanyi, *The Great Transformation* (Beacon Press 1944).

2 As political scientists have pointed out, reforms are difficult to adopt in crisis periods due to the extremely high costs and limited electoral benefits involved. However, it is true that crises also offer greater opportunities to bring about profound changes than exist in normal times: B. Guy Peters, Jon Pierre and Tina Randma-Liiv, 'Global financial crisis, public administration and governance: Do new problems require new solutions?' (2011) 11 *Public Organization Review* 13, 27.

3 Quotation from Gian Candido De Martin, 'Il disegno autonomistico disatteso tra contraddizioni e nuovi scenari problematici' (2014) 1 *Istituzioni del Federalismo* 29. This refers to the Italian context, but is also applicable in other European countries.

level. This tendency is particularly evident in countries that have chosen the French-Napoleonic model of administrative organisation. However, it is also found in other countries adopting different models, such as the federal states of Central Europe (based on a German-speaking model) and Scandinavian countries.[4]

Within new, multi-level, European-governance designs both levels of government should be involved in the bottom-up phase of European policy-making at state level as well as the top-down one of policy implementation.[5] As far as the local level is concerned, there has been a clear intent to strengthen municipal authority by: creating or enhancing large or metropolitan areas; attempting mergers; supporting management modes involving common administrative functions; and weakening second-level local authorities, such as the *Département* or Province (which has long been considered the Achilles' heel of political-territorial organisation in many states).[6]

The comparative landscape of public administration reforms offers various scenarios. In some cases, the number of municipalities and/or second-level authorities has been reduced, as in Denmark, Finland, Lithuania, Ireland, Latvia, Greece, and Portugal. In other cases, the merging or unification of first-level bodies has been opted for, as in France, Italy, and, again, Finland, Denmark, the Netherlands, and Iceland. In recent years, the Nordic countries have attempted local government reform, but have not always succeeded. Reforms in Denmark in 2007 led to a significant reduction in the number of municipalities there from 271 to 98. This followed the adoption of the criterion of having a minimum of 20,000 inhabitants per municipality; in addition, the country's 14 counties were supplanted by 5 new administrative regions.[7] An attempt was made to propose reform again in 2016, but debate on this did not persist. In Finland, a reform substantially similar to the Danish one

4 We employ the terminology and causality adopted by Giorgia Pavani and Lucio Pegoraro (eds), *Municipi d'occidente. Il governo locale in Europa e nelle Americhe* (Donzelli 2006). For political scientists, the point of reference for the classifications used is based on the typologies formulated during the golden decade. The initial elaboration of these is found in Edward C. Page and Michael J. Goldsmith (eds), *Central and Local Government Relations A Comparative Analysis of West European Unitary States* (Sage 1987).

5 On the relations between the European Union, regions, and local authorities in Member States, see Aurélie Noureau, *L'Union européenne et les collectivités locales* (La Rochelle 2011); Emmanuel Cherrier and Stéphane Guérard, *La régionalisation en Europe. Regards croisés* (Bruylant 2014).

6 Besides Italy, Spain has also had a long tradition of attempting provincial-level reform. When it seemed time to divest power in favour of *mancomunidades* (groups of municipalities) or consortia, the Parliament shifted gears once again in favour of the provinces (Ley 23/2017). On the role of *provincias* (provinces) in Spain, see María Teresa Salvador Crespo, *La autonomía provincial en el sistema constitucional español. Intermunicipalidad y Estado Autonómico* (Instituto Nacional de Administración Pública 2007).

7 Vibeke Normann Andersen, 'Denmark', in Edward C. Page and Michael J. Goldsmith (eds), *Changing Government Relations in Europe: From Localism to Intergovernmentalism* (Routledge 2010) 48, 49.

(reducing the number of municipalities) was attempted. However, this effort was supplanted in 2015 with a new project to create larger regions and due to the voluntary mergers of municipalities in the country, their number was reduced from 431 in 2006 to 317 in 2014.[8] In the Netherlands, the pace of reforms grouping municipalities together has remained constant year after year (by 2015, their number had dropped as a result by two-thirds compared to the 1970s). Meanwhile, in Iceland, there were 229 local authorities in 1950 versus 74 in 2013. In other countries, intermediate bodies have been eliminated (e.g. Greece and the Czech Republic).[9]

A common feature of local government reform laws in many European countries is the reorganisation of administrative functions. Usually, local government reforms have been conceived and developed based on the structure of local authorities (e.g. their apparatuses and entities) and, subsequently, their administrative functions. In contrast, the main objective of many reform laws passed during the economic and financial crisis was to reorganise functions to avoid duplication between local authorities. These reforms involved a variety of trajectories ranging from *New Public Management* modernisation to reorganising service provision between the public and private sectors.[10] Such reforms are characterised by a pull towards the centre in terms of functional ownership and an intensifying of cooperative mechanisms between local authorities. Downsized, transformed, and – in some cases – eliminated, local authorities emerged from the economic crisis in a way that clearly marked a reversal in the swing of the "pendulum". However, they were only to face another crisis that saw additional accentuated movement towards the centre, beginning with the initial regulatory and administrative acts used to manage the pandemic. Local authorities found themselves operating on the front line of the health emergency at its onset in the spring of 2020.[11] These authorities, however, were the product of a series of pre-pandemic reforms aimed at rationalising territorial organisation which were often only partly implemented quick responses to internal and/or supranational economic-financial demands. At the start of the new decade, the economic and financial crisis had thus, left behind all the necessary elements for the pandemic to set off explosive unresolved issues

8 Pekka Kettunen, 'The Finnish municipal reform' (2014) 11(1) *Public Policy* 61.

9 An analysis of reforms in various states can be found in Page and Goldsmith (n 7). For a financial perspective, see Carlos Nunes Silva and Ján Buček (eds), *Fiscal Austerity and Innovation in Local Governance in Europe* (Routledge 2014). See also Council of European Municipalities and Regions (CEMR), 'Decentralisation at a crossroads, Territorial reforms in Europe in times of crisis' (2013) at www.ccre.org.

10 In this regard, see the results of the COST Action project, *Local Public Sector Reforms: An International Comparison (LocRef)* in Sabine Kuhlmann and Geert Bouckaert (eds), *Local Public Sector Reforms in Times of Crisis: National Trajectories and International Comparison* (Palgrave McMillan 2016).

11 Their role is also referred to in the Council of Europe's *Human rights handbook for local and regional authorities* (2021) 2(16).

between centre and periphery as well as to reopen fresh wounds regarding the principle of local autonomy.

The synthesis reflected in the health emergency legislation was quite simple. The pandemic had a devastating impact on local authority autonomy both externally, in terms of exercising regulatory and administrative independence and links with other territorial authorities, and internally, in terms of the relationships between bodies or between an entity and its community. Despite a number of unresolved prior issues, local-authority pandemic management reaffirmed the importance of legal concepts such as subsidiarity and the proximity of the authority providing services to the local community. An administration that is, "'open' (not just digitally, but also physically), and which is approachable, nearby, and caring is more necessary than ever [since] the ethics of care cannot be remotely applied".[12] It is true that the autonomy of local governments was formally limited by the pandemic emergency legislation. In turn, this shifted decision-making power towards higher levels of government, leaving the lower level with only an executing power. Still, local governments have been major actors in terms of "taking care" of their communities. As such, the mayors of some large cities have overshadowed federal and state heads or regional leaders, particularly in some large federal states outside Europe. To summarise then, while the state above all ignored or limited local authority responsibilities with its emergency legislation, cities, in contrast, were protagonists duringthe pandemic and will continue to be so in its aftermath.

1.3 A change of focus: From local government to cities

The comparative panorama emerging out of the crisis legislation thus confirms that two levels of territorial government have been enhanced: the intermediate (regional) and lower (municipal) levels. This has entailed a reversal in the trend toward decentralisation policies and a clear acceleration of the pendulum swing towards the centre. The lower level, comprised almost everywhere of municipal authorities, has become a particular subject of interest within EU institutions and the legal literature.

1.3.1 The role of the scholarship formant[13] in the theoretical construction of the right to the city

In terms of the legal literature, there has been a progressive enhancement in the role of local communities in developing a theoretical concept of the

12 "Una administración que sea 'abierta' (no sólo digital, sino también físicamente), que sea próxima, cercana y atenta, es más necesario que nunca [porque] la ética del cuidado no se puede hacer a distancia".Rafael Jiménez Asensio, 'La autonomía olvidada: los ayuntamientos ante la crisis' at https://rafaeljimenezasensio.com/2020/08/09/la-autonomia-olvidada-los-ayuntamientos-ante-la-crisis/ (accessed 31 August 2023).

13 A leading scholar said that "living law contains many different elements such as statutory rules, the formulations of scholars, and the decisions of judges– elements [...] we will call

city. Faced with a scenario in which local authorities have suffered the regulatory effects of multiple crises, "living law" offers a different perspective which see the city as a protagonist and a new institutional legal entity.[14] Cities have become places where the goals of the *2030 Agenda* have taken on a European dimension, especially in the post-pandemic era. This has been the case in relation to: climate change challenges (e.g. clean energy production and sustainable mobility policies); the digitising of public administrations; using AI to step up service smartness; sustainable growth; cohesion via the innovative circular urban economymodel; social inclusion; and anti-poverty efforts.[15] These are all issues with a transnational bent, which feature a dimension that transcends municipal borders, and can thus only be addressed in a spirit of cooperation and dialogue between different states or entities within states.

There is, however, a terminological and legislative hurdle to indiscriminately using the terms "municipality" and "city". In fact, unlike the "municipality", which is regulated by local government laws in the various European states, the term "city" is absent in most of their laws. Historically, however, the city has been a relevant entity in terms of its legal organisation in many European states (e.g. think of city-state autonomy during the Renaissance). With the emergence of modern states, though, the city was replaced by an autonomous administrative entity – the municipality – that is regulated within the same state order. In some European states, the city is mentioned in local government laws only in relation to large municipalities. Such is the case in Spain with the *Ley 57/2003, de Medidas para la Modernización del Gobierno Local*, also known as the *Ley de Grandes Ciudades*. This law amended Title X of *Ley 7/1985, Reguladora de las Bases del Régimen Local*, which was dedicated to the "*Régimen de organización de los municipios de gran población*". In France, the cities of Paris, Lyons, and Marseille are subject to a special framework under the *Code général des collectivités territoriales*, while in Italy the term "city" corresponds to an honorary title issued by the President of the Republic under *Art. 18 del Decreto Legislativo 267/2000 Testo Unico delle leggi sull'Ordinamento degli Enti Locali*.

them, borrowing from phonetics, the 'legal formants'": Rodolfo Sacco, 'Legal formants: A dynamic approach to comparative law (installment I of II)' (1991) 39 *American Journal of Comparative Law*, 1–34.

14 The theoretical construction of the right to the city is a particularly complex topic. Scholarly debate on it was taken up again by Jean-Bernard Auby, *Droit de la ville: Du fonctionnement juridique des villes au droit à la Ville* (LexisNexis 2013).

15 The *2030 Agenda for Sustainable Development* is comprised of 17 goals states must fulfil with regard to sustainable development. SDG11 ("Make cities inclusive, safe, resilient and sustainable") refers directly to urban areas. For more on this, see the UN General Assembly resolutions: *A/RES/70/1 Transforming Our World: the 2030 Agenda for Sustainable Development*, 25 September 2015 and subsequent *A/RES/71/256 New Urban Agenda: Quito Declaration on Sustainable Cities and Human Settlements for All*, 23 December 2016.

The public law literature – with somewhat of a delay compared to the other social sciences – has begun to show interest in the urban dimension[16] and has come to make a conceptual distinction between the local authority in closest contact with the community – generally the municipality – and the city, understood as a new political-institutional subject.[17] Recognising, therefore, "a legal meaning for cities, which goes beyond the dimension of a sole administrative entity",[18] and defining it "as a unique socio-economic and political space",[19] entails a paradigm shift from the study of local authority law to the study of the right to the city.[20] Studies on the "right to the city" highlight the importance of legal literature on the theoretical construction of the concept of the city as distinct from that of the municipality. It can be said that this is one of the few new areas of scientific research in the social sciences in which the legal literature is making a fundamental contribution to the development of the subject practically in the absence of the legal formant. Indeed, the construction of the "right to the city" is nurtured from below – through a dialogue between cities – as well as at the European level. In contrast to positive state law, references to cities are increasingly found in European law and especially in many soft law documents.

1.3.2 Cities and urban policies within the European Union

Certainly, the COVID-19 pandemic has forced EU institutions and member state governments to question the sustainability of the EU's socioeconomic growth model. The war in Ukraine has also further intensified thinking about the energy crisis and the consequences of climate change. However, well before the European Green Deal and the Next Generation EU (NGEU) were approved, the European Union had viewed cities as the ideal actor for implementing its ecological and solidarity-based policies. The European Commission has adopted several communications over the years which address

16 Supported, for example, by the collectively written book: Ernst Hirsch Ballin, Gerard van der Schyff, Maarten Stremler and Maartje De Visser (eds), *European Yearbook of Constitutional Law 2020. The City in Constitutional Law* (T.M.C. Asser Press 2021).

17 See Jean-Bernard Auby, 'The role of law in the legal status and powers of cities' (2013) 2 *Italian Journal of Public Law* 302, 306 and Id., 'El papel de la ciudad como nuevo sujeto político institucional' (2019) 1 *Anuario del Gobierno Local* 189–202, and the bibliographical references therein. For a summary of the theory that sees the city as a new legal entity that might remain "within the state" or position itself "in place of the state", see Tomás Font, 'De la autonomía local al poder de las ciudades' (2019) Special Number *Istituzioni del Federalismo* 115.

18 Fabio Giglioni, 'Verso un diritto delle città. Le città oltre il comune' in Enrico Carloni and Fulvio Cortese (eds), *Diritto delle autonomie territoriali* (Wolters Kluwer 2020) 269.

19 Erika Arban, 'Constitutional law, federalism and the city as a unique socio-economic and political space', in Ballin, Schyff, Stremler and De Visser (n 16) 326.

20 Fulvio Cortese, 'Il nuovo diritto delle città: alla ricerca di un legittimo spazio operativo' in Giuseppe Franco Ferrari (ed), *Smart city. L'evoluzione di un'idea* (Mimesis 2020).

sustainable urban development, in particular, and begin to use the term "city". The basic idea has been to make cities more socially and environmentally liveable, thus combating social exclusion and setting high common standards for environmental protection. One of the first documents in this regard is the *Green Paper on the Urban Environment*.[21] This identified some of the main urban problems related to the negative effects of intense urbanisation within the territory considered purely in terms of urban planning and industrial concentration. However, these objectives have also evoked support for developing the Charter of European Cities and Towns for Sustainability.[22]

As well known, the Treaties do not assign any authority to the union on issues of urban policy, but this has not prevented its institutions from devoting specific attention to urban areas. So much so that the EU's defining of an "*Urban Acquis*" has gradually been established over time and aligned with the more general concept of an "*Acquis Communautaire*".[23] This was initially achieved by testing innovative funding modalities focussing on urban areas,[24] including the URBAN programme.[25] Through this, EU-financed "area-based" projects have been aimed at undertaking urban regeneration in deprived city areas. With this impetus from the European Union, Member States then began to commit themselves to defining a common strategy for European urban territories. The so-called 'informal ministerial meetings' between the ministers responsible for urban development (within the work of the Council) have been particularly crucial in adopting important documents dedicated to sustainable urban development. One of the main ones has been the *Leipzig Charter on Sustainable European Cities* adopted under the leadership of the German Council Presidency. This Charter's strategies were later reaffirmed in 2010 under the Spanish Presidency in the *Toledo Declaration on Integrated Urban Regeneration*. The latter was also the result of work done by the ministers responsible for urban development.

21 Communication from the Commission to the Council and Parliament, COM (90) 218 final, 25 July 1990.

22 The *Aalborg Charter* was approved by the participants at the first European Conference on Sustainable Cities and Towns held in Aalborg, Denmark on 27 May 1994. The Charter resulting from the conference was promoted by the European Commission and the municipality of Aalborg and had more than 3,000 local authority signatories in addition to the support of many other national and international bodies and NGOs.

23 For a detailed reconstruction of European sources on this see Fulvio Leonzio, 'Città e tutela dell'ambiente: quale ruolo all'interno dell'unione europea?' (2023) 4, *Diritto Pubblico Comparato ed Europeo*, 1065-1086.

24 This included funding for some pilot projects: Maria Tofarides, *Urban Policy in the European Union: A Multi-Level Gatekeeper System* (Ashgate 2003) 54, 66.

25 This was financed over the 1994-1999 period, renewed for a second one (URBAN II covering the 2000–2006 period), and then incorporated into the mainstreaming of the Union's cohesion policies: Ignazio Vinci, *Politica urbana e dinamica dei sistemi territoriali. Attori e strategie nell'Europa degli anni Novanta* (FrancoAngeli 2002) 162, 165; Tofarides (n 24) 67, 74.

One of the recurring aspects of documents produced during the first decade of the 2000s has been their inclusion of the principle of sustainable development, which has become key to the modernisation and transformation of urban territories. Sustainable development has been supported through a coherent strategy and clear methodology based on: a common system for evaluating the state of urban territories within the Union; innovative financing instruments geared toward territorial specificities and directly targeted at urban areas; local authority involvement via an effective exchange of best practices and the creation of city networks; and the pursuit of the multi-level management of urban phenomena.[26] In parallel with the EU's increased financial commitment to sustainable urban development, EU Institutions and Member States have also adopted further documents promoting the social and environmental sustainability of cities. Following upon important previous efforts by various actors, including the European Commission,[27] European Parliament,[28] European Committee of the Regions,[29] European Economic and Social Committee (EESC),[30] and the EUROCITIES association,[31] the ministers of the Member States responsible for urban and territorial issues approved the Pact of Amsterdam in 2016, better known as the European Urban Agenda[32]. This continues to represent the most accomplished result of European action in urban areas.

26 See: Robert Atkinson, 'The urban dimension in cohesion policy. Past developments and future prospects' (2015) 3(1) *European Structural and Investment Funds Journal* 21–31; Enrico Carloni and Manuel Pineiro, 'Le città intelligenti e l'Europa. Tendenze di fondo e nuove strategie di sviluppo urbano' (2015) 4 *Istituzioni del Federalismo*, 2015 881, 883; Giancarlo Cotella, 'The urban dimension of EU cohesion policy' in Eduardo Medeiros (ed), *Territorial Cohesion: The Urban Dimension* (Springer 2019) 138, 145; Martín Fernández-Prado and Luis Domínguez Castro, 'Introduction' in Martín Fernández-Prado and Luis Domínguez Castro (eds), *City Policies and the European Urban Agenda* (Palgrave Macmillan 2019) 3, 17.

27 See the Commission's report entitled Cities of tomorrow: Challenges, visions, ways forward (October 2011) and their Communication of 18 July 2014 on The urban dimension of EU policies-key features of an EU urban agenda (COM (2014)0490).

28 See the European Parliament Resolutions of 23 June 2011 on the European urban agenda and its future in cohesion policy and of 9 September 2015 on the urban dimension of EU policies (2014/2213(INI)).

29 See the opinion of the European Committee of the Regions of 25 June 2014, Towards an Integrated Urban Agenda for the EU and of 8 April 2016, Concrete steps for implementing the EU Urban Agenda.

30 See the opinion of the European Economic and Social Committee (EESC) of 21 September 2011, *Metropolitan Areas and City Regions in Europe 2020.*

31 See the EUROCITIES document, Strategic framework 2014–2020: towards an EU urban agenda for cities (December 2014).

32 *Pact of Amsterdam establishing the Urban Agenda for the EU.* Document adopted at the informal meeting of Member State ministers responsible for urban issues on 30 May 2016 in Amsterdam, the Netherlands.

In this context, the European Green Deal also marks a decisive moment for the EU's environmental ambitions.[33] As is well known, the Commission decided to launch the Green Deal in 2019 as

> a new growth strategy that aims to transform the Union into a fair and prosperous society, with a modern, resource-efficient and competitive economy, where there are no net emissions of greenhouse gases in 2050 and where economic growth is decoupled from resource use.

Furthermore, it specifically included this aim within a policy track initiated at the international level as "an integral part of this Commission's strategy to implement the UN 2030 Agenda and the sustainable development goals".[34] The Green Deal poses a goal for the other European institutions of profoundly transforming the EU's economic system in pursuit of a more sustainable future. This will thus have an impact on energy policies, overall industrial strategy, mobility, food systems, and biodiversity. Explicitly concretising the climate objectives of the Green Deal, Climate Regulation (EU) 2021/1119 enshrines the legal constraint of EU climate neutrality by 2050. In particular, Art. 2(1) of this Regulation sets the famous 2050 target that

> Union-wide greenhouse gas emissions and removals regulated in Union law shall be balanced within the Union at the latest by 2050, thus reducing emissions to net zero by that date, and the Union shall aim to achieve negative emissions thereafter.

While Art. 4(1) notes that,

> In order to reach the climate-neutrality objective set out in Article 2(1), the binding Union 2030 climate target shall be a domestic reduction of net greenhouse gas emissions (emissions after deduction of removals) by at least 55% compared to 1990 levels by 2030.

Although these European documents lack an explicit reference to cities, it is clear that the goal of eliminating climate impacts will not be attainable without the involvement of urban areas.[35] This recognition has resulted, in fact, in the

33 See the Communication from the Commission to the European Parliament, the Council, the European Economic and Social Committee (EESC), and the European Committee of the Regions entitled 'The European Green Deal' COM (640) 2019 final.

34 COM (2019) 640 final, Section 1, paragraph 2 and 7, respectively.

35 See Hannah Abdullah, 'Introduction', in Hannah Abdullah (ed), *Towards a European Green Deal with Cities. The Urban Dimension of the EU's Sustainable Growth Strategy* (CIDOB editions 2021) 12, 16.

amendment of the *Leipzig Charter*, leading to a 2.0 version[36], which focusses on the transformative power of cities in promoting sustainability and aligns with both the Green Deal and *UN 2030 Agenda*.

In addition to the policy objectives included in these documents, the European resources provided by the Multiannual Financial Framework (MFF) for the 2021–2027 seven-year period (in particular Regulation (EU) 2021/1058 on cohesion policies 2021–2027), and the Horizon Europe 2021–2027 programme, are specifically dedicated to supporting research and innovation projects. As such, they introduce new EU Mission[37] instruments which seek to tackle highly challenging problems that may have a strong impact on the daily lives of EU citizens. Mission 4, for example, on "climate-neutral and smart cities", has taken shape as a challenge to create 100 climate-neutral European cities by 2030. This goal anticipates the target set for all of Europe by 2050 under the European Climate Law. Among the crucial elements of Mission 4 is that the 100 cities will be called on to develop a key "Climate City Contract" to be adopted at the end of an idea gathering and sharing process involving citizens and stakeholders in the city.[38] In Chapter 1, Part III, of this book, the case of Bologna is analysed in this context in terms of both the application and contract drafting phases of this process.

1.4 Local authorities serving (green) cities in the NRRPs

In July 2020, the European Council endorsed the NGEU programme. This is a temporary instrument designed to stimulate recovery through a monetary package of approximately €750 billion. The main component is the Recovery and Resilience Facility (RRF), which will run for six years from 2021 to 2026, making approximately €700 billion in loans and grants available to support reforms and investments in Member States. In this context, the role of cities and local authorities emerges – or at least should emerge – out of the various NRRPs which have been submitted by governments to the European Commission under the NGEU since the spring of 2021. These NRRPs have been subsequently approved by the implementing decisions of the Council of the European Union and contain state strategies for channelling European funds into repairing the damage caused by COVID-19.

They do this through a series of reforms and investments aimed at building a more sustainable future. The objectives of the EU Regulation establishing

36 See the document, *The New Leipzig Charter. The Transformative Power of Cities for the Common Good*, adopted at the informal ministerial meeting of Member State Ministers responsible for urban issues on 30 November 2020.

37 Art. 8, Regulation (EU) 2021/695.

38 See Hanny Gronkiewicz-Waltz et al., *Proposed Mission: 100 Climate-Neutral Cities by 2030 – By and for the Citizens, Report of the Mission Board for Climate-Neutral and Smart Cities* (Office of the European Union 2020) and Sonia De Gregorio Hurtado, 'A green deal for the urban age: A new role for cities in EU climate action', in Hannah Abdullah (n 35) 27, 33.

the RRF include, in particular: the green transition; digital transformation; smart, sustainable and inclusive growth; social and territorial cohesion; economic, social, and institutional health and resilience; and policies for the new generation, children, and youth.[39] Based on the NRRPs, territorial authorities now find themselves involved in a new season of reforms, structural innovation, and implementing EU funding according to the above-mentioned objectives. Member state NRRPs must particularly allocate at least 37% of their budget to support the green transition. These percentages have reached 40% in Italy for financing investments to combat climate change, 46% in France for climate policy and energy transition, and 40% in Spain.[40] The involvement of local authorities in the *bottom-up* phase of NRRP drafting and the *top-down* one of realising them represents a privileged key, in constitutional terms, for understanding the implementation of local autonomy and vertical subsidiarity principles, i.e. the principles most limited by the health emergency's legal rules in various European states.

Based on a reading of the NRRPs and their preparatory documents, it seems the post-crisis legislative reforms of 2008 (responsible for the re-centralising of administrative functions, see Section 1.2 above) and the pandemic emergency regulations (characterised by the formal ousting of local authorities from health-policy decision-making) both had an impact on their drafting. With regards to the preparation phase of the NRRPs, the European Commission emphasised the importance of involving Local and Regional Authorities (LRAs) at an early stage, together with various civil society actors, stakeholders, etc.[41] The Commission did not express itself in a coercive way, but rather strategically asked the states to explain the modality of consultation to the LRAs using an outline of the process.[42] The Committee of the Regions also immediately emphasised the value of consultation and local authority involvement, insisting on the importance of LRA participation in the upstream planning as well as the downstream phase of policy implementation at the local level.[43] Together with the Council of European Municipalities and Regions

39 Art. 3 of EU Regulation No. 2021/241 of the European Parliament and of the Council of 12 February 2021.

40 For an analysis of some comparative non-legal elements see Patrick Bisciari, Wouter Gelade and Wim Melyn, 'Plans nationaux de relance et de résilience de la France et de ses principaux pays voisins' (2021) 3 *Revue Française d'économie* 19 and Davide Tentori and Antonio Villafranca, *Recovery and Resilience Facility: Una comparazione tra Paesi chiave dell'Unione europea* (ISPI 2021) 181.

41 This included indicating who was consulted, when, and how. See Art.18(4)(q) of the *Recovery and Resilience Facility (RRF)*.

42 European Commission, *Guidance to Member States. Recovery and Resilience Plans*, SWD(2021) 12 final PART 1/2, 22 January 2021, p. 47.

43 See the Opinion of the European Committee of the Regions – 'Recovery plan for Europe in response to the COVID-19 pandemic: Recovery and Resilience Facility and Technical Support Instrument' (2020/C 440/24).

(CEMR), the Committee of the Regions also monitored the preparation phases of the various NRRPs from the very beginning.[44]

Initial research was carried out by the Committee of the Regions on a sample of eight states (including Germany, Belgium, Spain, and Italy, characterised by strong political decentralisation and Poland, France, Croatia, and Romania, characterised by predominantly bureaucratic-administrative decentralisation).[45] The results attest to a very weak involvement of Local and Regional Authorities (LRAs), in particular, municipal authorities, in both the upstream preparation and downstream implementation phases. With the exception of Belgium, Germany, and Poland, which achieved the highest score for having consultations in line with the requirements indicated in Art.18(4)(q) of the RRF,[46] the other states were rather deficient in involving both the intermediate (e.g. *Regions*, *Comunidades Autónomas*, and *Länder*) and local government (municipality) levels.[47] In federal-regional states, the local level was consulted either after the intermediate level (e.g. in Spain) or was not directly involved. If the involvement of local authorities has been limited in the bottom-up phase, their top-down involvement can also be described as worrying, particularly with regard to reform proposals that see them as recipients in certain sectors (social services, urban planning, etc.). The (poor) consultation procedures led the authors of the Committee of the Regions Report to highlight that local and regional authorities risk being involved only as recipients or executing entities. The responsibilities of territorial authorities are evident in the context of cross-cutting topics such as green and smart city policies. However, these authorities have not been included in those sections of the NRRPs relating to smart housing, building, etc. in the regional and federal

44 They launched a consultation with national associations of local authorities and European state authorities between November 2020 and early January 2021. See COR-CEMR (2021), *The involvement of municipalities, cities and regions in the preparation of the national Recovery and Resilience Plans: Results of the CoR-CEMR targeted consultation.*

45 See European Committee of the Regions, *Regional and local authorities and the National Recovery and Resilience Plans*, 2021.

46 Alessandro Valenza et al., *Regional and local authorities and the National Recovery and Resilience Plans* (European Committee of the Regions 2021), Chart 1. Involvement of LRAs in preparation of the NRRP, 16.

47 Mere information – even if well structured – cannot be considered a form of involvement. Given that, in December 2020, the French ministries of Territorial Cohesion and Economy (*Ministère de la Cohésion des territoires and Ministère de l'Économie*) created a *Mayor's Guide to the Recovery Plan* (*Guide à destination des maires – Plan de reliance).* In this, the measures, available funding, and practical modalities of contracting facilitated by the recovery and ecological transition contracts (*Contrats de relance et de transition écologique–CRTE)* were indicated for each of the NPPR public policies involving municipalities. This was a sort of handbook provided by the government, which, in full transalpine style, states thus: "This guide has been designed to make the Recovery Plan measures readable and accessible to mayors in order to concretise and accelerate deploying them in your territories"(*Ce guide a été conçu pour rendre lisibles et accessibles les mesures du Plan de relance à destination des maires, afin de concrétiser et d'accélérer son déploiement dans vos territoires*).

states (the exception is Belgium which included the regions and capital of Brussels as a priority). Still, the numerous references made to the implementing legislator are noteworthy. In a few cases (Italy and Belgium), the NRRPs also provide for territorial resource allocations.

In summary, some critical findings emerge regarding NRRPs preparation and implementation from a territorial perspective. These include the observations that there has been a "lack of LRA involvement", [the] territorial dimension [was] partially addressed, [and there was] miscoordination with Cohesion Policy Analysis of the eight NRRPs".[48] In terms of governance, the European institutions have not provided any guidelines or guidance to states other than asking for reassurance on the effectiveness of national instruments in managing financial resources. However, the solutions adopted by the various European states have some common elements. Firstly, political responsibility for the implementation phases of the NRRPs is recognised at the state level and as being in the hands of the executive or ministry in charge of finance, which is, in any case, the direct point of contact for the European Commission. Governance formally envisages the involvement of the territorial level, yet the opportunity for state governments to engage in dialogue with other levels of government seems, in most cases, to have been wasted. This is because the information flow has moved from the NRRP steering committees (the State Executive) downward toward the territorial entities. This reflects a governance scheme in which the central level is the undisputed protagonist while the territorial authorities are excluded from the decision-making control room, regardless of their role. A later document of the European Committee of the Regions and the Council of European Municipalities and Regions(of27 April 2022) confirms the low participation of LRAs even in the later implementation phase of NRRPs. This document states:

> Comparison with the results of our 2021 consultation suggests that national governments did use the past months/year for providing information to, and seeking dialogue with, LRAs … Regarding implementation of the NRRPs, only a very small share of LRA respondents declare having an appropriate role in monitoring, or being sufficiently taken into consideration on the basis of their competencies.

1.5 Conclusion: Innovative approaches for a green urban future

The involvement of local authorities (regions and local governments) is indispensable for achieving the European Green Deal objectives and coping with the consequences of the pandemic by implementing the NGEU NRRPs. The objectives of the European Green Deal insist on a shift from a linear economic model to a circular and regenerative one, whereby economic growth does not

48 Valenza (n 46) 91.

entail environmental damage or over-exploitation of resources. It concerns a model for transforming "the European Union into a just and prosperous society". Accomplishing this requires a paradigm shift in terms of the citizen-authority relationship and multi-level governance of the transition. Cities play a key role in achieving these goals. They become circularcities when they promote this kind of transition by functioning in an integrated manner *and* "in collaboration with citizens, businesses and the research community" while "through this transition, cities seek to improve human well-being, reduce emissions, protect and enhance biodiversity, and promote social justice, in line with the Sustainable DevelopmentGoals".[49]

If the 2015 Commission Communication, "Closing the Loop – An EU Action Plan for the Circular Economy"[50] makes a generic reference to local authorities being involved in implementation, preventing food waste, and coping with the heterogeneous situations found in different regions and countries, the 2020 Communication, "A New Circular Economy Action Plan for a Cleaner and More Competitive Europe",[51] turns cities into protagonists in the circular economy policies. Many European cities have complemented their post-COVID economic recovery strategies with "green transition-oriented approaches"; these include everything from Amsterdam's investment in the circular economy, to Barcelona's digital and equitable transition and the "15-minute" city model promoted by Paris.[52] All these models are contributing to cities emerging from the pandemic with eco-solidarity profiles and features. Post-pandemic European cities, therefore, are developing urban environmental and climate change policies using national plans in a spirit of solidarity. They orient their actions according to international declarations that set climate targets with global impacts, albeit on an urban scale. They are also acting by implementing European soft law documents as well as state regulations and balancing the use of instruments for promotion and implementation.

There is no shortage of originality in developing new methods, tools, or entities, such as Climate Assemblies. Theseare a specific application of City Assemblies which draw on a representative sample of the population made up of residents and city users (people who use city services without residing there). The main feature of these assemblies is "deliberation" or the process by which citizens are directly involved in public decisions. Deliberation itself is not a new concept and dates back to the 1980s. Since then, related instruments have been tried out alongside typical representative democracy ones. The *European Charter of Local Self-Government* (Art.3) also mentions citizens'

49 This definition of a circular city is given on the Circular City Declaration site at https://circularcitiesdeclaration.eu/cities-and-the-circular-economy/what-is-a-circular-city.
50 COM (2015) 614.
51 COM (2020) 98.
52 Edoardo Croci and Tania Molteni, 'Il Green Deal e il Recovery Plan: un nuovo quadro per una riconversione urbana sostenibile, circolare e smart', in Giuseppe Franco Ferrari (ed), *Le smart cities al tempo della resilienza* (Mimesis, 2021) 379.

assemblies alongside elected ones. In the last ten years, "waves of deliberation" have started to swell. The Organisation for Economic Co-operation and Development (OECD) report, *Innovative Citizen Participation and New Democratic Institutions-Catching the Deliberative Wave*, analysed 289 cases of successful deliberation between 1986 and 2019, and this marks the first comparative international study on these practices.

Over time, citizens' assemblies have also become a tool serving complex problems that require lengthy processes, such as those addressing environmental and climate issues. An initial example of this is France's experience with the *Convention Citoyenne pour le Climat*, a citizens' assembly set up in October 2019 by the national government. This brought together 150 citizens randomly drawn from the population with the aim of defining structural measures to achieve, in a spirit of social justice, a reduction in greenhouse gas emissions by at least 40% by 2030 (compared to 1990 levels) (see Chapter 4, Part II of this book). The *Convention* was involved in the legislative process for the so-called *Loi Climat et Resilience 2021-1104* of 22 August 2021. Besides the French example, that of the city of Berlin is also interesting because of its experience with bottom-up participation. In the face of Berlin's declaration to set a goal for carbon neutrality by 2050, the *Klimaneustart Berlin* organisation gathered 30,000 signatures in 2020 (10,000 more than needed under the Local Direct Democracy Act) and established a City Climate Assembly to shape public decisions. This bottom-up participatory model is now inspiring the formation of a Climate National Assembly in Germany.

In Italy, the city councils of the cities of Milan and Bologna declared a Climate and Ecological Emergency in 2019, pledging to adopt a series of commitments fostering citizen participation on municipal-level environmental policy issues. Prominent among these instruments were the Climate Assemblies established in both cities which aimed to prepare recommendations and an opinion for delivery to their respective city councils. These participatory tools confirm that, despite the trend in the re-centralising of functions (which was confirmed by the governance of the NRRPs), cities are increasingly establishing themselves as laboratories of replicable innovation for higher levels of government. In urban planning law, "it is nothing new that instruments originating at the lower (or regional or even municipal) level are then transposed towards the national legislature or public administrations".[53] In the age of connectivity, the difference lies in the way of these instruments are elaborated and experimented with, given that cities more and more frequently define their own political-administrative guidelines. In doing this, they draw inspiration from the contents of agreements signed with other cities and Charters of Rights transposed into local regulatory and administrative instruments. Today,

53 Elena Buoso, 'Da Leonia a Ecotopia: il contributo delle città alla tutela dell'ambiente', in Filippo Pizzolato, Guido Rivosecchi and Antonino Scalone (eds), *La città oltre lo stato* (Giappichelli 2022) 263.

scholars of international relations observe that "in the digital age cities have returned as actors in the international system as they were in antiquity and the Middle Ages", as demonstrated by the case of Smart City Sweden. This is an example of paradiplomacy based on Sweden's innovative "triple helix" model which connects three sectors: academia, industry, and government at all levels to create sustainable cities.[54]

Bibliography

Abdullah H., 'Introduction', in H. Abdullah (ed), *Towards a European Green Deal with Cities. The Urban Dimension of the EU's Sustainable Growth Strategy* (CIDOB edicions 2021).

Andersen V.N., 'Denmark', in E.C. Page, M.J. Goldsmith (eds), *Changing Government Relations in Europe: From Localism to Intergovernmentalism* (Routledge 2010).

Arban E., 'Constitutional law, federalism and the city as a unique socio-economic and political space', in E. Hirsch Ballin, G. van der Schyff, M. Stremler and M. De Visser (eds), *European Yearbook of Constitutional Law 2020. The City in Constitutional Law* (T.M.C. Asser Press 2021).

Atkinson R., 'The urban dimension in cohesion policy.Past developments and future prospects' (2015) 3(1) *European Structural and Investment Funds Journal* 21.

Auby J.-B., *Droit de la ville: Du fonctionnement juridique des villes au droit à la Ville* (LexisNexis 2013).

Auby J.-B., 'The role of law in the legal status and powers of cities' (2013) 2 *Italian Journal of Public Law* 302.

Auby J.-B., 'El papel de la ciudad como nuevo sujeto político institucional' (2019) 1 *Anuario del Gobierno Local* 189.

Bisciari P., Gelade W. and Melyn W., 'Plans nationaux de relance et de résilience de la France et de ses principaux pays voisins' (2021) 3 *Revue Française d'économie* 19.

Bolgherini S., *Navigando a vista. Governi locali in Europa tra crisi e riforme* (il Mulino 2015).

Buoso E., 'Da Leonia a Ecotopia: il contributo delle città alla tutela dell'ambiente', in F. Pizzolato, G. Rivosecchi and A. Scalone (eds), *La città oltre lo stato* (Giappichelli 2022).

Carloni E. and Pineiro M., 'Le città intelligenti e l'Europa. Tendenze di fondo e nuove strategie di sviluppo urbano' (2015) 4 *Istituzioni del Federalismo* 865.

Cherrier E. and Guérard S., *La régionalisation en Europe. Regards croisés* (Bruylant 2014).

Cortese F., 'Il nuovo diritto delle città: alla ricerca di un legittimo spazio operativo', in G.F. Ferrari (ed), *Smart city. L'evoluzione di un'idea* (Mimesis 2020).

54 "Sweden has used its cities to build hubs that contribute to the creation of its own ecosystems and where the interrelationships of the three sectors have resulted in companies with high levels of innovation". (Mario Torres Jarrín, 'City diplomacy theory and practice of paradiplomacy: Smart city Sweden case', in Paulina Astroza, Giuliana Laschi, Nahel Oddone and Mario Torres Jarrín (eds), *Over the Atlantic. EU and Latin American Relations: between Diplomacy and Paradiplomacy* (Peterlang 2023) 167 and 172.

'COST Action Local Public sector reforms: An international comparison (LocRef)', in S. Kuhlmann, G. Bouckaert (eds), *Local Public Sector Reforms in Times of Crisis: National Trajectories and International Comparison* (Palgrave McMillan 2016).

Cotella G., 'The urban dimension of EU cohesion policy', in Eduardo Medeiros (ed), *Territorial Cohesion: The Urban Dimension* (Springer 2019).

Council of European Municipalities and Regions (CEMR), 'Decentralisation at a crossroads, Territorial reforms in Europe in times of crisis' (2013) at www.ccre .org.

Croci E. and Molteni T., 'Il Green Deal e il Recovery Plan: un nuovo quadro per una riconversione urbana sostenibile, circolare e smart', in G.F. Ferrari (ed), *Le smart cities al tempo della resilienza* (Mimesis, 2021).

De Gregorio Hurtado S., 'A green deal for the urban age: A new role for cities in EU climate action', in H. Abdullah (ed), *Towards a European Green Deal with Cities. The Urban Dimension of the EU's Sustainable Growth Strategy* (CIDOB edicions 2021).

De Martin G.C., 'Il disegno autonomistico disatteso tra contraddizioni e nuovi scenari problematici' (2014) 1 *Istituzioni del Federalismo* 21.

Fernández-Prado M. and Domínguez Castro L., 'Introduction', in M. Fernández-Prado, L. Domínguez Castro (eds), *City Policies and the European Urban Agenda* (Palgrave Macmillan 2019).

Font T., 'De la autonomía local al poder de las ciudades' (2019) Special Number *Istituzioni del Federalismo* 115.

Giglioni F., 'Verso un diritto delle città. Le città oltre il comune', in E. Carloni, F. Cortese (eds), *Diritto delle autonomie territoriali* (Wolters Kluwer 2020).

Gronkiewicz-Waltz H. et al., *Proposed Mission: 100 Climate-Neutral Cities by 2030 – By and for the Citizens, Report of the Mission Board for Climate-Neutral and Smart Cities* (Office of the European Union 2020).

Hirsch Ballin E., van der Schyff G., Stremler M., De Visser M. (eds), *European Yearbook of Constitutional Law 2020. The City in Constitutional Law* (T.M.C. Asser Press 2021).

Fulvio Leonzio, 'Città e tutela dell'ambiente: quale ruolo all'interno dell'unione europea?' (2023) 4 *Diritto Pubblico Comparato ed Europeo*, 1065-1086.

Jiménez Asensio R., 'La autonomía olvidada: los ayuntamientos ante la crisis', https://rafaeljimenezasensio.com/2020/08/09/la-autonomia-olvidada-los -ayuntamientos-ante-la-crisis/.

Kettunen P., 'The Finnish municipal reform' (2014) 11(1) *Public Policy* 55.

Noureau A., *L'Union européenne et les collectivités locales* (La Rochelle 2011).

Nunes Silva C. and Buček J. (eds), *Fiscal Austerity and Innovation in Local Governance in Europe* (Routledge 2014).

Page E.C. and Goldsmith M.J. (eds), *Central and Local Government Relations. A Comparative Analysis of West European Unitary States* (Sage 1987).

Pavani G. and Pegoraro L. (eds), *Municipi d'occidente. Il governo locale in Europa e nelle Americhe* (Donzelli 2006).

Peters B.G., Pierre J., Randma-Liiv T., 'Global financial crisis, public administration and governance: Do new problems require new solutions?' (2011) 11 *Public Organization Review* 13.

Polanyi K., *The Great Transformation* (Beacon Press 1944).

Sacco R., 'Legal formants: A dynamic approach to comparative law (installment I of II)' (1991) 39 *American Journal of Comparative Law* 1.

Salvador Crespo M.T., *La autonomía provincial en el sistema constitucional español. Intermunicipalidad y Estado Autonómico* (Instituto Nacional de Administración Pública 2007).
Tentori D. and Villafranca A., *Recovery and Resilience Facility: Una comparazione tra Paesi chiave dell'Unione europea* (ISPI 2021).
Tofarides M., *Urban Policy in the European Union: A Multi-Level Gatekeeper System* (Ashgate 2003).
Torres Jarrín M., 'City diplomacy theory and practice of paradiplomacy: Smart city Sweden case', in P. Astroza, G. Laschi, N. Oddone, M. Torres Jarrín (eds), *Over the Atlantic. EU and Latin American Relations: between Diplomacy and Paradiplomacy* (Peterlang 2023).
Valenza A. et al., *Regional and Local Authorities and the National Recovery and Resilience Plans* (European Committee of the Regions 2021).
Vinci I., *Politica urbana e dinamica dei sistemi territoriali. Attori e strategie nell'Europa degli anni Novanta* (FrancoAngeli 2002).

2 Green urban planning across Europe

Legal instruments, goals settled, and implementation throughout the National Recovery and Resilience Plans

Andrés Boix Palop and Clàudia Gimeno Fernández

2.1 Introduction: Key elements of green infrastructure planning in the European Union

The increasing global concern regarding the repercussions of human-induced global warming, coupled with a heightened environmental consciousness extending across various domains, has spurred noteworthy regulatory initiatives at the international, European, and national levels. These initiatives delineate key objectives aimed at mitigating the carbon footprint, curbing non-renewable energy consumption, regulating pollutant emissions, managing waste generation, and addressing a myriad of related challenges in order to respond to challenges that are now, fortunately, extremely topical. The United Nations Sustainable Development Goals, embodied in the 2030 Agenda,[1] which most European public institutions have embraced, at least formally and symbolically, are a good example of this change in attitude. On a more concrete level, the United Nations Framework Convention on Climate Change (UNFCCC) has established specific obligations for signatory countries.[2] This instrument is a good reflection of the international community's priority to drastically reduce emissions of gases which, in addition to significant

1 The Sustainable Development Goals on which the 2030 Agenda is based are 17 goals and 169 targets proposed as a continuation of the Millennium Development Goals with which the United Nations welcomed the 21st century. They were adopted by the United Nations General Assembly on 25 September 2015, and were embodied in the *Transforming our world: the 2030 Agenda for Sustainable Development*, which entered into force on 1 January 2016.

2 The United Nations Framework Convention on Climate Change (UNFCCC) was adopted in 1992 and has undergone several revisions that have gradually incorporated stricter obligations for the parties through subsequent agreements. The latest of these, the Paris Agreement, establishes specific measures for the reduction of greenhouse gas emissions and has replaced since 2020 the well-known Kyoto Protocol, which initiated the path of multinational agreements within the framework of the UNFCCC for the establishment of specific emission reduction targets to be met by the signatory parties. The Paris Agreement has been signed by some of the major emitting powers (e.g., China), but not by the world's largest per capita emitter, the United States.

DOI: 10.4324/9781032665184-4

air pollution and the associated public health problems, are responsible for human-induced climate change.

Correlatingly, the concurrent global climate and biodiversity crises have accentuated the pivotal role of the European Union's environmental and sustainable development competences and policies. This confluence has positioned these competences and policies as central elements within the broader framework of the EU's environmental and sustainable development policy.[3] The regulations stemming from these competences form an extensive body of secondary legislation, encompassing diverse areas such as integrated environmental assessment, noise pollution, nature protection, habitats and biodiversity, flood and soil pollution prevention, air and water protection, waste management, energy, and climate change. Beyond ensuring consistent environmental protection, these regulations also exert influence on urban and land-use planning instruments, introducing principles like non-regression in environmental protection and sustainable development and many considerations relating to urban environment and landscape protection.[4]

In general, these rules incorporate requirements, formalities, and obligations into Member States' spatial and infrastructure planning and regulation. Additionally, in some sectoral areas, the EU determines the obligation of Member States to draw up specific spatial plans (as, for example in relation to flood risks, in accordance with Directive 2007/60/EC on the assessment and management of flood risks). And even, in the case of the regulation of the Natura 2000 Network (a network of protected areas covering valuable and threatened species and habitats), we find rules at the European level that directly determine land uses, particularly on rural land, conditioning its classification as protected land for development purposes.[5]

Within the European environmental legal framework, noteworthy attention should be given to various communications from the European Commission that have contributed to advancements in this area, with a particular focus on environmental protection and land-use planning.[6] These include the

3 Alba Nogueira López, 'La transposición de directivas ambientales en el Estado autonómico', in Arzoz Santisteban (dir), *Transposición de directivas y autogobierno. El desarrollo normativo del Derecho de la Unión Europea en el Estado autonómico* (Institut d'Estudis Autonòmics 2013); Fernando López Ramón, 'La construcción del ordenamiento ambiental español' (2018) 46 *Cuadernos de Derecho Local*, 14.

4 Andrés M. González Sanfiel, *El principio de no regresión en el Derecho público* (Aranzadi 2022); Juli Ponce Solé, 'Derecho urbanístico y prevención y mitigación de desastres: la perspectiva española en el marco de la Unión Europea' (2013) 285 *Revista de Derecho Urbanístico y Medio Ambiente*, 3; and Jesús María Ramírez Sánchez, *Urbanismo para una nueva ciudad. El principio de desarrollo urbano sostenible* (Aranzadi 2021).

5 Marta Lora-Tamayo Vallvé, *The Europeanisation of Planning Law. The European – Land Use – Silent Revolution* (Thomson Reuters Aranzadi 2017).

6 Although the European Union does not have explicit competences in relation to the regulation of the territory or urban planning, it does have the power to determine planning through different sectoral competences and promotion policies, such as the environmental competence

European Union's (EU) Green Infrastructure Strategy, which was launched in 2013.[7] The EU strategy defines green infrastructure as "a strategically planned network of natural and semi-natural areas with other environmental features designed and managed to deliver a wide range of ecosystem services". Green infrastructure is conceived, in this sense, as a key element in spatial development, which reinforces and materializes in different policies, and from which social, environmental[8] and economic benefits are derived.[9]

Green infrastructure can refer to rural, peri-urban, or urban settings, covering terrestrial, coastal, and marine areas. Among its key principles are connectivity (between areas of green infrastructure), multi-functionality (areas that have multiple functions and social values attached to them), the need for multi-scale planning and coordination, and an increased greenery (e.g., the ambition to enhance the quantity and/or quality of green and blue areas).[10] One of its key elements is the achievement of zero net loss of biodiversity and ecosystem services. The achievement of zero net loss involves refraining from converting green infrastructure to grey, implementing compensatory measures in ecological and territorial domains, and recognizing that green

---

or the cohesion policies. In addition, the Union has carried out leadership in this matter through intergovernmental dialogue, although framed within what is understood as soft law (generally, agreements without binding effects).

7 Communication from the Commission to the European Parliament, the Council, the European Economic and Social Committee, and the Committee of the Regions, Green Infrastructure (GI) – Enhancing Europe's Natural Capital, COM(2013) 249 final.

8 The European Commission, 'Evaluating the Impact of Nature-Based Solutions: a Handbook for Pratitioners (Publications Office of the European Union 2021), https://op.europa.eu/en/publication-detail/-/publication/d7d496b5-ad4e-11eb-9767-01aa75ed71a1, and Alexander van der Jagt, Laura Tozer, Helen Toxopeus and Hens Runhaar, 'Policy mixes for mainstreaming urban nature-based solutions: An analysis of six European countries and the European Union' (2023) 139 Environmental Science & Policy, 51, establish the importance of nature-based solutions, and define them as solutions that are inspired and supported by nature, which are cost-effective, and that simultaneously provide environmental, social and economic benefits, and help build resilience. They must therefore benefit biodiversity and support the delivery of a range of ecosystem services. Nature-based solutions have been introduced into the EU policy agenda and identified as a key action in several EU policies, such as the European Green Deal, the EU Biodiversity Strategy, and the EU Adaptation Strategy.

9 Peter Massini and Henry Smith, 'Planning for green infrastructure – the green infrastructure factor and learning from Europe' (2018) *PERFECT Expert Paper*; Anastasia Chatzimentor, Evangelia Apostolopoulou, and Antonios D. Mazaris, 'A review of green infrastructure research in Europe: Challenges and opportunities' (2020) 198 *Landscape and Urban Planning*; and Rebecca Leigh Rutt and Natalie Marie Gulsrud 'Green justice in the city: A new agenda for urban green space research in Europe' (2016) 19 *Urban Forestry & Urban Greening*, 123.

10 Elin Slätmo, Kjell Nilsson, and Eeva Turunen, 'Implementing Green Infrastructure in Spatial Planning in Europe' (2019) 8(4) *Land 62*; and Simona R. Grădinaru and Anna M. Hersperger, 'Green infrastructure in strategic spatial plans: Evidence from European urban regions' (2019) 40 *Urban Forestry & Urban Greening*, 17.

infrastructure yields advantages not solely in climate, ecology, and biodiversity but also extends to social, cultural, and economic dimensions.[11]

The Strategy received added impetus through the European Green Deal (2019), which strengthens the commitment to the circular economy and solidifies Europe's trajectory towards a green transition. This alignment is further substantiated by the Biodiversity Strategy for 2030 – an extension of the Natura 2000 program (2021)[12] – alongside the European Urban Agenda (2016), the EU Climate Adaptation Strategy,[13] and several initiatives under Horizon 2020 and Horizon Europe. These projects not only bolster member states' engagement but also underscore their active participation in diverse strategic and applied Green Infrastructure initiatives.[14]

All these instruments highlight the need for green infrastructure planning to be developed in a multi-level manner, especially in urban settings, where more than 60% of Europe's population lives and where the benefits of green infrastructure can have the greatest impact.[15] In these urban environments, the Strategy recognizes the loss of ecosystem services that the impoverishment of the biodiversity of this ecosystem has entailed. In this sense, it highlights that the urban system has become dependent on other habitats and is unbalanced, and that, although adaptation to climate change is part of the political agendas of cities, additional efforts must be made to achieve real change. It, therefore, establishes the need for all cities with more than 20,000 inhabitants to develop Urban Greening Plans in which the above-mentioned principles are implemented by the end of 2021.

Despite this, the objective has not been met and the implementation of the Strategy, in general, and is being delayed.[16] Its development has catalyzed an increasing number of urban regions and cities to embrace strategic planning as a potent tool to address contemporary environmental challenges,[17] a trend elaborated in subsequent chapters of this work. This shift is embodied through the evolution of two key aspects: (1) the conceptualization of urban green infrastructure as an interconnected and complementary network of urban green spaces, encompassing elements of environmental, landscape, or heritage

11 Tüzin Baycan-Levent and Peter Nijkamp, 'Planning and management of urban green spaces in Europe: Comparative analysis' (2009) 135 *Journal of Urban Planning and Development.*

12 Communication from the Commission on the EU Biodiversity Strategy for 2030 – Bringing nature back into our lives, COM/2020/380 final.

13 Communication from the Commission on Forging a climate-resilient Europe – The new EU Strategy on Adaptation to Climate Change, COM/2021/82 final.

14 Raffaele Lafortezza and Clive Davies, 'Pandemic urban development is leading us away from nature' (2023) 217 *Environmental Research*, 114858.

15 Massini, Smith (No. 9).

16 Bettina Wilk, Andreas Vetter, and Alice Schröder, 'Tackling the climate and biodiversity crises in Europe through Urban Greening Plans. Recommendations for avoiding the implementation gap' (2021) *Scientific Opinion Paper German Environment Agency.*

17 Grădinaru, Hersperger (n 10), Massini, Smith (No. 9).

significance, along with their associated ecological processes and flows,[18] and which integrates green planning with other disciplines such as housing, mobility, infrastructure, and public health, with the aim of balancing the challenges of today's cities; and (2) specific urban green infrastructure schemes, which have emerged as a specific and concrete normative sector of green infrastructure aimed at creating and maintaining networks of green spaces in urban environments through the application of certain processes and visions to urban planning.[19]

Among the cities that stand out in terms of the approval of such plans are Utrecht, a pioneering city in green plan development since the 1990s;[20] Malmö, which in 2003 approved the first Green Plan for Malmö; Copenhagen, which adopted the Copenhagen Climate Plan in 2012; Barcelona, which adopted, in 2011, the Pla Verd i de la Biodiversitat (2011–2020), continued and reinforced in 2021 with the Pla Natura Barcelona 2030; Madrid, through the approval of the 2018 Green Infrastructure and Biodiversity Plan; Amsterdam, which in 2020 adopted the Amsterdam Green Infrastructure Vision 2050 and the Green Vision 2020–2050; and Valencia, which in 2023 adopted the Pla Verd i de la Biodiversitat de València, a case study analyzed extensively in a chapter of this book.

2.2 European cities as key players in the implementation of the European green agenda

Sub-national authorities, from a formal and legal standpoint, remain external to the European Union's legal framework. Neither the Treaties nor secondary legislation typically acknowledge them as subjects of law. Local authorities lack the capacity to contribute substantially to the development of European law; they are predominantly a domestic phenomenon. Consequently, they are not officially recognized as playing a role in the operational dynamics of the EU. For this reason, it has been said that the EU and the European legal order are blind to the presence of subnational authorities in the MS, and it is only through the relations between European and state institutions that European competences are usually articulated.[21]

From a functional point of view, however, sub-national authorities do play an active role in the EU. Over time it has become apparent that local authorities often act as direct allies of the EU in the realization of its objectives.[22] In

18 Maite Uriarte Ricorte, 'Planificar la infraestructura verde urbana' (2014) 99–100 *Revista Vasca de Administración Pública*, 2873.

19 Clive Davies, Raffaele Lafortezza, 'Urban green infrastructure in Europe: Is greenspace planning and policy compliant?' (2017) 69 *Land Use Policy*, 93.

20 Sybrand Tjallingii, 'Green and red: Enemies or allies? The Utrecht experience with green structure planning' (2003) 29(2) *Built Environment (1978–)*, 107.

21 Michele Finck, *Subnational Authorities in EU Law* (Oxford University Press 2017).

22 Ibid.

this regard, the presence of cities in the framework of European governance has witnessed significant growth over the last three decades.

The establishment of city-specific funding programs, the advocacy for city-driven consultation processes, the proliferation of networks fostering the exchange of good urban practices, as well as the development of numerous multilateral agreements and instruments – most of which emphasize the role of local governments – all highlight the pivotal role cities play in the EU. Furthermore, the introduction of principles such as subsidiarity within the EU framework, emphasizing the efficiency of decision-making and implementation at the level of government closest to the citizenry, has further solidified this recognition.

In addition, many regulatory provisions and specific actions introduced by the European institutions directly affect local authorities, as they fall within the purview of local responsibilities. Achieving the outlined goals demands a comprehensive and structural overhaul of policies, entailing a global reevaluation of planning, economic strategies, social initiatives, developmental approaches, and environmental considerations.[23] Thus, the European regulatory framework predefines the potential methods for organizing the provision of local public transport services,[24] the general traffic rules and the legal grounds for imposing limitations on the use of public space.[25] It is also unavailable to local authorities to establish pollution and environmental quality thresholds in cities, which today depend not only on state regulations on the matter but also, substantially, on the European regulations that frame them. For example, to date, it is still the Air Quality Directive (Directive 2008/50/EC of 21 May 2008 on ambient air quality and cleaner air for Europe and its subsequent amendments) that establishes these thresholds, which in principle must be met by the Member States, with a system of penalties in the event of non-compliance, leading to the existence of state legislation that imposes legal limits beyond which it is possible to establish restrictions that affect the performance of a wide range of activities.[26]

The responsibilities of local and metropolitan governments have also been emphasized at the international level. Thus, at the Habitat III Conference in Quito, the United Nations approved the so-called New Urban Agenda (NUA), which contains the global guidelines on the basis of which urban

23 Giorgia Pavani, 'From smart to sharing? Presente e futuro delle città (al di là delle etichette)' (2019) XL (4) *Le Istituzioni del Federalismo*, 849.

24 Enrique Guillén López, 'El Derecho de la movilidad sostenible en España', in Boix Palop and Marzal Raga (eds), *Ciudad y movilidad. La regulación de la movilidad urbana sostenible* (PUV 2014).

25 Juan Ignacio Cubero Marcos, 'Títulos habilitantes y normas de procedimiento', in Cubero Marcos and Lasagabaster Herrarte (dirs), *Espacio público y ordenanzas locales: estudio sobre su régimen jurídico* (IVAP 2019).

26 Antonio José Sánchez Sáez, *Las restricciones de tráfico en las ciudades por motivos ambientales y su afección a la libertad de circulación* (Comares 2019).

policies must be developed in many areas and also, of course, in environmental and planning issues.[27] In essence, all these changes have elevated the role of European cities in environmental matters, giving rise to increasingly complex agendas and promoting the strategic significance of local governments, and have reshaped how cities execute public actions, culminating in these levels of government becoming integral elements of European environmental and green policy, as elaborated further below.

2.3 European green cities, NRRP, and green local policies

2.3.1 Sustainable urban mobility and energy transition as key vectors for the transformation of European cities towards sustainability: The approach and use of new legal instruments

2.3.1.1 Motor vehicle restrictions

A noteworthy shift in the application of traditional legal instruments for environmental intervention and the enhancement of urban mobility sustainability lies in the recent acknowledgment that the Air Quality Directive's thresholds, or the corresponding national regulations adopted by Member States, can serve as a foundation for local councils to implement vehicle circulation restrictions extending beyond typical traffic regulations in cities. This marks a significant departure from the previous regime, as certain additional restrictions, especially if they entailed restrictions or effective limitations on the use of goods – in this case, certain types of vehicles – which in principle are consumer goods that can be bought and sold freely because they are within the margins set by national and international technical standards, were traditionally considered problematic and an issue that went beyond local competences for the regulation of traffic – and which went beyond possible restrictions on the freedom of movement of vehicles.

Indeed, concerns about potential constraints on the free movement of goods and the impact on competition, especially as restrictions intensified, cast doubt on the approval of regulations with such effects.[28] Nevertheless, the surge in environmental consciousness, coupled with the recurring breach of air quality thresholds in numerous European cities outlined in the European Directive

27 On the New Urban Agenda and its effects on the Law of the City, Juli Ponce Solé, 'El derecho a la ciudad, Gobernanza y la Nueva Agenda Urbana', in Ponce Solé, Migliari, Capdeferro (coords), *El derecho, la ciudad y la vivienda en la nueva concepción del desarrollo urbano. Desafíos transnacionales y transdisciplinarios de la gobernanza en la Nueva Agenda Urbana* (Atelier 2019).

28 In particular, the Commission defined in its Regulation 2016/646 emission limits for nitrogen oxides not to be exceeded during new real-world driving tests, supposedly much more stringent than the previous ones. But these limits were themselves less stringent than more advanced environmental standards such as the 2007 Euro 6 vehicle emission standard. It was therefore questionable whether local authorities should uncritically accept not being able to set limits under the more demanding standard.

on air quality, has paved the way for the explicit permissibility of restrictions affecting specific types of vehicles – notably, the most polluting ones before and with greater intensity than the others, in order to overcome a very basic analysis of proportionality.[29] These restrictions have been deemed acceptable provided (1) they don't extend to the entire metropolitan or regional area, rendering a consumer good practically obsolete within established technical standards; (2) the temporary nature of the measures, or (3) they respond to a need sufficiently supported by the aforementioned criteria of proportionality – which in addition to this internal coherence in the regulation must take into account the need for the measure, whether or not derived from the actual levels of pollution and emissions.

Highly relevant to this issue is the judgment of the Court of Justice of the European Union in the *Ville de Paris & Ville de Bruxelles & Madrid* case.[30] Even in the face of objections from the European Commission itself regarding the imposition of limits by these cities on vehicles that conformed to European technical standards within emissions limits, the Court determined that such restrictions, as long as they are proportional and necessary, fall within the purview of local authorities and must be decided by them. This decision unequivocally signals a direct expansion of local regulatory authority that extends beyond the mere management of road traffic in cities since, although using this instrument, the aim is not to establish more orderly or fluid traffic conditions but to pursue another public interest, the reduction of pollution and emissions, which in a classic understanding would have depended on the competence title in the matter of emissions – as, after all, the Commission's approach was intended to do.

Similarly, the Belgian Constitutional Court has explicitly affirmed that such local regulatory initiatives do not impede the free movement of goods, establishing their perfect compatibility with European and constitutional rules governing the free market.[31]

29 For an example of a study on the operation of proportionality analysis in these matters (albeit in relation to the conflict with freedom of movement), see Sánchez Sáez (n 27) 133–155.

30 The Court of Justice of the European Union, in its Judgment of 13 December 2018, joined cases T-339/16, *City of Paris v Commission*, T-352/16, *City of Brussels v Commission*, and T-391/16, *City of Madrid v Commission*, upholds these municipalities on the grounds that the Commission could not modify the emission thresholds already established in the Euro 5 and Euro 6 standards with the practical effect of increasing the permitted margins and that the municipalities of the cities concerned were therefore not obliged to comply with the new standard set by the Commission in their traffic rules and the restrictions they had introduced for the circulation of certain types of vehicles. Environmental, jurisdictional, and legal certainty considerations are intertwined in an analysis that ends up significantly expanding the capacity of municipalities to establish effective restrictions on the use of certain types of vehicles.

31 Thus, the Brussels Low Emission Zone has recently been endorsed by the Belgian Constitutional Court in a decision of 28 February 2019 (*Arrêt 37/2019 de la Cour constitutionnelle de Belgique*).

With heightened legal standards and propelled by citizen and judicial activism, some European Union countries now perceive local authorities' adoption of such policies not merely as a legal possibility within the scope of their powers but as actual legal obligations. Consequently, these are viewed as planning obligations for urban green infrastructure. Notably, the European Commission has previously initiated infringement proceedings against multiple Member States for failing to implement public policies at all levels, including regional and local levels, to ensure compliance with the provisions of the Air Quality Directive. These actions suggest that the broad discretion now afforded to local authorities is not just optional; in specific circumstances – particularly when there is a persistent breach of the maximum air quality thresholds – it is considered mandatory.[32]

Based on these actions, it can be contended that the broad discretion granted to local authorities is not only optional but, in specific circumstances – particularly in instances of repeated breaches of maximum air quality thresholds – it becomes mandatory. The juridification of these obligations has substantial implications for the formulation and approval of Green Urban Planning instruments. More recently, the approval of European recovery and resilience funds and the introduction of conditionality measures have further reinforced these obligations in many cases. This reinforcement is achieved by linking fund disbursement to the establishment of urban low emission zones and equivalent measures. As a result, air quality linked to vehicle traffic in cities and measures related to sustainable urban mobility have become integral components of any successful urban green planning.

2.3.1.2 Environmental taxation and urban tolls

Another possibility for local intervention facilitating the advancement of urban public policies geared towards enhancing sustainable urban mobility lies in the implementation of fiscal incentives for green mobility and exploring the feasibility of taxation models that integrate environmental considerations into their structure. By incentivizing and aligning financial structures with environmentally conscious mobility choices, cities can actively promote and contribute to

32 The European Commission, on the basis of the Air Quality Directive (Directive 2008/50/EC) and its specific thresholds and limits (which, although varying and adapting, have traditionally been set out in Annexes I to XI), has taken action against several member states in recent years on these issues (Germany, France, Hungary, Italy, the United Kingdom, and Romania) on the grounds that their national, regional and local regulations were not achieving a situation in line with the limits set. More recently, action has also been taken against Spain following recent changes and amendments to previous plans to reduce air pollution in cities such as Madrid. See in this respect Jaime Doreste, 'A la Comisión Europea se la ha acabado la paciencia con España' (2019), *Agenda Pública*, http://agendapublica.elpais.com/a-la-comision-europea-se-le-ha-acabado-la-paciencia-con-espana/.

the broader goals of sustainable urban development,[33] thus enshrining Pigou's theories related to how some social problems caused by certain negative externalities could be solved in this way.[34] Due to the importance of these externalities in environmental issues, this instrument is of great use in this field and green urban planning; therefore, it is not surprising that its use has become widespread in recent decades.[35]

Beyond mere legal considerations, which have alleviated traditional reluctance towards tax measures due to their strict adherence to the principle of economic capacity – a customary condition for the constitutionality of tax measures in European countries – the impetus for this shift is notably associated with the acknowledged efficacy of Pigouvian taxes. Interestingly, these policies often fall within the purview of local authorities, affording them a greater degree of flexibility than would be otherwise attainable. This latitude empowers local authorities with increased maneuverability in the implementation of such measures, aligning with a broader recognition of the benefits and adaptability that localized governance can bring to environmental and economic concerns.[36] Pigouvian logic, together with a whole series of tax exemptions or incentives that depend on state and regional regulations – reductions in road tax, especially – is also being clearly imposed in the establishment of public prices – reductions and even free use of public roads for certain vehicles that are otherwise subject to the payment of a public price, especially regulated parking – generally with good results. Hence, it emerges as a compelling tool within the purview of municipalities, presenting an interesting lever for action at the local level. Consequently, it should be an integral component of the array of measures considered within the green plans of cities. These measures can range from those with less ambition, such as tax rebates and incentives, to those with greater ambition, including the establishment of planning and management measures for all motor vehicle traffic in urban environments, subject to criteria of economic efficiency and environmental protection. This diverse spectrum allows municipalities to tailor their approaches based on the specific needs and aspirations of their communities, contributing to the multifaceted objectives of sustainable urban development.

33 Iñaki Bilbao Estrada, 'Transporte colaborativo, medioambiente y beneficios fiscales: especial referencia al ordenamiento jurídico español', in Boix Palop, De la Encarnación, Doménech Pascual (eds), *La regulación del transporte colaborativo* (Aranzadi Thomson Reuters 2017).

34 Christopher R. Knittel and Ryan Sandler, 'The welfare impact of indirect pigouvian taxation: Evidence from transportation' (2013) 18849 *National Bureau of Economic Research Working Paper Series*, 20; Jonathan S. Masur and Eric A. Posner, 'Towards a pigouvian state' (2015) 164 *University of Pennsylvania Law Review*.

35 Roxana J. Javid and Ali Nejat, Katharine Hayhoe, 'Selection of CO2 mitigation strategies for road transportation in the United States using multi-criteria approach' (2014) 38 *Renewable and Sustainable Energy Reviews*, 960.

36 Cubero Marcos (n 26) 77–83.

Indeed, a particularly advanced manifestation of this green planning model, already implemented in several European cities on a large scale – and on a small scale or in trials in many other cities around the world[37] – concerns urban tolls. The first and most important experience to date, and therefore the best known, that of the London city center, has been operational for two decades.[38] It is noteworthy that this model combines certain legal elements, which might pose challenges in implementation because of the need of a particular previous legal framework. For instance, in the case of London and other European countries, a prerequisite was the enactment of a prior law thus enabling the city of London to establish and manage the model. Despite these legal complexities, the London experience provides valuable insights into the outcomes and possibilities of ambitious local policies on urban mobility, serving as a case in point. In comparison to the initial objectives of the model, which aimed not only to restrict traffic in central London but also to generate funds for improving public transport, the outcomes in London reveal a noteworthy discrepancy. The reduction in traffic within the city center surpassed initial expectations, largely due to the prevalence of vehicles exempt from tolls. Consequently, the funds raised by the toll were less than anticipated. This discrepancy highlights the dynamic and nuanced nature of implementing such models and underscores the importance of continual assessment and adaptation in urban planning and mobility strategies.[39]

In summary, it appears that urban tolls of this nature, as demonstrated by the successive expansions of the perimeter in London and the model's extension to other cities, prove highly effective in reducing traffic in city centers. However, their primary impact may be rather on traffic reduction than achieving the projected significant increase in funding for public transport. This latter objective may need to be pursued through alternative revenue sources, primarily a combination of fares – although some regions, like Luxembourg and certain cities, are successfully experimenting with fare abolition to promote use and

37 Cities such as Stockholm, Milan, Hong Kong, and Singapore, as well as New York, San Francisco, and especially Beijing, in addition to London, have all had experiences in this sense. See Andrés Boix Palop, 'Los desafíos internacionales de la regulación de la movilidad urbana y la Nueva Agenda urbana', in Fortes Martín (dir), *Movilidad urbana sostenible y acción administrativa* (Thomson Reuters Aranzadi 2019).

38 Introduced definitively in 2003, following the passing of the Greater London Authority Act 1999 and the Greater London Congestion Charging Order of 2001, it is the best-known and most studied experience. On its effects, Michael Fehling, 'Movilidad sostenible en áreas urbanas: conceptos e instrumentos', in Boix Palop and Marzal Raga (eds), *Ciudad y movilidad. La regulación de la movilidad urbana sostenible* (PUV 2014); Stephen Glaister and Daniel J. Graham, 'Pricing our roads: Vision and reality' (2005) 59 *IEA Research Monograph*.

39 In addition to the effects already studied for London, the conclusions seem to be similar for Beijing: Jun Yang, Avralt-Od Purevjav, and Shanjun Li, 'The marginal cost of traffic congestion and road pricing: Evidence from a natural experiment in Beijing' (2020) 12 *American Economic Journal: Economic Policy*, 418.

address climate change[40] – and, increasingly, direct contributions from public budgets. This recognition emphasizes the multifaceted and evolving nature of urban planning strategies and the need for a comprehensive approach to address the challenges of sustainable urban mobility.

2.3.1.3 Other traditional instruments

In the design of urban mobility policies and sustainable green planning at the local level, both the management of public transport services and the planning and distribution of urban space to prioritize the various modes of mobility are becoming increasingly important. In relation to both vectors, the current guidelines for the fight against pollution and climate change must lead us to a more decisive commitment to public transport – initiatives such as free public transport are, in fact, aligned seamlessly with this imperative – and to a distribution of public space consistent with this idea, both guidelines being fully compatible with the principles established by the New Urban Agenda and its commitment to a more socially inclusive mobility model that promotes public transport, on foot or by human-powered means rather than private vehicles.[41] This entails very relevant changes in terms of the most efficient and socially and environmentally sustainable designs, so that local authorities must organize their uses in a coherent and compatible way with the aforementioned purposes and, obviously, include all these considerations and a specific decision and management in this regard in their urban green planning.

2.3.2 The realignment of urban planning tools to attain and enhance environmental sustainability goals

2.3.2.1 The extension of supra-municipal land use planning

The evolution of spatial policies in the EU has been shaped by three pivotal factors. Firstly, the recognition, dating back to the Treaty of Rome, of the imperative to foster the harmonious development of the European Community, particularly in response to urban challenges arising from deindustrialization

40 Since 1 March 2020, public transport in Luxembourg City is free of charge. See the explanation on the official website of the city of Luxembourg: https://www.vdl.lu/en/news/introduction-free-public-transport-luxembourg-1-march-2020.

41 The considerations contained in the current international framework for sustainable urban mobility are radically contrary to the idea underlying many Spanish legislations that the work of public authorities should be limited to establishing a "neutral" legal regime between the various possible forms of urban mobility so that citizens can choose the one they prefer. On the contrary, certain forms of urban mobility should be enhanced and benefit from a differential legal framework and public investment in their favor. In this sense, Andrés Boix Palop, 'La Ley Valenciana de Movilidad de 2011 y algunas experiencias y ejemplos de su aplicación', in Boix Palop and Marzal Raga (eds), *Ciudad y movilidad. La regulación de la movilidad urbana sostenible* (PUV 2014).

and globalization. Despite the inherently supra-local nature of these challenges, cities, experiencing signs of decline, proactively engaged in their control and resolution. Secondly, successive enlargements of the Union revealed numerous territorial imbalances, emphasizing the necessity to establish mechanisms for equalizing European economies. Many times, this was accomplished through programs specifically targeting cities. Lastly, the elevation of environmental concerns as an integral element in European territorial development, marked by the full assumption and exercise of environmental competencies, a domain initially lacking in the EU's purview. These circumstances have prompted both the EU and its Member States to recognize the importance of giving special attention to the spatial dimension, even at the supranational level.

As a result of the extension of European territorial policies and, above all, of the various agreements and agendas adopted within the Council of the EU, there has been a deepening of territorial (supra-municipal) planning, especially in countries with an urban planning tradition, such as Italy and Spain.[42] This type of planning is a characteristic feature of countries with a Germanic and Nordic tradition, but not of models based on a "hard law" urban planning tradition, which depend heavily on legal provisions materialized through local urban planning figures. Together with intergovernmental commitments, these instruments have helped to develop and introduce urban policies in many Member States where such frameworks were previously absent. Simultaneously, they have fostered a convergence of spatial planning systems across Member States.[43] In this sense, an increasing number of countries have developed an integrated national urban policy, often referred to as the urban agenda, modeled after the European paradigm. This convergence has been facilitated in part by common features shared among existing urban planning systems within the EU (i.e., the distribution of power between the different

42 European Commission 'The EU compendium of spatial planning systems and policies' (Publications Office 1997), and ESPON Project, *Governance of Territorial and Urban Policies From EU to Local Level. THIRD INTERIM REPORT* (2006) https://www.espon.eu/sites/default/files/attachments/3.ir_2.3.2_final.pdf.

43 The conjunction of these circumstances and the development of these principles has determined what is known as the Europeanisation of planning or territory. Europeanisation has been defined as those processes of (1) construction, (2) diffusion, and (3) institutionalisation of formal and informal rules, procedures, policy paradigms, styles, "ways of doing", and shared beliefs and norms that are first defined and consolidated in EU decision-making and then incorporated into the logic of internal discourse, identities, political structures, and public policies. Claudio M. Radaelli, 'The Europeanization of public policy', in Featherstone, Radaelli (eds), *The Politics of Europeanization* (Oxford University Press 2013); Lora-Tamayo Vallvé, (n 5); Erich Dallhammer, Roland Gaugitsch, Wolfgang Neugebauer and Kai Böhme, 'Spatial planning and governance within EU policies and legislation and their relevance to the New Urban Agenda' (Publications Office of the European Union 2018), and David Evers and Joost Tennekes, *The Europeanisation of Spatial Planning in the Netherlands* (PBL Netherlands Environmental Assessment Agency 2016).

levels of government in urban planning regulations), enabling coordination and the adoption of shared proposals.

2.3.2.2 *The incorporation of the sustainable development paradigm in urban planning*

Furthermore, the influence of the sustainable development paradigm has underscored the imperative nature of addressing the climate crisis and conserving natural resources, particularly in the domain of cities and urban planning. Within the urban sphere, the intricacies and significance of the relationship between urban planning and the environment take center stage. This not only involves the critical necessity of curtailing the consumption of scarce natural resources but also arises from the anticipation of an increase in climate disasters and extreme weather events. Consequently, it becomes paramount to devise urban planning instruments that bolster the city's resilience, ensuring its capacity to adapt to and recover from a spectrum of situations, disasters, or incidents expected to unfold over time.[44]

In this context, anchored in the principle of sustainable urban development, particularly drawing from the international domain, the formulation and execution of strategies have been actively pursued. These strategies encompass a spectrum of measures, including the prioritization of judicious land and resource utilization in urban and territorial planning, the effective administration of public services, rehabilitation and regeneration of structures, and the integration of green planning. Facilitated by engagement in international networks of sustainable cities, these endeavors foster the exchange of experiences, contributing to a collective and globally informed approach.[45] However, while these strategies have reinforced the importance of taking into account environmental issues and the effects of climate change and environmental degradation in urban planning, it has been noted that the driving effect of the principle of sustainability (and more recently, the term "green infrastructure")[46] has been to reduce the environmental impact of urban planning in the articulation of these strategies and has ended up being used, sometimes, as a mantra.[47]

44 Judith Gifreu i Font, 'Ciudades adaptativas y resilientes ante el cambio climático: estrategias locales para contribuir a la sostenibilidad urbana' (2018) 52 *Revista Aragonesa de Administración Pública*, 102; Peiwen Lu and Dominic Stead, 'Understanding the notion of resilience in spatial planning: A case study of Rotterdam, The Netherlands' (2013) 35 *Cities* 200.

45 Ramírez Sánchez (n 4); Walter Musakwa and Adriaan Van Niekerk, 'Implications of land use change for the sustainability of urban areas: A case study of Stellenbosch, South Africa' (2013) 32 *Cities*, 143.

46 Stephan Pauleit et. al., *Advancing urban green infrastructure in Europe: Outcomes and reflections from the GREEN SURGE project* (2019) 40 *Urban Forestry & Urban Greening*, 4; Slätmo, Nilsson, Turunen (n 10).

47 Judith Gifreu i Font, 'Las actuaciones sobre el medio urbano como nueva frontera de las políticas públicas al servicio de la sostenibilidad territorial y urbanística', in García Rubio, Camp i Batalla, Vandelli, (coords), *Las nuevas perspectivas de la ordenación urbanística y del*

Hence, there is an imperative to encourage a paradigm shift across all echelons, recognizing that the climate emergency situation necessitates citizens and stakeholders engaged in city planning and management to intensify and radicalize their approaches and expectations. This entails conditioning urban developments on their ecological viability, thereby subordinating human activities and economic growth to the availability of resources. This approach mandates a conscientious evaluation of the environmental impact of these activities on the territory, materializing such considerations in urban plans. Central to this shift is the objective of minimizing the consumption of undeveloped land within the city, thereby promoting sustainable and ecologically responsible urban expansion,[48] but also the establishment of criteria that promote biodiversity and improve the quality of the soil in all types of infrastructures and spaces in the city.

It is also necessary to incorporate measures in urban planning that have a reducing effect on the consumption of fossil fuels and atmospheric pollution (regulations that de facto prevent the carrying out of certain particularly polluting activities or those with a negative impact on the environment, that reduce and eliminate mono-functional spaces and areas, in which the land is totally sealed off or oriented towards private vehicles). This means, for example, promoting and extending more accessible and walkable city models, in which the various uses and needs are closer together, such as the 15-minute city.[49] Moreover, there is a need to integrate the stipulation that land use regulation must be responsive to the imperatives of compactness, space reuse, enhanced mobility, and inclusivity through a blend of spatial and temporal functions, promoting multifunctionality and intensification of use, while accounting for

paisaje, smart cities y rehabilitación: una perspectiva hispano-italiana (Fundación Democracia y Gobierno Local 2017), 87.

48 Through solutions such as brownfield redevelopment, urban reconversion, or densification practices, as pointed out by Tomas Hartmann and Jean-David Gerber in 'Land, scarcity, and property rights', in Hartmann, Gerber, Hengstermann, (eds), *Instruments of Land Policy: Dealing with Scarcity of Land* (Taylor & Francis 2018). In this sense, the development of mechanisms such as that provided for by French law concerning the principle of zero net artificialization of soil, which requires that any artificialization of soil must be compensated by a corresponding de-artificialization of soil, provided for in art. 69 of the Loi n 2016–1087, pour la reconquête de la biodiversité, de la nature et des paysages, that Camille Mialot, *La ville au changement climatique: Nouveaux instruments juridiques* (Berger Levrault 2020), analyzes.

49 The 15-minute city is based on the concept of "chronourbanism", which states that the quality of urban life is inversely proportional to the amount of time spent on transport. This concept advocates an urban configuration where citizens can access all their basic needs in distances of no more than 15 minutes on foot or by bicycle, and for the repairing of urban and social fragments by restructuring the urban built landscape to ensure that it complies with components such as proximity, diversity, density and ubiquity. In this regard, Carlos Moreno, et. al., 'Introducing the "15-Minute City": Sustainability, Resilience and Place Identity in Future Post-Pandemic Cities' (2021) 4(1) *Smart Cities*, 93.

temporal variations.[50] In this sense, strategies such as temporary or adaptive urban uses and regulations must be incorporated, which adapt and change to the risks posed by the environment.

Ultimately, urban planning instruments must be reoriented to incorporate environmental sustainability objectives in a more effective way. Urban planning is an essential tool for ensuring the long-term well-being of our communities, and can play a transformative role in shaping the places we live in and the quality of life of our societies, enabling efficient use of resources and infrastructure, with multiple benefits for society, the environment, and the economy.

2.4 Conclusion

As we have tried to show in these reflections, a number of very positive regulatory and policy initiatives can be detected in the last years in the fields of environmental, territorial and urban planning, sustainable urban mobility, and energy transition. All of them, theoretically, have been reinforced by the creation of the Next Generation EU fund as a revulsive instrument for the recovery of the Member States' economies from the coronavirus pandemic, and whose priority objective is to build a greener, more digital, and resilient future for all European citizens.

However, the current implementation of recovery and resilience plans funded by this initiative reveals a contrary trend. Post-pandemic, there has been a promotion of models prioritizing economic and urban development to swiftly revitalize the local economy. Regrettably, in many instances, these models overlook the advancements discussed earlier. This observed trend, noticeable in various countries,[51] entails an acceleration of inappropriate and unsustainable development. In numerous cases, there is a revival of urban transformation plans that were previously discarded or deactivated years before the onset of the pandemic. Consequently, the impetus behind numerous projects in different states needs reconsideration to prevent regression in urban development policies. It is imperative to avoid giving unequivocal priority to recovery and economic development, and instead, reclaim previous approaches rooted in respect for biodiversity, nature, and the environment.

The so-called "collaborative economy" and, especially, the technological progress that has led to the irruption in practically all goods and services markets of highly efficient digital platforms and services when it comes to bringing supply and demand into contact, as is inevitable, have also had an

50 Eric Hoppenbrouwer and Erik Louw, 'Mixed-use development: Theory and practice in Amsterdam's Eastern Docklands' (2005) 13(7) *European Planning Studies*, 967, give the example that a school can be used as a community center in the evening and a theater can be used for lectures during the day and as a cinema in the evening. Mixed land use tends to increase the kinds of combinations and interactions that also sustain urban vitality and quality.

51 Lafortezza, Davies (n 14).

impact in better brokerage models on mobility markets and must therefore be taken into account in the necessary urban planning schemes which are to be developed by European local powers duly coordinated with the recovery and resilience plans. If we take into account that, for a number of reasons, and in more or less restrictive variants, traditional regulation across Europe reserved urban transport to public authorities, preventing or significantly restricting the private provision of such services on a free market basis, it is easy to understand the major legal disruption brought about by the emergence, initially outside Europe, of delivery models such as Uber or similar.[52] A forthcoming urban strategy for sustainable urban mobility regulation, led by cities, should empower them to make decisions on these intricate issues. To achieve this, there is a need to integrate these considerations into a comprehensive and cohesive design, harmonizing them with other aspects of urban mobility planning, such as the utilization of public space and the pivotal influence of public transport systems. This integration should also account for the interplay between public regulation and supply while managing the contributions from private providers.[53]

Bibliography

Baycan-Levent T. and Nijkamp P., 'Planning and management of urban green spaces in Europe: Comparative analysis' (2009) 135 *Journal of Urban Planning and Development*.

Bilbao Estrada I., 'Transporte colaborativo, medioambiente y beneficios fiscales: especial referencia al ordenamiento jurídico español', in Boix Palop, De la Encarnación and Doménech Pascual (eds), *La regulación del transporte colaborativo* (Aranzadi Thomson Reuters 2017).

Boix Palop A., 'La Ley Valenciana de Movilidad de 2011 y algunas experiencias y ejemplos de su aplicación', in Boix Palop and Marzal Raga (eds), *Ciudad y movilidad. La regulación de la movilidad urbana sostenible* (PUV 2014).

Boix Palop A., 'Los desafíos internacionales de la regulación de la movilidad urbana y la Nueva Agenda urbana', in Fortes Martín (dir), *Movilidad urbana sostenible y acción administrativa* (Thomson Reuters Aranzadi 2019).

Boix Palop A., 'The challenges of urban mobility regulation and the new urban agenda', in Davidson, Tewari (ed), *Law and the New Urban Agenda* (Routledge 2020).

Chatzimentor A., Apostolopoulou E., and D. Mazaris A., 'A review of green infrastructure research in Europe: Challenges and opportunities' (2020) 198 *Landscape and Urban Planning*.

Cubero Marcos J. I., 'Títulos habilitantes y normas de procedimiento', in Cubero Marcos and Lasagabaster Herrarte (dirs), *Espacio público y ordenanzas locales: estudio sobre su régimen jurídico* (IVAP 2019).

52 Rozen Noguellou and David Renders (eds), *Uber & Taxis. Comparative Law Studies* (Bruylant 2018).

53 Andrés Boix Palop, 'The challenges of Urban Mobility Regulation and the New Urban Agenda', in Davidson, Tewari, *Law and the New Urban Agenda* (Routledge 2020).

Dallhammer E., Gaugitsch R., Neugebauer W. and Böhme K., *Spatial Planning and Governance within EU Policies and Legislation and Their Relevance to the New Urban Agenda* (Publications Office of the European Union 2018).

Davies C. and Lafortezza R., 'Urban green infrastructure in Europe: Is greenspace planning and policy compliant?' (2017) 69 *Land Use Policy*, 93.

Doreste J., 'A la Comisión Europea se la ha acabado la paciencia con España' (2019) Agenda Pública, http://agendapublica.elpais.com/a-la-comision-europea-se-le-ha-acabado-la-paciencia-con-espana/.

ESPON Project, *Governance of Territorial and Urban Policies from EU to Local Level. Third Interim Report* (2006) https://www.espon.eu/sites/default/files/attachments/3.ir_2.3.2_final.pdf.

European Commission, 'Evaluating the Impact of Nature-Based Solutions: a Handbook for Pratitioners (Publications Office of the European Union 2021), https://op.europa.eu/en/publication-detail/-/publication/d7d496b5-ad4e-11eb-9767-01aa75ed71a1.

European Commission, 'The EU compendium of spatial planning systems and policies' (Publications Office 1997).

Evers D. and Tennekes J., *The Europeanisation of Spatial Planning in the Netherlands* (PBL Netherlands Environmental Assessment Agency 2016).

Fehling M., 'Movilidad sostenible en áreas urbanas: conceptos e instrumentos', in Boix Palop, Marzal Raga (eds), *Ciudad y movilidad. La regulación de la movilidad urbana sostenible* (PUV 2014).

Finck M., *Subnational Authorities in EU Law* (Oxford University Press 2017).

Gifreu i Font J., 'Ciudades adaptativas y resilientes ante el cambio climático: estrategias locales para contribuir a la sostenibilidad urbana' (2018) 52 *Revista Aragonesa de Administración Pública*, 102.

Gifreu i Font J., 'Las actuaciones sobre el medio urbano como nueva frontera de las políticas públicas al servicio de la sostenibilidad territorial y urbanística', in García Rubio, Camp i Batalla, Vandelli, (coords), *Las nuevas perspectivas de la ordenación urbanística y del paisaje, smart cities y rehabilitación: una perspectiva hispano-italiana* (Fundación Democracia y Gobierno Local 2017), 87.

Glaister S. and Graham D.J., 'Pricing our roads: Vision and reality' (2005) 59 *IEA Research Monograph*.

González Sanfiel A.M., *El principio de no regresión en el Derecho público* (Aranzadi 2022).

Grădinaru S.R. and Hersperger A.M., 'Green infrastructure in strategic spatial plans: Evidence from European urban regions' (2019) 40 *Urban Forestry & Urban Greening*, 17.

Guillén López E., 'El Derecho de la movilidad sostenible en España', in Boix Palop and Marzal Raga (eds), *Ciudad y movilidad. La regulación de la movilidad urbana sostenible* (PUV 2014).

Hartmann T. and Gerber J.-D., 'Land, scarcity, and property rights', in Hartmann, Gerber and Hengstermann, (eds), *Instruments of Land Policy: Dealing with Scarcity of Land* (Taylor & Francis 2018),

Hoppenbrouwer E. and Louw E., 'Mixed-use development: Theory and practice in Amsterdam's Eastern Docklands' (2005) 13(7) *European Planning Studies*, 967.

Javid R. J., Nejat A. and Hayhoe K., 'Selection of CO_2 mitigation strategies for road transportation in the United States using multi-criteria approach' (2014) 38 *Renewable and Sustainable Energy Reviews*, 960.

Knittel C. R. and Sandler R., 'The welfare impact of indirect pigouvian taxation: Evidence from Transportation' (2013) 18849 *National Bureau of Economic Research Working Paper Series*, 20.
Lafortezza R. and Davies C., 'Pandemic urban development is leading us away from nature' (2023) 217 *Environmental Research*, 114858.
López Ramón F., 'La construcción del ordenamiento ambiental español' (2018) 46 *Cuadernos de Derecho Local*, 14.
Lora-Tamayo Vallvé M., *The Europeanisation of Planning Law. The European – Land Use – Silent Revolution* (Thomson Reuters Aranzadi 2017).
Lu P. and Stead D., 'Understanding the notion of resilience in spatial planning: A case study of Rotterdam, The Netherlands' (2013) 35 *Cities* 200.
Massini P. and Smith H., 'Planning for green infraestructre – The green infrastructure factor and learning from Europe' (2018) *PERFECT Expert Paper*.
Masur J.S. and Posner E.A., 'Towards a Pigouvian State' (2015) 164 *University of Pennsylvania Law Review*.
Mialot C., *La ville au changement climatique: Nouveaux instruments juridiques* (Berger Levrault 2020).
Moreno C., et. al., 'Introducing the "15-minute city": Sustainability, resilience and place identity in future post-pandemic cities' (2021) 4(1) *Smart Cities*, 93.
Musakwa W. and Niekerk A., 'Implications of land use change for the sustainability of urban areas: A case study of Stellenbosch, South Africa' (2013) 32 *Cities*, 143.
Nogueira López A., 'La transposición de directivas ambientales en el Estado autonómico', in Arzoz Santisteban (dir), *Transposición de directivas y autogobierno. El desarrollo normativo del Derecho de la Unión Europea en el Estado autonómico* (Institut d'Estudis Autonòmics 2013).
Noguellou R. and Renders D., (eds), *Uber & Taxis. Comparative Law Studies* (Bruylant 2018).
Pauleit S., et. al., Advancing urban green infrastructure in Europe: Outcomes and reflections from the GREEN SURGE project (2019) 40 *Urban Forestry & Urban Greening*, 4.
Pavani G., 'From smart to sharing? Presente e futuro delle città (al di là delle etichette)' (2019) XL(4) *Le Instituzioni del Federalismo*, 849.
Ponce Solé J., 'Derecho urbanístico y prevención y mitigación de desastres: la perspectiva española en el marco de la Unión Europea' (2013) 285 *Revista de Derecho Urbanístico y Medio Ambiente*, 3.
Ponce Solé J., 'El derecho a la ciudad, Gobernanza y la Nueva Agenda Urbana', in Ponce Solé, Migliari and Capdeferro (coords), *El derecho, la ciudad y la vivienda en la nueva concepción del desarrollo urbano. Desafíos transnacionales y transdisciplinarios de la gobernanza en la Nueva Agenda Urbana* (Atelier 2019).
Radaelli Claudio M., 'The Europeanization of public policy', in Featherstone and Radaelli (eds), *The Politics of Europeanization* (Oxford University Press 2013).
Ramírez Sánchez J. M., *Urbanismo para una nueva ciudad. El principio de desarrollo urbano sostenible* (Aranzadi 2021).
Rutt R. L. and Gulsrud N. M., 'Green justice in the city: A new agenda for urban green space research in Europe' (2016) 19 *Urban Forestry & Urban Greening*, 123.
Sánchez Sáez A.J., *Las restricciones de tráfico en las ciudades por motivos ambientales y su afección a la libertad de circulación* (Comares 2019).
Slätmo E., Nilsson K. and Turunen E., 'Implementing green infrastructure in spatial planning in Europe' (2019) 8(4) *Land 62*.

Tjallingii S., 'Green and red: Enemies or allies? The Utrecht experience with green structure planning' (2003) 29(2) *Built Environment (1978-)* 107.
Uriarte Ricorte M., 'Planificar la infraestructura verde urbana' (2014) 99–100 *Revista Vasca de Administración Pública* 2873.
Van der Jagt A., Tozer L., Toxopeus H. and Runhaar H., 'Policy mixes for mainstreaming urban nature-based solutions: An analysis of six European countries and the European Union' (2023) 139 *Environmental Science & Policy* 51.
Wilk B. and Vetter A., Schröder A., 'Tackling the climate and biodiversity crises in Europe through urban greening plans. recommendations for avoiding the implementation gap' (2021) *Scientific Opinion Paper German Environment Agency.*
Yang J., Purevjav A-O. and Li S., 'The marginal cost of traffic congestion and road pricing: Evidence from a natural experiment in Beijing' (2020) 12 *American Economic Journal: Economic Policy*, 418.

Part II

Right to the city and NRRPs

1 The path towards green and inclusive cities

Points of reference on the case of France

Jean-Bernard Auby and Camille Mialot

1.1 Introduction

(Jean-Bernard Auby and Camille Mialot)

The mission I was assigned in the Bologne meeting was a bit tricky, since it required putting together the right to the city, the law on cities, the green city, the solidarity city, the French *Plan National de relance et de resilience* (PNRR) and above all these, the French point of view. I endeavoured to mix all this together and what came up are the following comments, which, I hope, will bring some kind of input into the excellent SHINE project.

The approach I propose is to touch upon three general issues (§ 2): 1) the consequences of the recent crises on the city and the law on cities, with a specific orientation towards the case of France; 2) the prospects for a revival of green and solidarity cities, in particular under the effect of the PNRR, again focussing on French cities; and 3) the right to the city and solidarity cities in French law, discussing the current situation and perspectives. And then, to focus on a specific ongoing process: the moving from climate strategies at the state level to cities' urban climate action (§ 3).

1.2 The path towards green and inclusive cities: General comments on the French case

(Jean-Bernard Auby)

1.2.1 Consequences of the crises on cities, in brief

What crises? The one we have mainly on our mind is the coronavirus one, which had very strong consequences on the functioning of cities and their law. But, before that, there was the economic crisis of 2008,[1] which also affected the administrative and legal functioning of cities. It is also important not to

1 Jean-Bernard Auby, 'Le droit administratif et la crise' (2014) 1 *Droit administratif* 1.

DOI: 10.4324/9781032665184-6

neglect the potential and current crises linked with climate change, even if, for now in our countries, these are still latent crises, or micro-crises – for example, tensions created by the receding coastline in coastal cities – specially, in the expectation of big climate crises that have must be feared in the future.

Beyond the images of deserted cities, Covid had strong consequences, obviously, on local economies and on local public finances. In fact, this negative evolution had started before, with the 2008 financial crisis, but the health crisis accentuated it.

There were also consequences on planning: among other issues, renewed debates emerged in the aftermath of the pandemic on the advantages and disadvantages of urban density, as well as how to adapt planning to the evolution of remote working, which imposes urban transformations concerning the relationship between workplaces and homes.

There were consequences on mobility, including those related to the growth of Uber-type services, green transport, car sharing, and new ways of conceiving mobility in cities. The need for an adaptation of urban policies to these new needs led, for example, in France in 2021, to the issuing of a new statute on mobility which significantly innovated in the organisation of local public transport.

In general, the crisis and especially the health crisis created new dynamics in the dialectical management of public and private spaces: the border between what is private and what is public were altered in relation with containment, with both practical and legal relevance.

Significant consequences could also be observed in the relations between cities and other levels of government.[2] Typically, in France, the Covid crisis led to strong tensions between state and local governments, especially in cities. These tensions were in the first instance financial and about determining who should bear the burden of public finance problems. Actually, these tensions were already present pre-Covid, but Covid made everything more complex in the relations between municipalities, and more generally local authorities and the state.

There were also tensions between the state and local governments regarding measures more closely related to the pandemic emergency, such as who had the authority to adopt police measures, limits on movement and containment, or who had authority over hospitals and the healthcare system. All this was problematic in France. On police measures, the state decided to assume most of the decision making, asking local authorities not to intervene.[3] In a few cases, local authorities tried to defend their powers in courts, but this

2 Jean-Luc de Boissieu (et al.), 'Les collectivités territoriales face à la crise' (2021) *Semaine Juridique, édition Administration et Collectivités Territoriales – GRALE, Droit et Gestion des Collectivités Territoriales, L'administration locale face à la crise sanitaire, Le Moniteur*.

3 Pierre Villeneuve, 'Le retour de l'État d'urgence' (2020) *Semaine Juridique édition Administrations et Collectivités Territoriales*.

litigation was generally resolved in favour of the state.[4] In relation to hospitals, in the past, large competences were attributed to local authorities, whereas since Covid, the healthcare system is now entirely in the hands of the state.

There have been tensions in the management of local urban life; for example, the management of local public procurement has become somewhat chaotic, some public contracts having become impossible to perform by either the administration or private parties, or both.

Finally, social assistance systems at the local level had to react to the Covid crisis: for example, it was necessary to increase significantly the services already offered by the municipalities, such as bringing food to the elderly.

1.2.2 The prospects for a relaunch of green and inclusive cities:[5] The French PNRR

The French PNRR[6] is not especially city orientated. Cities do not appear in it either as a specific objective of action nor as a specific instrument for its implementation actions. By and large, it is the general concept of territory, and not the city, which constantly emerges. Moreover, the concept of territories as targets for national policies emerges, with no particular reference to corresponding local communities.

The recent crises, in fact, have reintroduced statist and centralist tendencies traditional in the French context, after a previous period (since 1980) of fairly strong decentralisation. This move backwards started to be apparent in the aftermath of the 2008 crisis, but it received a strong new impulse with the Covid crisis.

That said, even if cities are not especially targeted by the French PNRR, nor supposed to be prominent vectors of its implementation, there are, obviously, actions in the plan that particularly concern urban areas. The three basic priorities of ecology, competitiveness, and social cohesion cannot be retained without referring from time to time to cities. This applies particularly to the first priority, ecology.

Then, the French plan is articulated in a series of investment programmes: correspondingly, some allocations of funds are specific to cities and their urban problems. Once again, however, this allocation is indirect, without the plan making explicit reference to cities. Actions in favour of energy refurbishment of buildings and in favour of biodiversity and the fight against soil sealing (densification and urban renewal, etc.), are not reserved exclusively for cities although affecting mainly their territories. This is also the case for actions in favour of the modernisation of waste sorting and recovery tools or for those related to the development of green infrastructure and mobility, to the development of energy and green technologies and to the digitalisation of public services.

4 Sébastien Hourson, 'Aux confins du confinement' (2020) 5 *Droit Administratif* 3.

5 Marie-Christine Steckel-Assouère (dir), La résurrection des villes face à la Covid-19. Les opportunités de la revitalisation et de la régénération urbaines (L'Harmattan 2021).

6 https://www.economie.gouv.fr/plan-national-de-relance-et-de-resilience-pnrr.

1.2.3 The right to the city and solidarity cities in French law: Current situation and prospects

The concept of the right to the city has not yet become commonplace in France, even though the first author who proposed that concept – Henri Lefebvre – was French.

In terms of the development of direct local democracy mechanisms – which are a crucial contribution to the right to the city – the French landscape is contrasted. There are cities that are further ahead than others, such as Grenoble or Nantes, for example. Paris now has participatory budgeting and a series of neighbourhood bodies in its districts. Some of the other main cities are less concerned by the issue.

There is a national debate about participatory democracy and how to move in the direction of more direct democracy. But it has probably to be accepted that there is no French city where direct democracy would be as welcome as it is in Bologna, for example.

There is a slow movement of opening data (open data). Actually, this corresponds nowadays to a legislative obligation for municipalities of a certain importance. Unfortunately, this obligation is frequently ignored in practice, even if there are, in contrast, virtuous cases such as the one of the city of Nantes, which has made a great deal of its data accessible, subject to the respect of confidentiality and secrets, and susceptible to be freely reused.

There are also some initiatives to directly involve citizens in local governance. Among the most significant cases, here, is the one of Grenoble, where, recently, it has been made possible for groups of citizens to contractually manage public spaces and/or services mismanaged by the administration. This type of scheme is not easy to install in the French context, where the most frequent view is that services qualified as public must be operated by the public administration. In comparison with other countries, such as Italy, France lags on issues such as the management of common goods and collaborative pacts. However, there is a recent collective debate at the local level as well as the national one, on how to improve democracy by fostering means for direct expression of the people. The national tension in that direction was strongly visible during the crisis of the so-called "gilets jaunes". Thus, a more positive evolution could prevail in the near future.

1.3 The path towards green and inclusive cities: from climate strategies to cities' climate action

(Camille Mialot)

After these very inspiring comments by Jean-Bernard Auby, I would like to address the very broad issue of the city and climate change,[7] which impacts all

7 Camille Mialot, *La ville face au changement climatique, nouveaux instruments juridiques* (Berger Levrault 2020); Catherine Ribot, 'Les collectivités territoriales face à la justice cli-

the legal dimensions of the city,[8] through the narrow approach of land use and the current changes in urban planning in France.

By way of background, I would first like to explain how this issue relates more generally to the question of moving from climate strategies, which set distant and uncertain horizons, to climate action, i.e. the concrete climate achievements of cities.

This question of action through land use seems to me to be closely related to the question of the right to the city, which has points of intersection with the broader but more recent notion of climate justice.

1.3.1 Climate strategies, urban planning, and the right to the city

How can these three issues, which are *a priori* distant or even opposing, be linked? As Jean-Bernard Auby points out above, the right to the city was created by the French philosopher Henri Lefebvre in the late 1960s. Climate strategies are relatively new, although the first climate strategies for cities can probably be traced back to the Aalborg Accords of 1994, following the Rio Earth Summit of 1992. For a long time, urban planning has remained separate from the right to the city and climate concerns, if urban planning has not simply organized urban segregation and the consumption of natural agricultural and forest areas. It could even be said that urban planning in France has long been the enemy of both the climate and the right to the city.

1.3.1.1 The transition from climate strategies to actions: What role for cities?

The prevention of climate risks and the reduction of emissions are eminently relevant to cities, which are responsible for 70% of greenhouse gas emissions[9] and where the majority of the population, and therefore the vulnerability, is concentrated.

However, as Jean-Bernard Auby pointed out above, cities are not clearly identified in the various national climate strategies. The French NRRP is a strategy and a fund that adds to the many existing climate strategies and does not really bring coherence.

In fact, there are about 15 national climate strategies in France, adopted in "silos" according to different timetables. These include the national low-carbon strategy, the multi-year energy programme, the strategy for managing

matique' (2021) 2200 *Semaine Juridique édition Administration et Collectivités Territoriales*; Observatoire National sur les Effets du Changement Climatique, *Villes et adaptation au changement climatique* (La Documentation Française 2011).

8 Jean-Bernard Auby, 'La Ville nouvelle frontière du droit administratif' (2017) 853 *AJDA*.

9 Intergovernmental Panel on Climate Change, 'Assessment Report 5 Climate Change 2014: Mitigation of Climate Change' (2014) https://www.ipcc.ch/report/ar5/wg3/ 930 and following.

coastal retreat, the national green and blue grid guidelines, the national waste prevention plan, the national circular economy strategy, etc.

The confusion is so great that, as of July 7, 2022, a General Secretariat for Ecological Planning[10] attached to the Prime Minister will beresponsible for ensuring the coherence of all ecological strategies. One of the tasks of this secretariat will be to translate the strategies into action plans. The creation of this general secretariat reflects an awareness at the state level of the incoherence of current national strategies and the lack of government action to date.

The state's inaction on climate change was sanctioned by the Conseil d'État[11] in a decision dated July 1, 2021, on the initiative of the City of Grande-Synthe, with the cities of Paris and Grenoble joining the action. In this decision, the Council of State noted the insufficient action of the state and asked the Prime Minister to take all the necessary measures to kerb the curve of greenhouse gas emissions. However, I am cautious about the expected effects of climate litigation: it does not seem to me that it is up to judges to determine the content of climate policies, as these are political choices that must be subject to the mechanisms of democracy, participation, etc. But it is quite revealing that in the case of climate litigation, the Council of State found that the state had not acted sufficiently. Besides, it is also revealing that in this case it is the cities that are attacking the state for its climate inaction.

The crucial issue highlighted in the Intergovernmental Panel on Climate Change (IPCC) reports is the transition from climate strategies to climate actions.[12] In other words, from "saying" to "doing". According to the final Summary for Policymakers of the IPCC's Sixth Working Group, "There is a rapidly closing window of opportunity to secure a liveable and sustainable future for all (very high confidence)".[13] In other words, according to the IPCC, there is an urgent need for action.

Action on climate change is undoubtedly much more than a purely legal issue. There is undoubtedly an "ontological brake" on climate action in the sense that Philippe Descola[14] understands it, i.e. a civilisational inability to imagine a relationship with non-humans and the Earth that is not one of subordination and exploitation of the planet. This brake is very important and undoubtedly explains in part the general climate inaction.

Going back to the law, we might think that perfect coordination of climate policies at all levels of government would be the way forward for climate action, and indeed it is on this top-down model that the 2015 Paris Agreement is based. The goal of carbon neutrality by 2050, and the translation of the Paris Agreement into the European and national order with the

10 Décret n° 2022-990 du 7 juillet 2022 relatif au secrétariat général à la planification écologique.
11 Conseil d'État, 1er July 2021 Commune de Grande Synthe req n° 427301 https://www.conseil-etat.fr/fr/arianeweb/CE/decision/2021-07-01/427301.
12 Intergovernmental Panel on Climate Change, 'Assessment Report 6: Climate Change 2023' (2023) https://www.ipcc.ch/report/sixth-assessment-report-cycle/ 8.
13 Ibid. 25.
14 Philippe Descola and Alessandro Pignocchi, *Ethnographie des mondes à venir* (Seuil 2022).

European "fit for 55" pact. However, this vertical diagram omits an element of discontinuity: the climate issue is divisive at all levels.[15] Thus, it is not certain that the relative ease with which ambitious quantified targets are set at the international, European, and national levels will allow for their effective implementation. This is particularly the case because these ambitious targets entail major changes in lifestyles that are not well understood, or expressed, by national and international policymakers. In other words, the accounting or technocratic vision of the efforts required to adapt to and mitigate climate change at the national and international levels does not reflect the efforts that need to be made at the local level. The top-down process at work seems to shift the task of imagining a "livable future" to the intrastate levels, and especially to the cities.

In this respect, in the absence of clear decisions at the state level, cities are "on the front line" and "at the end of the line" in imagining lifestyles that are compatible with the limits of the earth and the climate, and in making the hard choices that fall within their competence. This is a very important practical difficulty that I have observed in the development of local climate plans: how to translate accounting statements about greenhouse gas (GHG) emission reductions into action. It is much easier to say that GHG emissions must be reduced by 55% by 2030 than it is to implement in a coordinated way the various levels of action such as waste management, mobility, land use, renewable energy production, and so on.

And moreover, these traditional instruments of public action do not make it possible to assess the climatic consequences of their implementation. In this sense, they are undoubtedly the product of a naturalistic ontology in which humans and non-humans live separately in the sense that Philippe Descola[16] understands it, in other words, humans are unaware of the consequences of their actions on the planet and on non-humans. In order to assess the climatic consequences of public actions, it is therefore necessary to establish relevant impact and monitoring indicators. However, the development of impact and monitoring indicators is an extremely complex process: it is necessary to combine environmental impact indicators that have existed for many years, particularly under the impetus of EU legislation; to add to these environmental impact assessments that evaluate carbon emissions over the entire life cycle of policies and projects; and finally, social impact and monitoring, etc.

To get an idea of the complexity of climate action by cities, it is probably useful to take the example of the fight against urban heat islands.[17] There is a wide range of possible actions: changing floor coverings, changing the colour of buildings, changing their location, insulating and exposing buildings,

15 François Gemenne, *L'écologie n'est pas un consensus* (Fayard 2022).
16 Descola, Pignocchi (n 14).
17 Jean-Jacques Terrin, *Villes et changement climatique îlots de chaleur urbain* (Parenthèses Editions 2015).

planting trees, etc. If we can see the expected results of an approach that combines these different tools, there are many dangers: Can we plant trees if the ground is artificial? How to mobilize water resources in case of drought? Who will bear the costs of the various developments, what will be the impact on mobility, etc.? More generally, as we will see below, cities are experimenting with how to make the necessary trade-offs between densification to build the city of the quarter-hour and reduce mobility, building social housing while promoting the recycling of existing buildings, creating green corridors while prioritizing so-called active mobility in limited public spaces, etc.

Paris is a good example of these difficult choices between densification and greening in a very limited urban context. For example, in 2021, the Paris Administrative Court[18] cancelled the building permit for two apartment buildings overlooking the Boulevard périphérique, an urban highway that encircles Paris. According to the Administrative Court, the inhabitants of these future buildings, although planted and called "Project Thousand Trees", would be exposed to too much pollution. The appeals were brought by environmental associations, Friends of the Earth and France Nature Environnement, which are very close to the environmental parties that participate in the government of the city of Paris. In other words, in the words of François Gemene ecology is not a consensus.

Like other intrastate actors, I believe that the city is at the "end of the chain" of climate action and that it is up to the city to make the hard choices, at least when other levels of decision-making are content to set numerical targets.

1.3.1.2 The right to the city and climate justice: Meeting points

I would like to highlight one central element, that of climate justice, with which I believe the right to the city can be linked.

The right to the city is older than climate justice, since it emerged with Henri Lefebvre in 1968, as mentioned above, but it undoubtedly finds correspondences under the term "urban climate justice" or "climate just city".[19] The right to the city can be conceived in its essentially political dimension as a right to participate in the governance of the city,[20] but it can also be conceived as a set of fundamental rights in an urban environment: the right to housing, the right to health, the right to the environment etc., or even the right to urban amenities and services.

18 TA Paris requête 2 juillet 2021 n° 1920927/4-3 http://paris.tribunal-administratif.fr/Actualites-du-Tribunal/Espace-presse/Projets-Mille-arbres-et-Ville-multi-strates-le-tribunal-annule-les-permis-de-construire.

19 Wendy Steele, Jean Hillier, Donna Houston, Jason Byrne, and Diana MacCallum, 'The climate-just city' in Jafry T. (ed.), *Routledge Handbook of Climate Justice* (Taylor & Francis Group 2018), 267.

20 David Harvey, *Rebel Cities: From the Right to the City to the Urban Revolution* (Verso 2013).

It is undoubtedly important to emphasize the plasticity of the concept of "climate justice", which reflects the plasticity of the concept of the right to the city. Climate justice has been present in the debates since the beginning of the Conferences of the Parties, and it appears constantly in the IPCC reports. Most recently in the Summary for Policymakers adopted in March 2023, according to which "adaptation and mitigation actions that prioritize equity, social justice, climate justice, rights-based approaches and inclusiveness will lead to more sustainable outcomes, reduce trade-offs, support transformative change and advance climate-resilient development".[21] This general statement by the IPCC obviously has particular resonance in urban environments.

A precise legal definition of climate justice seems difficult to give. Climate justice is both a legal concept and an ethical philosophy. From its origins, climate justice has undoubtedly had a social and spatial dimension in the form of the militant "environmental justice" that emerged in the early 1980s in the United States under the impetus of ethnic groups segregated in polluted urban spaces.[22] Environmental justice is thus linked to spatial justice from the outset.

To this social and spatial dimension, which climate justice undoubtedly shares with the right to the city, we can add a temporal dimension, in the past (we are thinking here of the responsibility for past emissions of certain developed and industrialized countries over the last two centuries, of fossil fuel companies in particular, but also of cities such as London, which was long lit by coal gas).[23] Climate justice extends into the future, with the key concept of the right of future generations, which has recently been developed in German and French constitutional law, and which also finds very concrete applications in the city with the implementation of the pedestrianization of "school streets".[24]

There are therefore many links between climate justice and the right to the city. In the urban environment, climate justice at least partially covers the right to the city, at least in its dimensions of participation in the governance of the city and its amenities and in its dimension of equal access to the city's amenities. However, as the IPCC indicates, climate justice is not only an element to be taken into account in climate action, but climate justice is a condition for the success of climate action. Thus, in my view, the right to the city should be understood as a condition for the success of cities" climate action.

21 Intergovernmental Panel on Climate Change (n 12) 33.

22 David Schlosberg and Lisette B. Collins, 'From environmental to climate justice: climate change and the discourse of environmental justice' (2014) 5 *WIREs Climate Change* 3.

23 Christophe Bonneuil and Jean-Baptiste Fressoz, *L'évènement anthropocène, la terre l'histoire et nous* (Seuil 2016).

24 https://www.paris.fr/pages/57-nouvelles-rues-aux-ecoles-dans-paris-8197.

1.3.1.3 The inherent limits of urban planning as a tool for climate action

Given the close links between climate justice and the right to the city, and its character as a crucial condition for successful climate action, I would like to make some general observations about urban planning as an instrument for climate action.

In my view, urban planning is first and foremost an illustration of the "spatialization of public law".[25] The spatialization of public law takes on special significance in the context of climate change, which I see as an important lever for spatialization, as Auby has pointed out above. Indeed, the issues of adaptation and resilience to climate change arise differently from one territory to another, depending on the exposure to the various climate risks identified: coastal erosion, drought and scarcity of water resources, urban heat islands, floods, forest fires, etc. The urban configuration: metropolis/medium city/suburbs and surrounding rural areas pose very different questions and actions in terms of food or energy autonomy, vulnerability, etc.

Urban planning is probably not the most direct form of climate action, as it is a set of rules that determine future land use. The implementation of urban planning depends on many factors, first and foremost a temporal factor: planning is essentially directed towards future land use and it relies on the action of many actors, including the private sector and market logics. These actors, these logics, will determine the realization of the operations during which the urban project inscribed in the urban plan will be implemented. Urban planning as an instrument of public climate action has a limited impact on cities that have already been built, as the IPCC points out[26]. This is because the structure of the city, its buildings and its infrastructure are to some extent set in stone for a period of more than 30 years, a period that is incompatible with effective climate action in the short and medium term. This is obviously the case for European cities, to which we should add a significant cultural dimension, with the constraints inherent in the protection of the built heritage.

Urban planning as an instrument of public climate action is therefore not a panacea! It can, however, have an impact on reducing artificialization of soils if it prevents urban expansion and requires the city to be considered within its current urban envelope, as we will see below.

25 Jean-Bernard Auby, 'Peut-on parler d'un «tournant spatial» dans le droit public?' (2022) *Chemins Publics* https://www.chemins-publics.org/articles/peut-on-parler-dun-tournant-spatial-dans-le-droit-public.

26 Intergovernmental Panel on Climate Change, 'Climate Change 2022. Mitigation of Climate Change, Working Group III contribution to the Sixth Assessment Report of the Intergovernmental Panel on Climate Change' (2022), Chapter 8 fig. 8.20, 8.21, 8.87, 8.88.

1.3.2 Towards a climate land use

One of the questions raised by the transition to climate action is the following: can we use the classic tools of public action: land use planning, public procurement, administrative police powers, expropriation, etc. for climate objectives for which they were not designed, or on the contrary, when they have contributed to climate change, or should we imagine new specific tools?

In France, we are witnessing both logics: the creation of new instruments and the modification of the content and objectives of classic legal tools.

1.3.2.1 The hybridization and coupling of strategic urban planning and climate planning

The changes in urban and climate planning in France are very recent and still ongoing. These changes reflect a certain sense of urgency and a certain legislative frenzy directed at the local level and, in particular, at cities.

The 2015 law on energy transition and green growth[27] requires all intermunicipal bodies with more than 50,000 inhabitants and their own tax system to develop territorial climate and energy plans. These plans must describe the diagnosis of the territory's and the municipality's CO2 emissions and the strategy and actions to achieve carbon neutrality in 2050. The section of these plans describing actions to reduce emissions and adapt to climate change is often very limited, as in the case of Paris, Rennes Métropole, Métropole Aix Marseille, etc. In addition to the weakness of the action component of these plans, there is a lack of normativity. They are often drawn up as "guidance plans" that do not contain any binding rules and have not yet been applied in practice. Despite these shortcomings, these plans were conceived in an emergency and have the merit of being the first truly binding climate plans for cities with more than 50,000 inhabitants.

A legislative ordinance of June 20, 2020 significantly changed the role of strategic urban planning, the schémas de cohérence territoriale (SCOT), at the intermunicipal level. This text put at the heart of the strategic planning project, projet d'aménagement stratégique (PAS), the limitation of land artificialisation, the energy and climate transition, the circular economy, mobility and local food autonomy etc. The ordinance of June 20, 2020 opened up the possibility of coupling strategic urban planning with the territorial climate air energy plan mentioned above. It remains to be seen how this new tool will be implemented. Knowing that the entry into force provisions of the aforementioned legislative ordinance allow for the deferral of the entry into force of these provisions, their actual implementation is postponed for several years and left initially to the "goodwill" of the intermunicipal bodies.

27 Loi n° 2015-992 du 17 août 2015 relative à la transition énergétique pour la croissance verte.

Previously, the Law of August 7, 2015 on the new territorial organization of the Republic[28] had unified the various regional planning in terms of spatial planning, climate, air, waste, biodiversity, mobility, circular economy into a single document, the Regional Plan for Sustainable Development and Territorial Equality. This single regional plan has forced the regions to unify their different climate strategies.

At the regional and inter-municipal level, a double movement seems to be taking place: on the one hand, classical strategic urban planning is addressing climate issues, and on the other hand, climate planning can be integrated into classical urban planning. This double movement should allow both the simplification of tools and a greater efficiency of action.

1.3.2.2 Towards the end of soil artificialization

The French government has not yet taken any real action on climate change, but the Climate and Resilience Law, adopted on August 22, 2021, opens up new perspectives in the fight against greenhouse gas emissions and adaptation to climate change, particularly in cities. This law was adopted through a very original process. One hundred and fifty citizens, selected by lot, met within the framework of the Citizens' Climate Convention[29] and formulated 149 proposals. These proposals were amended and adopted by Parliament in the Law of 22 August 2021 on Combating Climate Change and Strengthening Resilience to its Effects. This law includes specific provisions to limit land artificialization and manage coastal erosion, for which cities are primarily responsible.

The Climate Resilience Law of 24 August 2021 establishes the principle of ending net soil artificialization by 2050. The adoption of this objective is not a revolution in itself, as several European countries have already set this objective, or an even more ambitious one, such as Germany, which has planned to end land artificialization in 2040.[30] However, France consumes much more natural agricultural and forest land than its European neighbours, 1.5 times more, mainly because of an urban model that favours individual housing and individual automobile mobility (in France, 74% of working people go to work by car every day[31]).

It is not so much the objectives that are of interest, but rather the way in which the law has planned its implementation. In this sense, the law is quite innovative because it assigns responsibilities to each level for the formulation and implementation of the end of land artificialization. In fact, the law did not simply set two targets: a 50% reduction in land consumption over the period

28 Loi du 7 août 2015 portant nouvelle organisation territoriale de la République.

29 https://www.conventioncitoyennepourleclimat.fr/.

30 EU Soil Strategy for 2030 Reaping the benefits of healthy soils for people, food, nature and climate COM(2021) 699 final.

31 https://www.statistiques.developpement-durable.gouv.fr/la-mobilite-locale-et-longue-distance-des-francais-enquete-nationale-sur-la-mobilite-des-0.

2021–2031 compared with the previous decade and the end of soil artificialization by 2050. The 2021 Climate and Resilience Law developed an indicator to measure soil artificialization, which was established by decree, an obligation for local authorities to measure and report every three years. And the law organized the declination of the objective in all regional, intermunicipal, and local planning, imposing a deadline for adoption and implementation: 2024 for the regional level, 2026 for the intermunicipal level, and 2027 for the local urban planning level.

At first glance, this is a top-down logic from the national to the local level. However, the objective of reducing artificial land use by 50% by 2030 is imposed only at the regional level, which must then determine a trajectory for reducing artificial land use and the distribution of artificial land use envelopes expressed in hectares at the intermunicipal level. The regional plans are currently being revised. Not all regions have taken care to define criteria for the distribution of the envelopes. For example, the Provence Alpes Côte d'Azur region has not territorialized differentiated targets, whereas the Grand Est region has made this effort. According to the law of August 22, 2021, the modalities of this distribution must be carried out by the region in agreement with the intermunicipal level, which must make proposals during the conference of the communities in charge of strategic urban planning at the intermunicipal level. The purpose of this conference is to establish the criteria for determining the artificialization envelopes. This is not a strictly top-down logic, but a more collaborative logic between the different levels.

The room for manoeuvre left to each level is reinforced by the "light" normative relations, which do not imply full compliance between the different planning levels, but rather a consistency or compatibility normative relationship. The leeway left to each level can also be counterproductive by preventing the effective implementation of net zero land artificialization. In fact, because of the constitutional principle that prohibits the tutelage of one territorial authority over another, the decisions taken by a higher territorial authority can only be imposed in a relationship of compatibility-consistency and not of full compliance.

The objective of zero net artificialization is undoubtedly a major evolution in French urban planning. In fact, since the 1960s, urban planning has been mainly orientated towards low-density construction and urban expansion. Low density, and therefore urban sprawl, was even encouraged by the mechanism of the "legal density ceiling", accompanied by a financial compensation mechanism in case of over-density. The general principle of combating urban sprawl, established more than twenty years ago by the Solidarity and Urban Renewal Act of 2000, put an end to this system. However, far from limiting artificialization and urban sprawl, the Law of 2000 merely provided a framework for a practice that continued until the adoption of the aforementioned Law of August 22, 2021.

All the legal consequences of the principle of zero net artificialization have not yet been drawn. Local urban plans are still conceived as tools for the development of construction and urban expansion, with tools such as urbanization zones (future urbanization zones), development and programming guidelines, etc. For example, there are no provisions in the Urban Code requiring public transport services in areas to be developed or densified, which does not prevent urbanization that favours the use of cars. There is no obligation to ensure the availability of water resources before building, etc. Some mayors of municipalities in the department of Pyrénées Orientales have decided not to issue any more building permits because of the extreme drought. However, this local initiative does not have a solid basis in the urban planning code. The legislator has not yet reformed building permits. The building permit should undoubtedly become an authorization to artificialize the soil. In a climatic logic of soil conservation, the right to build should no longer be considered as an attribute of the right of ownership, which finds its limit in the rules of urban planning, but as a violation of the ecosystemic functions of the soil, which must be preserved.

In short, not all legal consequences of the end of soil artificialization have been drawn and many developments are still to come. But the principle has been established and will undoubtedly be reinforced by the implementation of the EU Soil Strategy.[32]

Despite the progress made, in my opinion, the 2021 Climate and Resilience Act suffers from a serious shortcoming. The question of the right to the city or urban climate justice has not really been considered in the law. The law of August 22, 2021 provides for the creation of local land observatories that can be coupled with housing observatories, but it does not provide for a social impact study of the plans, and this is undoubtedly a major shortcoming. Indeed, it is likely that cities that are constrained in their urban envelope, where land is scarce and expensive, will become unaffordable for people with the lowest incomes. This is already the case in many French metropolises such as Paris, Lyon, Bordeaux, Rennes, Nantes, Caen, Lille, etc. And this will undoubtedly exacerbate the tensions between cities, their suburbs and the surrounding rural areas, as Auby pointed out above.

There are some emerging mechanisms aimed at making land accessible, such as the solidarity real estate lease. This mechanism makes it possible to separate the ownership of the land, which belongs to a solidarity land office, from the ownership of the housing, which is reserved for qualified low-income buyers.[33] A rent control system, initiated by the cities most affected by real estate speculation, was introduced by two laws in 2014 and 2018. However, it is not certain that these mechanisms will moderate the rise in land prices, and the subsequent social exclusion.

32 https://ec.europa.eu/commission/presscorner/detail/en/QANDA_21_5917.
33 Camille Mialot, 'Affordable and workforce housing in France' (2020) 4 *Journal of Comparative Urban Law and Policy* 456.

In my opinion, in the medium term, the control of land prices will have to be considered so that the increase in land prices resulting from the artificialization of net zero does not become an obstacle to the right to the city and to the climate policies of cities. Indeed, the creation and restoration of green and blue infrastructures, the construction of social housing, etc., will require massive land acquisitions by cities, which will now be obliged to develop real land acquisition strategies.

These profound changes in the management of land use in French cities have only just begun. If we look at the prospects for development, the obstacles are numerous and mainly of an ideological nature: the real estate market can certainly no longer be considered a free market.

1.3.2.3 Management of coastal retreat

With regard to the management of coastal retreat, the Climate Resilience Law of 22 August 2021 seems to have organized adaptation to sea level rise in a more coherent and pragmatic way than that of artificialization.

The provisions of the aforementioned 2021 Law on Climate and Resilience impose on the intermunicipal bodies in charge of strategic planning the identification of areas for the relocation of public facilities affected by the retreat, and in the local urban plan, the integration of a local strategy for the retreat of the coastline with the design of a specific zone for retreat within 30 years and a subsequent zone for retreat between 30 and 100 years.

In addition to these mechanisms, a specific right of priority for public acquisition is available to allow targeted land intervention, and the recent LOI n° 2022-217 of February 21, 2022 on differentiation, decentralization, deconcentration mentioned above allows the use of expropriation to create land reserves for adaptation to the retreat of the coastline. Two mechanisms that were not foreseen by the law of 2021 in the case of zero net artificialization.

It is true that the legislator has been able to draw on local experience, such as that of the inter-municipal body Communauté Pays Basque, which has been working in this direction since 2012 with the implementation of a local strategy for coastal risk management, in conjunction with the adoption of the national strategy for the management of the coastline.[34] Since 2017, the inter-municipal local urban plan includes specific provisions to anticipate the retreat of the coastline.

The example of the community of the Basque Country is a case of application of the Plan France Relance, of which the French NRRP is an element. The Development Partnership Project (PPA) "Adaptation to the retreat of the coastline in Saint Jean de Luz North" was signed with the state in October 2021 and provides funding of 2.6 million euros to help relocate public facilities.

34 https://www.communaute-paysbasque.fr/a-la-une-2/actualites/actualite/recul-du-trait-de-cote-un-dispositif-inedit-signe-a-saint-jean-de-luz.

In a way, in the case of coastal management, the legislator has benefited from local experiments and incorporated them into national legislation according to a bottom-up model of climate risk management.

1.4 Conclusion

Cities are increasingly at the centre of public life and the public apparatus. But one source of current and future crises lies in the tensions between cities, their suburbs, and surrounding rural territories. These tensions generate an anti-metropolitan atmosphere, more widely some aggressivity against cities, while these are more and more the real centres of economic development and innovation. Tensions, also, with the state, whose power has been strengthened by the crises. Nevertheless, it will appear every day more necessary to involve cities as key levels to future democracy and as essential places where to fight for environmental protection and to combat climate change. Despite its naturally centralist orientation, the French system cannot ignore that necessity.[35]

In this sense, the situation in France may appear uncertain. The confusion of national climate strategies, for which the NRRP did not provide a solution, is matched by the state's climate inaction. In this context, cities must consider their climate actions in an evolving legislative context that tends to link local climate strategies and urban planning, opening new perspectives but also constraints. Climate justice in its urban dimension, which has much in common with the right to the city, has not really yet been taken into account by the legislator in France, and it is up to the cities to make hard choices. In our opinion, this is a serious risk for the failure of cities' climate action or, on the contrary, a condition for success, to quote the IPCC's warnings.

Bibliography

Auby J-B., 'Le droit administratif et la crise', (2014) 1 *Droit administratif* 1.

Auby J-B., 'La Ville nouvelle frontière du droit administratif' (2017) *AJDA* 853.

Auby J-B., 'Peut-on parler d'un «tournant spatial» dans le droit public?' (2022) *Chemins Publics* https://www.chemins-publics.org/articles/peut-on-parler-dun-tournant-spatial-dans-le-droit-public.

Bonneuil C. and Fressoz J-B., *L'évènement anthropocène, la terre l'histoire et nous* (Seuil 2016).

De Boissieu, J-L. (et al.), 'Les collectivités territoriales face à la crise', (2021) *Semaine Juridique, édition Administration et Collectivités Territoriales – GRALE, Droit et Gestion des Collectivités Territoriales, L'administration locale face à la crise sanitaire, Le Moniteur*.

Descola P., Pignocchi A., *Ethnographie des mondes à venir* (Seuil 2022).

Gemenne F., *L'écologie n'est pas un consensus* (Fayard 2022).

35 Jean-Marc Offner, 'Coronavirus at après? Pour de nouveaux compromis urbains' (2020) *Métropolitiques*.

Harvey D., *Rebel Cities: From the Right to the City to the Urban Revolution* (Verso 2013).
Hourson S., 'Aux confins du confinement' (2020) 5 *Droit Administratif*, 3.
Intergovermental Panel on Climate Change, 'Assessment report 5: Climate change 2014: Mitigation of climate change' (2014) https://www.ipcc.ch/report/ar5/wg3/.
Intergovermental Panel on Climate Change, 'Assessment report 6: Climate change 2023' (2023) https://www.ipcc.ch/report/sixth-assessment-report-cycle/.
Intergovermental Panel on Climate Change, 'Climate change 2022. Mitigation of climate change, Working Group III contribution to the Sixth Assessment Report of the Intergovernmental Panel on Climate Change' (2022).
Mialot C., 'Affordable and workforce housing in France' (2020) 4 *Journal of Comparative Urban Law and Policy*, 453.
Mialot C., *La ville face au changement climatique, nouveaux instruments juridiques* (Berger Levrault 2020).
Observatoire National sur les Effets du Changement Climatique, *Villes et adaptation au changement climatique* (La Documentation Française 2011).
Offner J-M, 'Coronavirus at après? Pour de nouveaux compromis urbains' (2020) *Métropolitiques*.
Ribot C., 'Les collectivités territoriales face à la justice climatique' (2021) *Semaine Juridique édition Administration et Collectivités Territoriales* 2209.
Schlosberg D. and Collins L. B., 'From environmental to climate justice: climate change and the discourse of environmental justice' (2014) 5 *WIREs Climate Change* 3.
Steckel-Assouère M-C. (dir), *La résurrection des villes face à la Covid-19. Les opportunités de la revitalisation et de la régénération urbaines* (L'Harmattan 2021).
Steele W., Hillier J., Houston D., Byrne J. and MacCallum D., 'The climate-just city' in Jafry T. (ed.), *Routledge Handbook of Climate Justice* (Taylor & Francis Group 2018).
Terrin J-J., *Villes et changement climatique îlots de chaleur urbain* (Parenthèses Editions 2015).
Villeneuve P., 'Le retour de l'État d'urgence' (2020) *Semaine Juridique édition Administrations et Collectivités Territoriales*.

2 The city and its law

A Spanish perspective on solidarity and sustainability

Tomàs Font i Llovet

2.1 Introduction: The city and its law

The current state of local government in Spain, from the point of view of its legal-institutional regime, presents three characteristics that hinder its evolution towards emerging realities: it is too *uniform*, it is too *rigid*, and it is too *static*. Thus, the attention to the current needs of European and Spanish local governments involves increasing three aspects in the local legal order: a) diversity and regulatory *differentiation*, b) the *flexibility* of normative and organizational instruments and c) the *dynamic* and relational dimension of local institutions.

Regulatory diversity is especially imperative to cope with the characteristics of the city. There are several ways of "being" a city, but their functions exceed the classic ones of municipal power, to face new realities:

The self-government of its own interests, but in a situation of fragmentation, diversity and even opposition of interests, so that the function of mediation and composition of interests prevails, as well as the creation of a legal space itself.

Codecision in the formulation of general national and even transnational policy, which proposes an expansion of international subjectivity and a real sharing of the representation of sovereignty.

The external projection of the collective aspirations of the community and the capture of sufficient resources not available in state structures, so that cities compete with each other (and not only cooperate, Article 10.3 European Charter of Local Self-Government).

Along with the above, cities, large agglomerations, metropolises, are assuming classic tasks typical of classical state power, such as public security, justice and legal security, income redistribution, the definition of rights (social solidarity, housing, immigration), the delimitation of the market, large infrastructures, even foreign or international relations. In reality, cities have gone from collaborating with the state to competing with the state and, finally, to supplying the state. They therefore need to exercise state powers.

DOI: 10.4324/9781032665184-7

Ferdinand Braudel has pointed out that the history of Europe is a race of the city against the state.[1] Basically, today we are faced with the task of determining the scope of a fundamental dilemma: should the city be given legal form "within" the state or the city "instead" of the state?

This general approach requires a rethinking of the content and form of city law. However, the approach must be made from very specific experiences, needs and possibilities. Three aspects of Spanish law are analyzed below: local entities and the Next Generation EU Fund, the ecological city and, finally, the instruments of co-administration, in particular the Regulation on Common Property and Collaboration Pacts.

2.2 Local entities and the Next Generation EU fund

2.2.1 Limited local participation in the National Plan for Recovery, Transformation and Resilience

The National Plan for Recovery, Transformation and Resilience (*Plan Nacional para la Recuperación, Transformación y la Resiliencia/*PRTR) is the main conduit for *Next Generation EU* (NGEU) funds in Spain. However, local Spanish governments have played only a limited role in this plan, acting mainly as receiving or executing agencies.[2] As such, the Royal Decree-Law 36/2020 regulating the Recovery Plan has resulted in centralised activity. Yet, this is no longer generally focused at only the national level, but specifically within the presidency of the government and the Department of Economic and G20 Affairs (*Departamento de Asuntos Económicos y G20*) in the cabinet of the prime minister.

Still, the measures envisaged in the PRTR involve areas which undoubtedly fall within the responsibilities and interests of municipalities (e.g. the urban agenda, housing and sustainable mobility). Still, participation by local governments, and, to a large extent, the autonomous regions, has been limited to simply being involved in the consultation process during the plan's initial drafting stage. Alternatively, local representatives have been able to attend the Plan's New Sector Conference thanks to the activity of the Spanish Federation of Municipalities and Provinces (*la Federación Española de Municipios y Provincias/FEMP*). However, local entities have had no real ability to influence the plan's content.

The government's December 2021 *Report on the implementation of the Recovery Plan* notes that:

1 Ferdinand Braudel, *Le modèle italien* (Flammarion 1994) 34.

2 This critical assessment is shared by, among others, Alfredo Galán Galán, 'Los gobiernos locales ante el reto de los fondos europeos de recuperación' (2021) 63 *Revista Catalana de Dret Públic* 101, 109, and Jesús Colas Tenás, 'Los Gobiernos locales intermedios en la gestión de los fondos europeos para la recuperación' (2021) 55 *Cuadernos de Derecho Local* 37, 38–39.

> prior to the Plan's publication, two additional meetings were held in which the government formally presented the draft to the Autonomous Communities, Autonomous Cities and the FEMPP. Likewise, in February 2021, the FEMP and the Ministry of Transport, Mobility and Urban Agenda agreed to set up a permanent Advisory Council on mobility and transport, which falls within the scope of the Recovery Plan and European funding.

The *report*, dated April 2022, does not provide further information on participation by local authorities.

Recovery Plan investments are being deployed through three mechanisms: (i) Strategic Projects for the Recovery and Transformation of the Economy (*Proyectos Estratégicos para la Recuperación y Transformación de la Economía/PERTE*) worth €30.30 billion; (ii) transfers to regional governments of over €13.3 billion for financing projects within their purview; and (iii) calls and tenders for general programmes at the national level.

Participation by local governments in the now well-known *PERTE* projects has been very limited. This is partly because the Council of Ministers (under Article 8.2 of the Royal Decree-Law 36/2020 of 30 December) is responsible for approving these projects. In addition, most of the PERTE projects approved to date are more clearly business-orientated and have therefore not integrated any significant involvement of local authorities in their governance mechanisms.

A PERTE project for the digitalisation of the water cycle, for example, approved on 22 March 2022, does not foresee any local participation in the working group that is supervising and promoting the activity. In contrast to other previously approved projects, collaboration between the state administration and local entities is mentioned, however, via the Federation of Municipalities and Provinces, yet the scope of this is not specified.

As for project implementation linked to the PRTR, local entities appear to be the most relevant actors, but only as recipients of aid and they are treated as private entities in most cases.

Some other relevant notable programmes include the awarding of grants for implementing low-emission zones and transforming urban transport. These activities are valued at €1 billion and involve a call for proposals to refurbish publicly owned buildings. Similarly, the Economy of Care Pilot Projects focus on modernising and improving social service care models for children and adolescents, dependent elderly persons and homeless people. These projects are also largely the responsibility of local authorities. Urban Agenda Pilot Projects support drawing up local action plans for implementation in municipalities, groups of municipalities and provincial councils. As such, these Urban Agenda projects effectively integrate social, economic and environmental sustainability objectives within territorial urban development policies.

2.2.2 The PRTR and public subsidies

The legal regime for implementing the PRTR raises many questions for local authorities. We address only a few of them below.

We can affirm that once a plan's "*leitmotif*" is to have powerful executive units, this can significantly modify the classic idea of a subsidy relationship. As a result, these relationships will be driven by either public-private collaboration via commitments to co-financing action or by public-public collaboration via administrative cooperative mechanisms. A subsidy then becomes a tool that defines a mainly organisational relationship. This relationship then guides and promotes the creation of new referral centres that the subsidising administration then maintains permanent and continuous contact with.

One of the ways these kinds of relationships have emerged is via the *beneficiary groups* created under the Royal Decree-Law 36/2020 of 30 December. These groups are also mentioned in Article 11.3 of Law 38/2003 of 17 November, which is the General Law on Subsidies (*Ley general de Subvenciones*/LGS). According to this:

> when the regulatory basis specifically provides for it, groups of natural or legal persons, whether public or private, communities of property or any other type of economic unit or separate entity, although lacking a legal profile, may carry out projects, activities or behaviour or be able to receive a grant, thus qualifying as beneficiaries.

Article 67 of the above Royal Decree-Law rounds out the scant regulation provided for in the LGS. It stipulates that members of a group must enter into an internal agreement governing their operation prior to applying for aid. However, they do not need to be in any way legally constituted to do this.

If public entities, and specifically local entities, form part of these beneficiary groups, the related agreement must take the form of a pact, or properly speaking, a *collaboration agreement* between a public administration, a public law entity, or one or more private parties, as referred to in Article 47.1 c) of the Law 40/2015 of 1 October on the Public Sector Legal System (*Régimen Jurídico del Sector Público*/LRJSP).[3] All the above will require streamlining the procedures and legal system governing such agreements. Articles 7 and 59 of the Royal Decree-Law 36/2020 of 30 December have already established

3 For these agreements see: Marc Vilalta Reixach, 'Los convenios administrativos a la luz de la nueva Ley de Contratos del Sector Público' in José María Gimeno Feliu (ed.), *Estudio sistemático de la Ley de Contratos del Sector Público* (Thomson Reuters Aranzadi 2018) 325 and idem 'Los convenios interadministrativos (locales) y la Ley de Contratos del Sector Público: Convenio o contrato?' (2019) 12 *Anuario de Derecho Municipal* 53; Diana Santiago Iglesias, 'Cooperación horizontal: los convenios interadministrativos' in Eduardo Gamero Casado and Isabel Gallego Córcoles (eds.), *Tratado de Contratos del Sector público – Vol. I* (Tirant lo Blanch 2018) 618; Carlos Alberto Amoedo Souto, 'La colaboración público-público en el ámbito local tras la Ley 9/2017, de contratos del sector público' (2018) *Anuario del Gobierno Local* 263.

certain measures to this end. However, deadlines become critical for local entities when agreements have to be signed by a company's plenary body.

2.2.3 The Recovery Plan and local cooperation

Certain aspects of local territorial organisation and inter-administrative cooperation will likely have to adapt, on the other hand, to the Recovery Plan's implementing logic. Order TMA/957/2021 of 7 September, for example, approved the regulatory basis for granting aid to develop pilot projects for local action plans under the Spanish Urban Agenda. It also supported a competitive call to apply for subsidies.

This kind of call is clearly aimed at local entities which the order sees as municipalities, regardless of their size or population, as well as Pprovincial, island and other councils (*Cabildos*). Thus, local entities of an "inter-municipal" nature remain somewhat outside the scope of such calls, i.e. counties (*comarcas*), commonwealths (*mancomunidades*) and metropolitan areas.

Instead of relying on the cooperative or joint action typical of local systems, the above Order refers to adopting another common mechanism in applying for subsidies, that is the beneficiary group noted above. In this way, beneficiary status is given to:

> groups of Local Entities which have at least two members and are constituted in accordance with Article 11.3 of the General Law on Subsidies and Article 67 of Royal Decree-Law 36/2020 of 30 December. These groups must also agree to draw up a similar action plan aimed at defending common territorial, cultural, social, environmental and economic interests. This, in turn, will enable these groups to be linked to a functional area sharing similar characteristics whether or not the components are part of the same province or Autonomous Community.

This then results in a new form of local inter-administrative cooperation.

In other cases, the beneficiary groups are envisaged as a mechanism for both public-private partnership and inter-administrative cooperation. However, these beneficiary groups are always under the leadership of a municipality, which is considered like a *city* to this end. For example, Order TED/1018/2021 of 20 September approved the regulatory basis for granting subsidies from the Fundación Biodiversidad, F.S.P. These subsidies were then aimed at promoting land renewal and resilience in Spanish cities and were approved as part of the 2021 call within the PERTE framework. Article 26 of the related Order states that beneficiary status may be granted to town councils of provincial or municipal capitals with more than 50,000 inhabitants or municipalities with more than 20,000 inhabitants, non-profit organisations, universities, research bodies, technology centres and the like. However, these entities must form beneficiaries groups together with at least one municipality which must comprise a provincial capital or have more than 50,000 inhabitants.

The idea of a *leading territorial and project city* then emerges in relation to beneficiary groups. The group is thus a new form of cooperation which plays out in and is represented by its lead city. The municipalities that encompass a beneficiary group also need to be neighbouring ones involved in a common project.

2.3 The ecological city

2.3.1 Spatial planning

Within the field of spatial planning and urban studies, planning technique is a fundamental tool for defining the essential characteristics of a climate-sensitive city. The most advanced climate change and ecological transition laws offer a new vision of how such tools and climate objectives may interact. Such laws have been enacted, for example, in the Autonomous Communities of Catalonia, the Balearic Islands, Andalusia, the Community of Valencia, the Canary Islands and the Basque Country among others. Also relevant here is state action under Law 7/2021 on Climate Change and the Energy Transition, which has modified land and urban planning legislation.

At the local level, some of these new laws have led to climate planning, designing energy sustainability studies within urban planning, giving local powers the ability to impose restrictions, banning polluting vehicles from circulation and converting municipal consumption toward using alternative non-fossil fuels.

As a whole, such laws facilitate dynamics that encourage less urban expansion. This is because they are based on a compact city model which limits land use and promotes the rejuvenation and renewal of the urban fabric. These laws present a new idea of a compact polycentric city, or the so-called "fifteen-minute city" as Carlos Moreno has noted with reference to Paris.[4] The COVID-19 crisis has highlighted as well the need for new and more extensive public spaces, whether through the so-called "superblocks" approach in Barcelona or via connections with peri-urban areas.

Promoting bioclimatic and sustainable construction, energy upgrading and city land restoration are also relevant objectives that involve improving the number and quality of green areas. In any case, these and many other issues are conditioned by the planning responsibilities of Autonomous Communities, which are only partly shared with local authorities.[5]

4 Carlos Moreno, *Droit de cité, de la "ville-monde" à la "ville du quart d'heure"* (Éditions de l'Observatoire 2020).

5 José Francisco Alenza García, 'Planificación climática local: ordenación del territorio, urbanismo y movilidad' (2021) *Anuario del Gobierno Local* 91 and Inmaculada Revuelta Pérez, 'La actividad de los gobiernos locales en el ámbito de la energía limpia: marco normativo' (2021) *Anuario del Gobierno Local* 171

2.3.2 *Energy and climate change*

2.3.2.1 *The international context*

The 2015 Paris Agreement marked a widely recognised turning point in global climate change policy, but its direct impact on local and citizen-level policies has seemed still too generalised. In contrast, the Global Covenant of Mayors for Climate & Energy has become the most important city and local government alliance working to fight climate change. More than 3,000 out of the total 8,000 municipalities in Spain have joined the Covenant, albeit many have only small populations. The Covenant is based on making commitments to strengthen climate change adaptation, achieve a just transition and keep greenhouse gas emissions below the 2°C global temperature-rise limit set for the end of the century. To join, local governments have to adopt a compliance-monitored climate action plan that has mitigation and adaptation measures and an energy access plan.[6]

The *C40 Cities* movement, in turn, brings together almost a hundred major cities, all allied against climate change. This group participated in the United Nations Climate Conference (COP26) in Glasgow in 2021. The mayors of London and Barcelona (Sadiq Khan and Ada Colau) have assumed leadership in this group and are acting as president and vice-presidents for Europe, respectively. Significantly, cities have played a role in the United Nations, which is, in fact, a "seat of states". Indeed, when Trump abandoned the Paris Agreement, the *Climate Mayors* filled his spot.

The role of cities in the fight against climate change is also apparent in EU law. Directive 2018/2001 of the European Parliament and Council of 11 December 2018 promotes energy efficiency and the use of renewable energy resources.[7] It also calls on local regulatory powers to set minimum requirements in these areas for new and renovated buildings. It further addresses local planning and urban planning, in particular. The aim is to design build and renovate: urban infrastructures; industrial, commercial and residential zones; energy infrastructure; urban heating and cooling systems; and natural gas and alternative fuel networks.

This directive also stresses the central role played by local authorities in promoting a decentralised energy model via local economic initiatives. Furthermore, it considers energy production related to personal consumption and the renewable energy communities municipalities participate in.[8] Directive 2019/944 incorporates the concept of citizen-based energy communities.

6 Alexandre Peñalver i Cabré, 'El rol de los gobiernos locales frente al cambio climático en el Derecho internacional y en el derecho de la Unión Europea' (2021) *Anuario del Gobierno Local* 51.

7 *Ibid.*

8 Joan Herrera and Pilar Navarro, 'Las comunidades energéticas como nuevo sujeto del derecho energético en España: del falanasterio a la transformación' (2021) *Anuario del Gobierno Local* 203.

This new type of entity might be described also as a "local energy community" (LEC) since local authorities participate in them, as we discuss further below.[9]

2.3.2.2 National regulation: Local energy communities (LECs)

Spanish local legislation during the financial crisis, and the related Law 27/2013, addressed Rationalisation and Sustainability in Local Administrations. As such, it restricted municipal authority in the environmental and clean energy areas. The concurrent Law 24/2013, addressing the electricity sector, also marked a step forward in transforming energy models. That being said, the partial transposition of the aforementioned Directive 2018/2001 (and 2019/2001), aimed at restoring the role of local authorities in the energy transition, has yet to be realised.

The Royal Decree-Law 23/2020 of 23 June (RDL 23/2020) approved measures addressing energy resources and other aspects of economic recovery. This law partially amends the Electricity Sector Act 24/2013 and introduces the innovative topic of regulating compensation systems. These measures all involve "renewable energy communities".[10] The latter are defined as legal entities based on the open and voluntary participation of neighbouring individuals in local renewable energy projects. Their primary purpose is to provide environmental, economic and social benefits to community members and the local operative area rather than any financial gain.

Alternatively, the "citizen energy communities" provided for in Directive 2018/944 have not yet been developed within the above Royal Decree-Law and are thus pending regulation. However, Article 2, paragraph 11 of the Directive, which concerns definitions, presents a citizen energy community as a legal entity which:

a) is based on the voluntary and open participation of and effective control by partners or members who are natural persons, small enterprises or local authorities, including municipalities;
b) has the primary objective of providing environmental, economic or social benefits to members, partners or the operative area rather than generating financial returns;
c) is involved in energy generation (including renewable energy) as well as energy distribution, supply, consumption, pooling and storage. It also

9 Isabel González Ríos, 'Las "Comunidades energéticas locales": un nuevo desafío para las entidades locales' (2020) 117 *Revista vasca de Administración pública* 147 and ibidem, *Los entes locales ante la transición y sostenibilidad energética. Nuevos desafíos jurídicos-administrativos para 2030/2050* (Thomson Reuters Aranzadi 2021); Isabel Gallego Córcoles, *Comunidades de energía y transición energética* (Thomson Reuters Aranzadi 2021).

10 Isabel Gallego Córcoles, 'Las comunidades de energías renovables: retos pendientes' in Francisco Delgado Piqueras et al. (eds.), *Los desafíos jurídicos de la transición energética* (Thomson Reuters Aranzadi 2022) 597–622.

entails providing energy efficiency services or electric vehicle recharging facilities and other energy services to members or partners.

The LEC issue has been subject to a prior public consultation organised by the Institute for Diversification and Energy Savings (*Instituto para la Diversificaciòn e Ahorro de la Energìa*/IDAE) and the Ministry of Ecological Transition and Demographic Challenges (*Ministerio para la Transición Ecológica y el Reto Demográfic*/MITERD). This consultation was held from 17 November to 12 February 2020 and aimed to gather contributions in order to draft a corresponding legal framework.[11] The resulting document indicates that local energy communities should encompass the two types set out in the European Directives, i.e., renewable energy and citizen energy communities.

These communities and their objectives may form a part of any project in the electricity sector, including those involving the activities indicated in c) above.

Private industry or service companies, local authorities and citizens may all be involved in local energy communities (LECs). As such, they have tools available to them for promoting their energy community and also a capacity for financing it via subsidies and tax breaks. Such energy communities, moreover, bring an objective and unifying approach to the table when engaging with different actors.

Given the inability to postpone the programme's deadlines, Herrera and Navarro point out that NGEU funding has been launched without a complete legal framework in place.[12] These authors further suggest the correct transposition of the Directive will involve, among other things, "explicitly indicating local authority responsibilities with respect to energy efficiency or savings and climate change measures in basic local government laws and the local regulations of each Autonomous Community". It should also account for approving the Municipal Ordinances that regulate LECs in any local entity.

2.3.2.3 LEC Implementation

The set-up of local energy communities is becoming widespread, particularly in the wake of NGEU support. To this end, Herrera and Navarro give a first-hand account of the situation underway in the municipality of Prat de Llobregat (located in the province of Barcelona and with a population of 65,000). On 3 February 2023, the Town Council, companies, residents and

11 This follows the explanation given by Joan Herrera and Pilar Navarro (n 8) 203.

12 Joan Herrera and Pilar Navarro (n 8) 203, 221. They report on the use of NGEU Funds by Local Energy Communities. See also Fundación Renovables, *Democratizar la energía como proyecto de país: los Fondos Next Generation EU y las infraestructuras del sistema eléctrico* (2021).

other organisations in the municipality officially set up *"Energía del Prat"*, a LEC which aims to be the largest in Spain.

The municipal government heads this LEC which integrates organisations, SMEs and individual residents. Its set-up has involved €300,000 of capital distributed amongst: the El Prat de Llobregat City Council (with 40% of the shares); a citizen user organisation, *El Prat Energía Asociación Ciudadana*, (with 20% of the shares as given to them by the city council); and private capital (accounting for the remaining 40% of the shares and linked to individuals and companies who became members during the competitive bidding process).

Once this LEC has been fully established, it will compete for the "*CE Implementa*" funding announced by the Institute for Energy Diversification and Savings . This programme facilitates access to subsidies for installing renewable energy resources and deploying energy demand management programmes or energy-saving and efficiency strategies in households, businesses and companies. The programme concurrently works to offer and gradually roll out energy services aimed at "democratising access to basic supplies for households and businesses in El Prat." For the time being, the LEC's community service offer consists of individual access and consumption of solar energy produced on the rooftops of municipal buildings.

From a legal point of view, this activity is seen as a local economic initiative and open competition (not a public service). It is also linked to creating a single LEC to provide the services again indicated in c) above. In terms of format, the municipality has opted for creating a new, local, mixed-capital company with the LEC. Local government is participating to some extent in this innovative company which aims to ensure free competition and equal opportunities to private capital from the start.

2.3.3 Sustainable mobility: Low emission zones (LEZs)

In the context of green cities and the fight against climate change, one of the most controversial local policies is that of allowing municipalities to define low emission zones (LEZs) that restrict or ban polluting vehicles from certain areas. Environmental legislation related to air quality or public health legislation was initially used as a basis for this activity. However, this gave rise to some doubts about the legitimacy of municipal activity in this area. Now, Article 14.3 of Law 7/2021 of 20 May on climate change and the energy transition explicitly provides for this kind of action, making it even mandatory in certain cases. The Autonomous Community laws on climate change have also integrated this kind of municipal power. These so-called low emission zones (LEZs) are addressed under Article 14.3 which states:

> Municipalities with over 50,000 inhabitants and island territories shall adopt aligned sustainable urban and air quality plans that introduce mitigation measures to reduce mobility-related emissions. These should include at least: a) establishing low emission zones by 2023.

Subsequently, the Royal Decree 1052/2022 of 27 December regulates LEZs in compliance with the mandate set out in Article 14.3 of the Climate Change Act. As such, Spanish municipalities with over 50,000 inhabitants, island territories and municipalities of over 20,000 inhabitants that exceed pollution limits must adopt sustainable urban mobility plans by 2023. These plans should introduce mitigation measures that reduce mobility-related emissions and include, at a minimum, setting up LEZs.

Prior to this Law, in fact, city councils in Madrid and Barcelona had already tried to institute ordinances establishing LEZs. Consequently, both cities have been subjected to rigorous judicial control which has counteracted these city regulatory provisions.

It is appropriate to note here that Barcelona has a responsibility and obligation to regulate LECs. Despite this, Judgement 970/2022 of 21 March 2022 by the High Court of Justice of Catalonia annulled its LEZ ordinance and the articles approved in 2019 which signalled the city's attempt to live up to its responsibilities. Articles 9 and 10, in particular, provided for a general ban on the circulation of the most highly polluting vehicles in the Rondas de Barcelona LEZ area. This ban was to apply to workdays from Monday to Friday, 7.00 a.m. to 8.00 p.m., and exceptions could only be made via compulsory registration or individual authorisation.

The High Court maintained at the outset, however, that:

> The ban is a maximum restriction measure that implies no access to LEZs [for vehicles with a certain environmental sticker]. It also prevents some vehicles within a LEZ from circulating during prohibited days and times. The extent of these limitations may render such vehicles in question useless.

Based on this, the judgment by the Court implied the need to carry out a thorough analysis of the fairness of the measure adopted, as it covered practically the entire municipal area. Furthermore, this study had to include considering alternative measures, etc. The Court at the same time actually annulled the existing municipal LEZ ordinance on the grounds that the background analysis done beforehand had been inadequate. The Court thus argued:

> It can be concluded from the above that the intensity and general scope of the restrictions imply compliance with the general requirements according to the statement of reasons set out in Art. 4.1 of the Public Sector Legal Regime Act (*Ley de Régimen Jurídico del Sector Público*) and Art. 5.2 of the Law on the Guarantee of Market Unity (*Ley de Garantía de la Unidad de Mercado*). These indicate the need to assess the impact of any measures on competitiveness and markets linked to transport and automotive-related businesses in the LEZ.

The case does not reflect sufficient analysis of alternatives or the economic, social, market and competitive consequences of the measures. It also does not sufficiently assess the cost-benefits of the draft provision for the targeted groups or the administrative burdens involved in implementing the Ordinance.

The High Court's judgment, in effect, annulled the city ordinance on the grounds that there had not been adequate prior studies and analyses carried out by the city council during the Ordinance's drafting and approval procedure. However, it did not counteract it on the grounds of the material illegality of its content or its being contrary to the legal system in place, e.g. due to any possible infringing on free access to economic activity or market integrity.

Something similar also occurred in the case of the Madrid City Council. Here, the Judgement of the Madrid High Court of Justice (*Tribunal Superior de Justicia/TSJ*) of 27 July 2020 annulled similar Ordinances relating to the "Madrid Central" LEZ. This annulment was also due to insufficient prior economic evaluation.

Thus, in the wake of local anti-pollution and global warming measures, it seems there is once again widespread debate in Spain over the annulling of regulations, ordinances and urban development plans on the procedural grounds or because of insufficient motives.[13] All the while, Spain has been the subject of related proceedings before the CJEU, which ended with a Judgment on 22 December 2022. This judgment ruled on the appeal against Spain for its non-compliance with Directive 2008/50/EC on ambient air quality and cleaner air for Europe.

In view of this situation, the national Recovery Plan has given special consideration to LEZ policies and urban transport transformation. The plan provides for a €1 billion block of aid to speed up carbon emission reductions in cities, improve air quality and mitigate noise levels by promoting low-emission zones (LEZs) and the sustainable transformation of urban and metropolitan transport. It also seeks to promote the deployment of reliable, attractive, accessible and affordable public transport systems and more modern, efficient and zero-emission fleets in urban areas. It further aims to encourage sustainable urban freight services and a smart digital concept of mobility. Each measure of the plan has undergone a targeted assessment to estimate its contribution to climate objectives. The resulting overall conclusion was that the plan allocates approximately 40% of its total resources to counteracting climate change.

13 See Fernando López Ramón, 'La calificación de los vicios de los reglamento' (2018) 205 *Revista de Administración Pública* 13 and Joaquín Tornos Mas, 'La nulidad de normas por vicios procedimentales. La necesidad de nuevos planteamientos legislativos y jurisprudenciales' (2019) 210 *Revista de Administración Pública*, 123. See also the other articles contained in the "Debates" section of the same *Revista de Administración Pública* issue.

2.3.4 Climate cities and European legitimacy

LEZ activities in Spanish cities have spurred further efforts in the field of European justice. These are of great interest from a procedural point of view and in terms of defining the legitimacy of cities in relation to European jurisdiction.

The Judgment of the General Court of the European Union No. 927 of 13 December 2018 (Joined Cases T-339/16, T-352/16 and iT-391/16) effectively recognised that the municipalities of Paris, Brussels and Madrid could legitimately lodge an appeal to annul Commission Regulation 2016/646. This regulation amended the emission ceilings set under Euro Law 6, making these limits less stringent. The previous ceilings had been laid down under Regulation 715/2007 of the European Parliament and Council in the wake of the so-called "Dieselgate" case. Madrid had previously approved a LEZ ordinance more strictly regulating the circulation of polluting vehicles, as noted above. However, a new European standard left this municipal regulation without force.

The General Court had recognised that cities may legitimately make an appeal. It did this by reiterating its position that if an EU act keeps a public person from exercising their power as they see fit, this directly affects their legal position. In turn, this is precisely the kind of situation needed under Article 263.4 of the TFEU in order to make an appeal. The General Court emphasised that what occurs in this case is:

> An act by the Union affects an infra-State entity *even more directly* if it impacts on its own *regulatory* powers [in this specific case, it does this with regard to regulating the movement of vehicles in an LEZ]. It also impacts on its power to adopt individual decisions within a pre-established framework.

Accordingly, the General Court's decision of 13 December 2018 continued as follows:

> The legal elements and circumstances considered above particularly refer to the claimant's power to restrict motor vehicle use to protect air quality. Based on this, it is clear that the Regulation under question affects the claimant's legal position and thus directly affects them pursuant to Article 263, paragraph 4 of the TFUE. Furthermore, the contested regulation is an act which does not include implementing measures as defined in the noted provision. Thus, as indicated above in paragraphs 38 and 40, the actions brought by the Cities of Paris, Brussels and Madrid are admissible and any objections against them by the Commission are not acceptable.

In this case, or that of annulment, the action taken by cities in making an appeal has general effects that go beyond re-establishing the legal violations against them. This is because they assume a role as guarantors of European environmental law. It is not the states, but the cities – the "infra-state entities", according to the judgement – that are the subjects which develop "discretionary" policy options. These options include a regulatory power over the so-called low emission zones (LEZs) which has been limited by an amendment to a community regulation (which was approved, moreover, via the "comitology" procedure).[14]

Indeed, an appeal against the above judgment was lodged by the Commission, Germany and Hungary. In this, the Advocate General took the view that the municipalities were not directly affected by the judgment under appeal because the regulation involved was aimed at approving types of vehicles. However, the Advocate General did maintain that the municipalities also had some legal standing based on a balanced interpretation of the need for a direct effect, pursuant to the principle of respecting local autonomy under Article 4.2 of the TJUE and the role of local governments in EU law.

The appeal was settled finally by the Court of Justice of the European Union Judgment of 13 January 2022 (C-177/19 P to C-179/19 P). This upheld the rejection of the judgment which admitted legality and, in turn, did not uphold the Advocate General's second argument in favour of admitting it. Consequently, it set aside the judgment by the General Court of the European Union based on the lack of standing.[15]

I point to this case merely as an indication that the process of recognising how city policies increasingly determine transnational ones, in this case at the European level, has already begun. As such, cities are directly involved actors that will need to achieve a legal-institutional status corresponding to their role.

2.4 The instruments of co-administration, in particular the Regulation on Common Property and Collaboration Pacts

2.4.1 Introduction

The city of Barcelona has historically enjoyed a special legal regime that is different, in important respects, from those common to the other Spanish municipalities (under Law 7/1985, on the Basis of Local Government/*Ley 7/1985, de Bases del Régimen Local/LBRL*). It is also different from other special systems in municipalities with a large number of inhabitants or "large cities" (Title X of the LBRL). At present, Barcelona's special legislation consists

14 See Beltrán Puentes Cociña, 'Las ciudades como garantes de la legalidad europea en materia de calidad del aire' in Fernando Lopez Ramon and Julián Valero Torrijos (eds.), *20 años de la Ley de la Jurisdicción contencioso-administrativa* (AEPDA-INAP 2019) 179 ff; Fabio Giglioni, 'Le città e l'inquinamento atmosferico nel diritto europeo' (2019) four *Giornale amministrativo* 447; Tomás Font i Llovet, 'La ciudad inteligente como actor global' (2021) two (1) *European Review of Digital Administration & Law* 19 (discussed further here as well).

15 See Peñalver i Cabré (n 6) 84.

of the Catalan Law 22/1998 of 30 December, addressing the Barcelona Municipal Charter (*Carta Municipal de Barcelona/CMB*), and the State Law 1/2006 of 23 March, on Barcelona's Special Regime. Within the framework of these laws, the Barcelona City Council has approved various additional municipal regulations that logically form part of the city's special regime as well.

One of the aspects regulated by the Barcelona Municipal Charter Law is the different instruments involved in administrative decentralisation and citizen participation. These measures are the result of Barcelona's long tradition of having special sensitivity for and paying special attention to citizen movements as well as to strengthening the relationship between social groups and municipal institutions. As the preamble to the Charter Law explains, it is:

> A Charter that responds to the desires of citizens who, through their participation and collective involvement, have made Barcelona what it is. The Charter deepens the mechanisms of citizen participation, reinforces democratic practice and stimulates cooperation between the city council, associative movements and social agents, seeing these as elements of progress and cohesion.

2.4.2 Civic management of municipal services and facilities

The instruments relating to the above cooperation between citizens and institutions, and the chapter referring to citizen participation (Article 34 of the Municipal Charter), integrate an innovative element – *the civic management of municipal services and facilities*. The rule linked to this management indicates:

> Non-profit entities, organisations and citizen associations may exercise municipal powers or participate on behalf of the City Council in the management of services or facilities whose ownership corresponds to other public administrations. The civic management of municipal authorities can be used also for activities and services that can be managed indirectly. This activity is always voluntary and non-profit in nature. It is awarded by public tender if there are several entities or organisations with identical or similar characteristics.

Although the legal formula used is somewhat misleading, what is actually proposed is that citizens participate in making public decisions by means of various consultation and co-decision-making mechanisms regulated by the Municipal Charter itself. However, citizens can also participate in the execution of public policies in terms of the management or provision of services as well.

Moreover, the allowing of these civic management mechanisms conveys another message in terms of the indirect management of services and facilities. That is, it is possible to offer the same not-for-profit services and facilities on the free market too or in areas where private economic actors generally operate. Community facilities such as youth, civic and social and neighbourhood centres and cultural spaces, etc. have been managed in this way for years.

With time, the initial foresight towards civic management has expanded considerably, based on the idea that "something public" can become "something communal". As such, Barcelona City Council has promoted:

> new forms of interaction between municipal public institutions and community citizen initiatives. This has centred on recognising the citizen and the community rights to manage and use facilities and services or public heritage in general.

The city council has pointed this out in its document, *Bienes Comunes: hacia el uso y la gestión comunitaria de lo público* (*Common Goods: Towards community use and management of the public*) (2022).

2.4.3 The transfer of public assets

Indeed, the city council has had a policy of ceding *publicly owned heritage assets* to associations and citizen groups. It has done this so that these groups can define ways of using and operating these assets rather than having their use predetermined as a public service or by an already existing facility. In this way, various types of built premises, undeveloped plots of land, "empty spaces" and green or garden areas have been handed over to public groups to create vegetable gardens.

An important difference between this and the previous way of doing things is that the assets involved are not classified as being in the public domain. This is because they have never been previously assigned for a public purpose or service. Thus, involved real estate is seen as part of the municipal patrimony and not an asset pertaining to some public service, e.g. land or plots left over from urban development operations, urban renewal activity, etc.

2.4.4 Achievements

Both these two forms of citizen participation, i.e. the managing of community or civic services and the common use of public assets, have been widely disseminated in recent decades. Here, I would refer to Marc Vilalta's comprehensive work for specific data and documentation of this.[16] In brief, it can be said that a quarter of the more than 50 civic centres in Barcelona are managed via a civic mechanism. On the other hand, there are more than 60 activities

16 Marc Vilalta Reixach, 'Instrumentos de gestión ciudadana de bienes comunes en la ciudad de Barcelona: la cesión de espacios vacíos y la gestión cívica de equipamientos' in Chiara Alvisi et al. (eds.), *New policies and practices for European sharing cities* (University of Bologna 2019) 377.

underway for the use of empty spaces and the transfer of assets and a network of 130 urban vegetable gardens under similar management.

Updated data shows that in 2021 alone, seven agreements were signed for the civic management of facilities and the use of public spaces, and these activities were linked to municipal subsidies totalling almost €2 million.

2.4.5 Legal regime

The legal modes used to formalise the relationship between city councils and civic associations, or the groups that manage municipal facilities or spaces, have evolved over the years. At present, the civic management of facilities and services is in line with the "Base model" approved by Barcelona City Council in 2015 and modified in 2019. This model governs the multi-year tender process (where reference to direct awarding has been removed). Formalisation takes place by the signing of an agreement whereby the civic manager mainly assumes the right and obligation to occupy and make proper use of the space they are given to develop.

The specific agreements signed by the Barcelona City Council contain a justification of their legal appropriateness indicating:

> civic management involves the use or transfer of the assets needed for developing an activity in accordance with the provisions of Decree 336/1988, of 17 October. This approved the Regulations on local authority assets and, where appropriate, the granting of a subsidy to a civic manager. It is also in accordance with the provisions of the general regulations governing municipal subsidies in Barcelona, or Law 38/2003 of 17 November on general subsidies, and the regulations that govern them.
>
> Civic management is formalised through a collaborative agreement and, although it establishes bilateral obligations, it does not take on the legal aspect of a public sector contract. Consequently, it does not constitute a form of procurement for the management of public services. Nor can its scope imply any breach of the basic rules of public sector procurement or the Community directives applicable to this issue.

Again, since this is not a market activity, the exclusion of public procurement legislation does not prevent the application of any public subsidy regime.

A contract for the temporary free-of-charge use of a public space is used in the case of empty spaces. That is, there is essentially an authorisation to occupy the space on a temporary basis. This contract is not transferable without the municipality's consent and is not subject to public sector contract law. However, it is subject to public administration property law, and assignments are made by public tender.

2.4.6 Perspectives

A lack of general provisions regarding city councils exists in terms of the legal regulation of the civic management of common goods and municipal facilities. This includes a lack of any specific municipal regulations as well. Despite extensive administrative and citizen activity in this area, a real municipal policy on common assets has not yet emerged based on the standard legal instruments found elsewhere, e.g. regulations or the *Patti di Collaborazione* in Italian municipalities.[17]

The Barcelona City Council has promoted relatedly a Programme for the Promotion of the Special Regime of the Municipality of Barcelona (*Programa para el impulso del Régimen especial del municipio de Barcelona/IREMB*). The most important results of this effort have been published in Tomàs Font i Llovet (ed.), *La Carta Municipal de Barcelona i el dret de la ciutat. Bases per al seu impuls i actualització* (Ayuntamiento de Barcelona 2022). Vicenç Aguado has presented an array of interesting proposals in relation to regulations in his work, including in *Propostes normatives per al règim especial de Barcelona sobre els béns comuns, administració compartida i gestió cívica*. There he points out the need to advance the regulatory development of Article 134 of the Municipal Charter. Because of its undoubted interest, I cite his remarks on this at greater length below. According to him, this regulatory development could cover some or all of the following aspects:

a) Explicitly recognising *the right of citizens* to contribute to the management of the commons as appropriate or as a possible manifestation and development of the so-called "right to the city".
b) Making it a municipal duty to periodically *identify* and publish properties available for civic management through a Catalogue of Properties for Community Use and Management. The inclusion of a property in this Catalogue should entail its having an inalienable character and the prioritisation of civic management over other forms carried out by for-profit entities.
c) Stating the *principles* that should govern the civic management of the commons including: continuity, economic sustainability, trust, marketing and transparency, accountability, inclusiveness and openness, equality and non-discrimination, proportionality, adequacy and differentiation, informality, civic autonomy and proximity and territoriality.
d) Regulating the *requirements* that active citizens should have in order to assume the care, renewal and shared management of the commons.

17 See Giorgia Pavani and Claudia Tubertini, '*European sharing (and collaborative) cities*: l'esperienza delle città italiane' in Concepción Barrero and Joana M. Socias (eds.), *La Ciudad del siglo XXI: transformaciones y retos* (AEPDA-INAP 2020) 729. Gregorio Arena also strongly supports this dynamic in 'Un nuevo derecho para la administración compartida de los bienes comunes. La experiencia italiana' (2017) 203 *Revista de Administracion Pública* 423 and *I custodi della bellezza. Prendersi cura dei beni comuni. Un patto per l'Italia fra cittadini e istituzioni* (Touring Club Italiano 2020). See also Fabio Giglioni, 'Le città come ordinamento giuridico' (2018) one *Istituzioni del federalismo* 29.

e) Recognising *groups without a legal status* which can carry out civic management. This should be done with reference to the law in Article 3.c) LPC.
f) Regulating how citizens may *formulate collaborative proposals* for carrying out the civic management of the commons.
g) Regulating the minimum content of *collaboration pacts* between the dministration and citizens. This content may include: objectives; duration; modality and forms of action, roles and their respective commitments; tools for guaranteeing collective enjoyment; the definition of management and coordination instruments; ways to evaluate the pact; the provision of council personnel; causes for the exclusion of citizens due to non-observance of the common good; and the consequences of potential damages done.
h) Establishing *obligations of transparency and control* in collaborative agreements.
i) Clarifying when awarding by *public tender* is appropriate due to the existence of "several entities or organisations with identical or similar characteristics".
j) Establishing a set of criteria for the *attribution of financial benefits* and other forms of support within the framework of the partnership agreements.
k) Having a regulated system of *responsibility* in civic management involving the sharing of responsibility between the administration and an active citizenry.

2.5 Conclusion: The powers of the city

Looking beyond the concrete actions it may undertake, the city appears to have, above all, an institutional position as a service provider and executor of European, state or regional policies. However, cities have less capacity to establish their own policies in terms of ecological and social solidarity activity.

The European context is moving towards greater recognition of the city as an actor in environmental and energy policies, but the principle of institutional autonomy still weighs too heavily to allow this change to be more decisive. In fact, state legislation and jurisdiction actually delimit a city's fields of action.

In this sense, city powers are worryingly fragile. Thus, the *regulatory* power of cities is still too conditioned by the dogma of statutory limits, which are certainly in need of profound revision. *Administrative policing* powers, especially the mayor's authority as an elected official, also need to be reconsidered.

The powers of the city are subject to very strict *judicial scrutiny*, and this does not greatly favour the democratic basis of municipalities. Excessive formal types of judicial review all too often overturn local rules on procedural flaws. This points towards a more general problem within Spanish administrative justice with respect to controlling regulatory powers.

In some cases, the criminal justice system is even misused against mayors. This occurs not so much to counteract corruption, but rather the legitimate undertaking of public initiatives which may appear to restrict economic activity, mobility or traffic. This was the case with the mayor of Barcelona, who adopted traffic restriction measures (e.g. "superblocks" or "green axes"). I refer to Chapter 9 by Marc Vilalta Reixach in this book to this end.

In short, a change of perspective is needed. I might sum this up by quoting a line from the memorial tribute I wrote for the great Bolognese jurist, Luciano Vandelli. There, I noted that "perhaps the time has come to move from *local autonomy* to the *powers of the city*."[18]

Bibliography

Alenza García, J.F., 'Planificación climática local: ordenación del territorio, urbanismo y movilidad' (2021) *Anuario del Gobierno Local* 91.

Amoedo Souto, C.A., 'La colaboración público-público en el ámbito local tras la Ley 9/2017, de contratos del sector público' (2018) *Anuario del Gobierno Local* 263.

Arena, G., 'Un nuevo derecho para la administración compartida de los bienes comunes. La experiencia italiana' (2017) 203 *Revista de Adminstracion Pública* 423.

Arena, G., *I custodi della bellezza. Prendersi cura dei beni comuni. Un patto per l'Italia fra cittadini e istituzioni* (Touring Club Italiano 2020).

Braudel, F., *Le modèle italien* (Flammarion 1994).

Colás Tenas J., 'Los Gobiernos locales intermedios en la gestión de los fondos europeos para la recuperación' (2021) 55 *Cuadernos de Derecho Local* 37.

Font i Llovet, T., 'De la autonomia local a los poderes de la Ciudad: un cambio de perspectiva' (2020) Special Issue in honour of Luciano Vandelli, *Istituzioni del federalismo* 115.

Font i Llovet, T., 'La ciudad inteligente como actor global' (2021) 2 (1) *European Review of Digital Administration & Law* 19.

Font i Llovet T. (ed.), *La Carta Municipal de Barcelona i el dret de la ciutat. Bases per al seu impuls i actualització* (Ayuntamiento de Barcelona 2022).

Fundación Renovables, *Democratizar la energía como proyecto de país: los Fondos Next Generation EU y las infraestructuras del sistema eléctrico* (2021).

Galán Galán, A., 'Los gobiernos locales ante el reto de los fondos europeos de recuperación' (2021) 63 *Revista Catalana de Dret Públic* 101.

Gallego Córcoles, I., *Comunidades de energía y transición energética* (Thomson Reuters Aranzadi 2021).

Gallego Córcoles, I., 'Las comunidades de energías renovables: retos pendientes', in Delgado Piqueras, I. et al. (eds.), *Los desafíos jurídicos de la transición energética* (Thomson Reuters Aranzadi 2022).

Giglioni, F., 'Le città come ordinamento giuridico' (2018) 1 *Istituzioni del federalismo* 29.

Giglioni, F., 'Le città e l'inquinamento atmosferico nel diritto europeo' (2019) 4 *Giornale amministrativo* 447.

González Ríos, I., 'Las 'Comunidades energéticas locales': un nuevo desafío para las entidades locales' (2020) 117 *Revista vasca de Administración pública* 147.

18 Tomás Font i Llovet, 'De la autonomia local a los poderes de la Ciudad: un cambio de perspectiva' in (2020) Special issue in honour of Luciano Vandelli *Istituzioni del federalismo* 115.

González Ríos, I., *Los entes locales ante la transición y sostenibilidad energética. Nuevos desafíos jurídico-administrativos para 2030/2050* (Thomson Reuters Aranzadi 2021).

Herrera, J. and Navarro, P., 'Las comunidades energéticas como nuevo sujeto del derecho energético en España: del falanasterio a la transformación' (2021) *Anuario del Gobierno Local* 203.

López Ramón, F., 'La calificación de los vicios de los reglamentos' (2018) 205 *Revista de Administración Pública* 13.

Moreno Carlos, *Droit de cité, de la "ville-monde" à la "ville du quart d'heure"* (Éditions de l'Observatoire 2020).

Pavani, G. and Tubertini, C., 'European sharing (and collaborative) cities: l'esperienza delle città italiane', in Concepción, Barrero and Joana, M. Socias (eds.), *La Ciudad del siglo XXI: transformaciones y retos* (AEPDA-INAP 2020).

Peñalver i Cabré, A., 'El rol de los gobiernos locales frente al cambio climático en el Derecho internacional y en el derecho de la Unión Europea' (2021) *Anuario del Gobierno Local* 51.

Puentes Cociña, B., 'Las ciudades como garantes de la legalidad europea en materia de calidad del aire', in Fernando López Ramón and Julián Valero Torrijos (eds.), *20 años de la Ley de la Jurisdicción contencioso-administrativa* (AEPDA-INAP 2019).

Revuelta Pérez, I., 'La actividad de los gobiernos locales en el ámbito de la energía limpia: marco normativo' (2021) *Anuario del Gobierno Local* 171.

Santiago Iglesias, D., 'Cooperación horizontal: los convenios interadministrativos', in Eduardo Gamero Casado and Isabel Gallego Córcoles (eds.), *Tratado de Contratos del Sector público – Vol. I* (Tirant lo Blanch 2018).

Tornos Mas, J., 'La nulidad de normas por vicios procedimentales. La necesidad de nuevos planteamientos legislativos y jurisprudenciales' (2019) 210 *Revista de Administración Pública* 123.

Vilalta Reixach, M., 'Los convenios administrativos a la luz de la nueva Ley de Contratos del Sector Público', in José María Gimeno Feliú (ed.), *Estudio sistemático de la Ley de Contratos del Sector Público* (Thomson Reuters-Aranzadi 2018).

Vilalta Reixach, M., 'Los convenios interadministrativos (locales) y la Ley de Contratos del Sector Público: ¿Convenio o contrato?' (2019a) 12 *Anuario de Derecho Municipal* 53.

Vilalta Reixach, M., 'Instrumentos de gestión ciudadana de bienes comunes en la ciudad de Barcelona: la cesión de espacios vacíos y la gestión cívica de equipamientos', in Chiara Alvisi et al. (eds.), *New Policies and Practices for European Sharing Cities* (University of Bologna 2019b).

3 The role of cities in the Italian National Recovery and Resilience Plan

Claudia Tubertini

3.1 Recovery and resilience plans as national programmes for major reform: The role of states and cities

Among the many challenges facing modern nation-states is that of representing the demands, needs and desires of cities and their inhabitants. This situation is the result of the progressive administrative decentralisation of most European countries and the concurrent increasing attention that European and supranational bodies now pay to cities.

To understand how vital the contributions made by cities now are to states in implementing their renewal objectives and responding to new population needs, we need recall that the legally created nation-state itself, understood as the basic form of political organisation in society throughout the 19th and first half of the 20th century, is today in crisis. This has led to a rediscovery of cities, which are now called upon to respond to needs which were generally met by state measures in the past. With this city activism, states themselves have discovered new strength and legitimacy by recreating, in urban contexts, the bond between the societal and political levels which is the basis of democracy.[1]

A broad concept of the city[2] is used here and is understood as encompassing a spatial-geographical dimension, i.e. the city as a physical place characterised by a particular demographic concentration. (In the case of diffuse cities, as in Italy, it includes, moreover, actual metropolises, medium-sized cities and networks of cities). It also encompasses an associative dimension (i.e. the city as a community of citizens and the economic and social actors operating therein)

1 Among the extensive legal literature on the increased role of cities, Jean-Bernard Auby, *Droit de la ville: Du fonctionnement juridique des villes au droit à la Ville* (LexisNexis 2013); Tomás Font i Llovet, 'De la autonomía local al poder de las ciudades' (2019) Special Issue *Istituzioni del Federalismo* 123, and Fulvio Cortese, 'Il nuovo diritto delle città: alla ricerca di un legittimo spazio operativo', in Giuseppe Franco Ferrari (ed.), *Smart city. L'evoluzione di un'idea* (Mimesis 2020) 79.

2 Erika Arban, 'Constitutional law, federalism and the city as a unique socio-economic and political space', in Ernst Hirsch Ballin, Gerhard van der Schyff, Maarten Stremler and Maartje De Visser (eds), *European Yearbook of Constitutional Law 2020. The city in Constitutional Law* (Springer 2021) 326.

DOI: 10.4324/9781032665184-8

and institutional one (i.e. city governing bodies). Regarding the latter, we recognise the frequent lack of congruity between the phenomenon of citizenship and legal boundaries, whether they be traditional (e.g. capital municipalities, unions of municipalities and provinces) or more recently institutionalised ones (e.g. Metropolitan cities).

The relationship between the nation-state and the city was notably and particularly put to the test during the pandemic period. This trend occurred in all countries, but particularly those with federal or autonomist traditions. The health emergency called forth co-participation at all the involved decision-making levels to ensure the utmost coordination between measures and the effectiveness of their resulting activity. Given the need for absolute timeliness, however, the emergency also resulted in a re-expansion of conflicts and a crisis in the cooperative mechanisms forming the foundation of multilevel states. This subsequently led to a strengthening of the role of the state to a greater or lesser extent, depending on the country, due to the reintroduction of standard emergency measures, but also some of an authoritative nature. The latter included, for example, the government's exceptional revoking of actions taken by local autonomies. In other European countries, it involved declaring a state of emergency, a relic of a long-outdated notion of the state.

Still, in regulating the management of the Recovery and Resilience Facility (RRF),[3] and its use via the national plans submitted to the Commission for approval, the European Union recommended states consult with all territorial levels. This was to be done from the initial plan development phase through to implementation. This choice not only appears in line with the European practice of multilevel governance, but is connected, above all, to the desired objective of setting up long-term growth policies continuing beyond the health crisis. As such, this crisis was leveraged to create long-term development projects and seize the potential opportunities offered by the historical moment, e.g. the expected long deadline for loan repayments (up until 2058).

According to the RRF Regulations, the development goals within national plans envision multiple intervention areas (i.e. the green transition; digital transformation; smart, sustainable and inclusive growth; social and territorial cohesion; health and economic, social and institutional resilience; and policies for the next generation, children and youth)[4] and require a minimum percentage of funding to be allocated to the green (37%) and digital transitions (20%). A review of these conditions allows grasping the close links that exist, first and foremost, between the interests, objectives and related actions of European

3 For a full review of the related European Parliament Regulation (EU) 2021/241, and that of the Council of 12 February 2021, see, first of all, Federico Fabbrini, *Next Generation EU. Il futuro di Europa e Italia dopo la pandemia* (Il Mulino 2022).

4 Art. 3 of the related regulation.

cities, which have long played a leading role not only nationally but internationally and in Europe.[5]

National plans were thus conceived from the outset as a blend and expression of state needs and requirements, but of states that cannot do without cities given the new dimensions of Europe. Moreover, as rightly observed (about Italy, but also applicable to all European countries), the development envisaged under the Next Generation EU programme can only emerge with joint collaboration between different institutional levels, different public and private entities, different territorial spheres and a unitary vision of the national interest. The latter is the only one affording a strong presence in the European forum, which complements and reinforces national ones with a renewed modern type of sovereignty. This is the case in a world, which despite the pandemic, is increasingly globalised and reflects leadership approaches that no longer coincide with those of traditional western democracies.[6]

However, the ambition and vastness of the current European programme have been linked from the start to tight deadlines for submitting national plans to the Commission, gaining approval, and, above all, actually using the resulting grants and loans (by 2026). There are also mechanisms for periodically verifying the meeting of the required Milestones and Targets needed for approving biannual resource disbursements under the plans. These elements certainly force Member States to put a degree of stress on their institutional set-ups and the decision-making processes governed by plan regulations. In other words, all countries are being asked to make an extraordinary effort. Of course, this does not exclude regulatory changes and/or making adjustments in response to the actual actions taken centrally or in relation to the procedures naturally delegated onwards (to Parliaments through to consultation forums between the state and sub-state territorial levels) in order to define national objectives. The actual procedures (and instruments) typically used in emergency situations may also be applied.

In essence, this is where the ambivalence of the European project lurks. It calls for the utmost sharing, but, at the same time, places responsibility for respecting set timeframes on the state's shoulders. States thus run the risk of centralising decision-making, and, further downstream, actual programme and project activity as well. This may be done to the detriment, first and foremost, of cities. As such, European governance itself was particularly strengthened[7] with the application of the initial financial solidarity instruments among states. This occurred both upstream, as previously mentioned, in identifying

5 For an overview of these programmes from the perspective of the city as a main actor, see Giorgia Pavani, 'Comparare al tempo delle cities', in Giorgia Pavani, Stefania Profeti and Claudia Tubertini, *Le città collaborative ed eco-sostenibili* (Il Mulino 2023) 28.

6 Anna Romeo, 'Le misure amministrative per la ripresa e la resilienza economica. Il piano italiano' (2022) 2 *Istituzioni del federalismo* 400.

7 Marcello Cecchetti, 'L'incidenza del PNRR sui Livelli Territoriali di Governo e le Conseguenze nei Sistemi Amministrativi' (2022) 3 *Rivista AIC* 13 September 2022.

the priorities common to all countries, and downstream in the periodic verification mechanisms needed to achieve results as well as in monitoring and reporting. All this has had obvious repercussions on the nation-state form of government.[8]

It is interesting to examine, therefore, how the Italian state configured its relationship with cities in adopting its National Recovery and Resilience Plan (*Piano Nazionale di Ripresa e Resilienza* /PNRR)[9] from the drafting through to management and implementation phases. This kind of analysis affords some reflection on the PNRR's coherence and implementation mechanisms. It also affords thinking about the evolution of the role of cities within the national panorama and what may be anticipated as happening "beyond" the PNRR. The implementation effort required by Italy is considerable from a quantitative as well as qualitative point of view.[10] Medium to long-term policies are expected to be implemented which will increase Italy's overall national institutional capacity, the competitiveness of its economic fabric and the sustainability of its repayment obligations (in terms of fairness and equality). The reform and investment plan is intended to extend well beyond the PNRR time frame and resource use period, such that it represents an extraordinary opportunity for enhancing and relaunching certain sectors, particularly in cities. This is especially the case in the wake of the austerity policies, collapse in public investments and cuts in the current resources of local authorities which have characterised the last decade. As previously mentioned, all this occurred in a context in which the state has been regaining unprecedented space in terms of its involvement in planning. It has elaborated the goals and set the standards along the way, signalling a change from the recent past which was characterised by the state's progressive renunciation of planning activity.[11]

8 This point is highlighted by Antonella Sciortino, 'PNRR e riflessi sulla forma di governo italiana. Un ritorno all'indirizzo politico "normativo"?' (2021) 18 *Federalismi.it* 235.

9 The NRRP(*Piano Nazionale di Ripresa e Resilienza*/PNRR) adopted by Italy on 30 April 2021 (tellingly referred to as "*Italia Domani*" or "The Italy of Tomorrow") amounts to a total of €191.5 billion and was approved by the European Council following its proposal by the Commission on 13 July 2021. The drafting of the PNRR began during the extended Conte government, which fine-tuned an initial draft based on the European guidelines and internal ones developed by the Secretariat of the National Committee for EU Affairs (*Comitato Interministeriale per gli Affari Europei*/CIAE). This version was then revised, partly rewritten and substantially changed by the Draghi government and approved by Parliament within the set deadline.

10 As is now well known, Italy is the country that has benefited most from the Recovery and Resilience Facility, garnering support totalling €191.482 billion, mostly consisting of loans.

11 Marco Dugato, 'L'intervento pubblico per l'inclusione, la coesione, l'innovazione e la sostenibilità ed il ruolo del servizio pubblico locale nel piano nazionale di ripresa e resilienza' (2022) 1 *Munus* 1.

3.2 The contents of the Italian PNRR: The different dimensions of the cities

It has been noted that in the process of adopting the Italian PNRR, involvement by cities and their governing institutions was highly limited. This was certainly partly due to the tight approval schedule involved.[12] It is true that in accepting Italy's plan, the European Commission pointed out that the Italian Chamber of Deputies and Senate did hold a series of hearings in which various stakeholders took part, e.g. regional and local authorities, social partners, civil society organisations and institutional bodies. They also approved related *ad hoc* reports together with resolutions fundamentally guiding the plan's completion. However, the basic feeling remained that the plan was "dropped down from on high". This was the case despite the increased involvement of territorial authorities who perhaps could have promoted their own active assuming of responsibility more. The same problem has also been noted in other European countries, where, with the exception of a few praiseworthy examples,[13] most regional and local actors have been consulted only in a formal unilateral way.[14] So much so, that the Committee of the Regions recommended the Commission encourage Member states to actively and structurally involve local and regional authorities in the plan implementation process precisely in order to compensate for their lack of upstream participation.[15]

Despite this, cities – in their manifold dimensions – cut across all, or almost all, of the plan's missions. This is because many horizontal reforms, such as digitisation or the recruiting and training of public employees, concern all public administrations. It is also because much infrastructure, and many measures concerning the ecological transition and new forms of transport, social assistance, and education, are local-level ones targeting local communities. It is precisely the term "community", alongside "citizens" and "citizenship", that appears most frequently in the plan, as if the city's social dimension is referred to even before its institutional one. This has also been the case in naming new investments (such as the multifunctional social and health structures which

12 According to Stefania Profeti and Brunetta Baldi, 'Le regioni italiane e il PNRR: la (vana) ricerca di canali d'accesso all'agenda' (2021) 2 *Rivista Italiana di Politiche Pubbliche*, 453, there has been a progressive "slipping" away from established inter-institutional dynamics towards a decision-making structure which increasingly features state central governments taking a more decisively hierarchical approach and putting the regions on an equal footing with the remaining local autonomies, despite the legislative and planning responsibilities the former has in many crucial PNRR areas. This equal treatment reveals the recognised role local autonomies have, and within them, cities.

13 For example, the case of Belgium as examined by Lorenza Violini, 'La predisposizione e la prima attuazione dei Piani Nazionali di Ripresa e Resilienza in alcuni Paesi europei: il ruolo delle Regioni' (2022) 6 *Le Regioni* 1159 ff.

14 See the report commissioned by the European Committee of the Regions, *Regional and local authorities and the National Recovery and Resilience Plans*, June 2021.

15 See the Opinion of the European Committee of the Regions on *Implementation of the Recovery and Resilience Facility* (2022/C 97/05).

have been called "*Case di Comunità*"[16]) and by referring back to institutions typically found in shared administrations (e.g. co-designing and co-programming as used under the Mission 5 objectives on social inclusion). In identifying objectives and investments, then, community is sometimes expressed in terms of its various territorial dimensions. That is, in terms of being an "urban", "metropolitan", "medium-sized", or associative (in the case of social territorial settings) community. Communities may also be identified in terms of their differences compared to other so-called internal areas or smaller centres.

There are more limited and almost implicit references to local government institutions, i.e. municipalities, and more sporadically, provinces, in terms of their varying demographic sizes.[17] Meanwhile, metropolitan cities are frequently directly referred to. The PNRR clearly banks on the latter for implementing an important series of projects to strengthen network infrastructures and rapid mass transport, promote sustainable local transport, protect and enhance urban and suburban green areas and upgrade railway hubs and key national transport links. An important investment line within the Integrated Urban Plan's funding goes towards metropolitan cities which are considered as communities and territories (with the peripheries of metropolitan cities to be recovered through participatory urban planning). This funding concurrently also targets metropolitan cities as entities entrusted with the aim of transforming vulnerable territories into sustainable smart cities. This means limiting land conversion for building purposes and encouraging planning synergies between "main" municipalities and smaller neighbouring ones. Here, the objective is to repair the urban and suburban fabric while bridging infrastructure and mobility gaps.

From what has been said, therefore, it is clear there was a lack of direct participation by institutions representing cities during the plan's development phase. However, this has not prevented cities from drawing on their own experience, planning, and numerous ideas to elaborate the detailed mosaic of objectives and lines of intervention comprising the plan's distinct missions.[18] Greater conviction to actively involving local communities in defining and

16 Provided for under mission m6c1: proximity networks, structures and telemedicine for territorial health care.

17 This is, for example, the case with mission m1c1.1 digitalisation of the public administration, which refers to Municipalities of 25,000 to 250,000 inhabitants being defined as "medium-size local administrations", alongside the provinces. Meanwhile, other missions (such as m1c3.2 regeneration of small cultural sites and cultural, religious and rural heritage) are aimed specifically at small centres to counteract the impetus to focus cultural and tourism support measures only in large cities.

18 According to Alberto Zanardi, 'Il ruolo degli enti territoriali nell'attuazione del PNRR' (2022) 3 *Rivista AIC*, 240, there are 137 milestones (qualitative and/or procedural goals) and targets (qualitative objectives) whose implementation involves local authorities (and which are a condition for the dispersal of EU funding instalments). Among these, there is a clear predominance of targets (108 in total or 34.4% of all the PNRR objectives) over tilestones (29 in total or 13.6% of all).

implementing individual projects could have been shown by drawing on the so-called right of cities more as a starting point, as has been previously and correctly been noted.[19] Shared administration experiences also could have been more relied on given that Italian cities were the first to create and play a key role in this kind of activity which transforms communities from mere beneficiaries into the co-implementers of measures.[20]

A different question arises with regard to whether the plan has taken *all* cities equally into account or instead favours certain territorial areas over others. In that respect, it has already been amply emphasised that resource allocations between regions, between cities, between large and small municipalities and between urban and inland areas were only partly decided upstream in the PNRR. This allocation depended, for the most part, on the final outcome of the competitive selection of projects submitted by the public and private entities eligible to participate in the tenders issued by the central administrations.[21]

Views on how apt this approach has been vary widely in terms of how well it identified specific problems to solve and individual projects to implement. In particular, there are those who take a positive view of "consistently assuming a widespread programmatic perspective with a project-dedicated approach, the consequent repositioning of the relationship between politics and administration and promoting a prevailing administrative law 'of things'".[22] On the other hand, there are others who have complained that "the plan does not aim to provide all citizens and territories with new services and infrastructure in a balanced way". Therefore, the government, as such, is seen as not having taken responsibility for the territorial allocation of PNRR measures.[23] On the other hand, it must be recalled that, prior to the PNRR's approval, authoritative voices had opposed the purported "territorial division" of the Recovery Fund's resources, instead calling for a unitary national vision of its management.[24]

What is certain, however, is that the distributional mechanisms finally chosen in the PNRR seem to be in apparent conflict with its stated cross-cutting objective of breaching the territorial divide. For this reason, it is very

19 This refers to Fabio Giglioni, 'Consolidamento e futuro dell'amministrazione condivisa' (2022) 20 *Federalismi.it* 212 ff.

20 About the link (to be further developed) between the PNRR and shared administrations, see Claudia Tubertini, 'Gli strumenti del diritto', in Pavani, Profeti, and Tubertini (5) 99.

21 According to Gianfranco Viesti, Carmela Chiapperini, and Emanuela Montenegro, *Le Città italiane e il PNRR* (2022) 13 Working Papers – Urban@it (at https://amsacta.unibo.it), 10, about 45% of the entire amount of PNRR resources will be distributed on the basis of a call-for-tender mechanism targeting mainly local authorities. This compares to 15% of resources being allocated based on distribution plans, primarily among the various regions. These regions are then called upon to distribute resources within their territory.

22 Fulvio Cortese, 'Gestione dei fondi "RRF" e diritto amministrativo: sguardo di sintesi e di contesto' (2022) 2 *Istituzioni del federalismo* 382.

23 Viesti, Chiapperini and Montenegro (21) 11.

24 See *Recovery Plan: un Piano coerente e operativo per la coesione*, Astrid Policy Brief n. 5, January 2021, at www.astrid-online.it.

important to verify if and how the two main mechanisms linked to the PNRR, and aimed at ensuring territorial rebalancing in the final resource allocations, have worked. This territorial rebalancing has involved allocating 40% of the plan's "territorialisable" resources to the South, thereby complementing the 2021–2027 structural funds programming, the REACT-EU programme and territorial participation (by local authorities or other economic and social actors) in so-called PNRR Governance.

Regarding the first point, it should be immediately noted that shortly after plan's approval, the legislature fine-tuned the so-called "40% clause". It did this by assigning the central administrations in charge of the PNRR measures the task of ensuring that at least 40% of the resources available for territorial allocation went to southern regions in Italy. This was to be done when defining the procedures for implementing measures which could be territorially allocated. It was also done through calls for tenders, regardless of the financial source of origin, while respecting any already foreseen specific territorial allocations.[25] The Department for Cohesion Policies of the Presidency of the Council of Ministers was meanwhile entrusted with the task of tracking compliance with the aforementioned objective. This was to be done using the data collected by the monitoring system activated by the Inspectorates General of the PNRR. Any cases of discrepancy were to be submitted as needed to the so-called "*Cabina di Regia per il PNRR*" (PNRR Steering Committee) in order to identify possible corrective and compensatory measures. However, doubts and criticisms have not been lacking even on the functionality of this mechanism. This is a sign of the unyielding distance between those who see more fear than benefits in the competitive project mechanism driving much of the plan versus those who maintain such a mechanism is needed to achieve implementation by 2026.

3.3 The PNRR governance mechanism and its progressive evolution: What kind of relationships exist between state and city?

In fact, the referral to the steering committee just noted recalls the other mechanism introduced to guarantee a balanced relationship between the state, cities and territories in implementing and carrying out the plan; that is, the plan's governance mechanism. Governance was provided for in the plan as a way of ensuring "dialogue with the territorial authorities" and "constant interaction in the context of economic, social and territorial partnerships". It was also designed to strictly monitor the implementation phase of measures. This phase was subsequently designed with a highly centralised architecture based on the preponderant role played by the Presidency of the Council of Ministers, the Ministry of Economy and occasionally other responsible Ministries. These

25 See Art. 2, para. 6-a of the decree law of 31 May 2021, no. 77 (converted into the law of 29 July 2021, no. 108).

were flanked by the purposefully set up the Steering Committee, which was further aided by a permanent Roundtable for economic, social and territorial partnerships (*Tavolo per il partenariato*).[26] This centralised management has been formally justified on the basis of the state's direct responsibility towards the European institutions. In fact, the relevant decree sets out the overriding value of the national interest in implementing the plan's measures (Art. 1, paragraph 2). It also specifies that any provisions adopted are carried out under the sole legislative responsibility indicated in Art. 117, paragraph 2, letter a), concerning the state's relationship towards the European Union, and which directly "define[s], pursuant to Art. 117, paragraph 2, letter m of the Constitution, essential levels of services that must be guaranteed throughout the national territory in terms of civil and social rights" (Art. 1, paragraph 3). Numerous criticisms raised by regional and local governments have led to a progressive modifying of the Steering Committee's original makeup, initially conceived as being exclusively comprised of state entities. In fact, it has been integrated with the participation of the Presidency of the Conference of the Regions and the Presidents of the individual regions concerned. Only after strong protests by Local Government Associations, and with a further amendment, the representatives of the local administrations, i.e. the Presidents of the National Association of Italian Municipalities (*Associazione Nazionale dei Comuni Italiani*/ANCI) and Union of Italian Provinces (*Unione Province d'Italia*/UPI) have been included as effective members, together with the mayor of Rome, the capital city, since 2023. Social partner representatives from the productive and social sectors, the university and research systems, and civil society like active citizenship organisations, identified on the basis of their representativeness,[27] have also been integrated.

The latest change – which entailed the concurrent elimination of the Partnership Roundtable – represents a final attempt to revitalise a body that, in practice, has so far played a less incisive role than expected. In this respect, assigning the steering committee chairmanship to the Minister for European Affairs[28] also appears to be in line with the government's intention to make debate and dialogue with the territories and their representative institutions ongoing rather than occasional. It was also done to overcome the growing difficulties which have emerged during the plan's implementation. However, the fact remains that, up until now, there have been other forums for adopting the main guidelines for PNRR implementation, including the Inter-Ministerial Committees, on the one hand, and the individual technical roundtables within

26 See Art 2, Legislative Decree 77/2021.

27 See Legislative Decree of 24 February 2023, no. 13 converted into Law 21 of April 2023, no. 41, Art. 1.

28 Whose full entitlement is now "Ministro per gli Affari Europei, le Politiche di Coesione e il Piano Nazionale di Ripresa e Resilienza" (Minister for European Affairs, Cohesion Policy and NRRP).

the Ministries in charge of measures, on the other. These roundtables were often voluntarily started up to ensure prior technical debate among potential implementers with the aim of arriving at agreed content for calls for tenders and implementing decrees.[29]

One can speculate, at this point, whether, in the face of the PNRR's "special" governance difficulties, the framework of so-called ordinary inter-institutional governance bodies, namely the State-Regions Joint Conferences (*Conferenze Stato-Regioni ed Unificata*), will help or alternatively create further problems. In fact, it should be recalled that under Legislative Decree 281/1997, draft laws, legislative decrees and government regulations are subject to mandatory review by the Joint Conferences if they bring together areas of regional and local responsibility. Also, the State-Regions Conference (*Conferenza Stato-Regioni*) and the Joint Conference may be consulted regarding initiatives undertaken by Regions or local authorities which address topics of common interest. However, the same Legislative Decree 281/1997 also provides, in case of emergency, for the Council of Ministers to adopt acts falling under its responsibility, submitting them only afterwards to the conferences. Except in certain limited cases, this council may proceed even if there is a failure to reach agreement. The restricted timetable imposed by the PNRR facilitates this kind of unilateral decision-making. It is hoped, therefore, that any conflicts encountered have been exceptions and not the rule given the absolute necessity for having a link between all the levels of government involved in the plan's missions and objectives. What is certain is that, although the setting up of a dedicated PNRR steering committee was meant to circumvent the functional problems of the Conferences System, plan implementation is still, in the end, mainly entrusted to the conferences.[30]

3.4 Cities as executing actors in the plan: The burden of deadlines and the spectre of substitute measures

We now come to the role of cities during the plan's implementation phase. The previously mentioned Legislative Decree 152/2021 established a Technical

29 To get an idea of how relevant this informal discussion activity is, see the ANCI document *IL PNRR di Comuni e Città Metropolitane: lo stato di attuazione e il ruolo di ANCI*, presented in the context of the "*Missione Italia*" initiative held on 5–6 July 2023, at www.anci.it. This reports on every investment to date in which municipalities have been involved in the section "*Le interlocuzioni di ANCI con l'amministrazione titolare*" as well as the letters sent by ANCI to the Ministries overseeing investments, meetings held and the forms of collaboration started up.

30 Renewed awareness of the vital character of these venues can be seen in the recent initiative taken by the Minister of Regional Affairs to appoint a study commission to draw up proposals to amend Legislative Decree 281/1997 by May 2024 to ensure better functioning. When the Commission took office, particular emphasis was placed on the exponential increase in the number of acts submitted to the conferences in recent years and, in particular, following the PNRR's approval.

Unit (*Nucleo tecnico*) in the Department for Regional Affairs and Autonomies (*Dipartimento per gli affari regionali e le autonomie*) of the Presidency of the Council of Ministers to liaise with the regions and support small municipalities in carrying out the activities required for participating in the allocation of plan resources. This choice has stirred up some doubts among local administrations since the Technical Unit, which also provides assistance to territorial authorities, is comprised of officials and staff who are not appointed by local administrations. In any case, this unit represents a support measure that does not include local authorities in the decision-making process driving policy choices.

The state's entire organisational effort was aimed, above all, at preventing some cities from being entirely excluded from funding because they could not respond to calls for proposals. Emphasis was put, in particular, on small municipalities, as well as provinces and metropolitan cities, which severely lack staff and thus often have difficulty in carrying out the planning and document preparation needed to participate in such calls. The first monitoring exercises carried out regarding the status of PNRR implementation, beginning with those by the national Auditor's Court (*Corte dei Conti*),[31] indicated that in many cases, the regions had organised internal coordination amongst themselves through their own local systems. This was done to support their administrations and allow for a rational and coherent distribution of resources across the territory; a steering role for some metropolitan cities was also launched within their respective territorial areas.

Despite this, the initial findings of the Parliamentary Budget Office (*Ufficio Parlamentare di Bilancio*/UPB) an independent body responsible for analyzing macroeconomic and fiscal forecasts by the government on the impact of the first calls for proposals on the aim of bridging the territorial gap particularly revealed some obvious systemic flaws. The question was, "Did the calls reach who they were supposed to or did only already prepared administrations or those who were better equipped technically respond?" The UPB's response to this indicated, at least to a large extent, the latter was the case[32] as funds were, in fact, distributed to a greater extent in the capital cities. This was a sign of the likely insufficient size of the investments planned in periurban areas characterised by greater social difficulties and fewer public assets.

As noted above, if a certain disparity in territorial allocations was to be expected, and the focus on large Italian cities fully justified, it is equally true that many medium and medium-to-small size Italian cities appear to have benefited from much more limited-scale measures. 38% of plan resources have been allocated to cities in Southern Italy. However, there are clearly vulnerable urban territories in this region (especially in Calabria and Sicily) where

31 Corte dei Conti, Sezioni Riunite in sede di controllo, *Relazione sullo stato di attuazione del Piano Nazionale di Ripresa e Resilienza* (prepared pursuant to Art. 7, paragraph 7, of the Legislative Decree of 31 May 2021, no. 77), March 2022, at www.corteconti.it.

32 Ufficio Parlamentare di Bilancio, *I bandi PNRR destinati agli Enti territoriali: obiettivi specifici e vincoli territoriali*, Flash no. 1/2022, 20 January 2022, at www.upbilancio.it.

only modest investments appear to have been mobilised so far. Subsequent analyses conducted by other research centres regarding the reach of some key PNRR measures aimed at closing territorial gaps[33] (e.g. strengthening school and childcare services) have also not been very encouraging.

The poor planning-response ability of cities (or at least among some of them) was occasionally combined with structural shortcomings in relation to the calls for tenders. For example, the calls on digital transformation only identified municipalities as beneficiaries and excluded the Union of municipalities from directly implementing measures. In some cases, this risked preventing "diffuse cities" (precisely those which make up the Unions of municipalities) from funding access. In other cases, delays in the implementing procedures by central administrations, which form the basis for city actions and measures, are what generated negative territorial repercussions.[34] The excessive procedural time spent in identifying measures for financing also had a trickle-down effect at later stages.[35]

On 30 December 2022, the Italian government announced it had achieved 55 PNRR targets and objectives for the second half of 2022. It thus sent a request to the EU Commission for the disbursement of the third plan instalment of €21,839,080,460. This was made possible by the fact that the objectives during the first year (2021) mainly related to regulatory measures, and those for 2022 to publishing notices and calls for tenders. In 2023, however, the plan entered its most difficult phase, as the *Corte dei Conti* has certified.[36] It is no coincidence that the strict timetable concerned and the aftermath of the war have placed the need for revising NRRPs at the centre of public,

33 Associazione per lo sviluppo dell'industria del Mezzogiorno (Association for the Development of Industry in the South/SVIMEZ), *Asili nido e infrastrutture scolastiche. Il PNRR non colmerà i divari territoriali*, Collana Informazioni SVIMEZ, 2 May 2023, at *http://lnx.svimez.info/svimez/*.

34 This is the case for all the activities under the "Mobility as a service" (MaaS) objective aimed at implementing pilot projects in technologically advanced metropolitan cities. Slowdowns in implementing these were due to a lack of clarity in identifying "Data Sharing and Service Repository Facilities" at the central level. Implementation for this measure was entrusted to the Ministry of Infrastructure and Transport (*Ministero delle infrastrutture edei trasporti/* MIT) by Executive Decree 188 of 19 September 2022. This ministry represents a pivotal point of reference and hub for MaaS projects and all the marketing and public initiatives needed to ensure their full interoperability.

35 In the case of (nursery schools and kindergartens under the plan, the extension of deadlines for participating in the call for tenders led to the pushing forward of these dates. As a result, they now fall very close together (the milestone for the awarding of works in Italy is 31 May 2023). This may put meeting these deadlines in jeopardy and create a risk that some municipalities may abandon the process (as underlined by ANCI, *Il PNRR di Comuni e Città Metropolitane* (28) 11).

36 Corte dei Conti, Sezioni Riunite in sede di controllo, *Relazione sullo stato di attuazione del Piano nazionale di ripresa e resilienza*, March 2023.

national and European debate.[37] In the meantime, the European Commission has decided to extend the deadline for evaluating the required targets that need to be met for dispersing the third resource instalment. They did this in order to better assess Italy's proper implementation of reforms and investments to date under the plan. In this context, Italy's attention has now naturally more precisely focused on its cities since they are the main implementers of all the measures to which the obtained resources have so far have been directed.[38]

Further fine-tuning of the PNRR governance framework has occurred as result.[39] This has included making provisions aimed at allowing for substitute measures in the event of non-compliance by the cities (as well as the regions) relative to the obligations and commitments they assume as governing bodies in PNRR implementation. Such shortcomings may relate to a failure to adopt the actions and measures needed to launch projects or the stalling, delay or non-compliance of project implementation. Such stalling or delay may concern only several measures or the implementation of an entire programme.

What is involved is not something completely new. As already indicated, through Legislative Decree 77/2021, the PNRR governance mechanism already provides for wide-ranging substitution powers in line with the plan's top-down approach. These can be activated by the Council of Ministers when the achieving of intermediate and final PNRR objectives are at risk, after being proposed by the steering committee or the responsible minister and after setting a deadline for the implementing entity concerned to react within 30 days. Similar substitute measures had also already been provided for in the event of disagreements, refusals or oppositional procedures liable to prevent the implementation of PNRR measures (Art. 12–13 of the aforementioned Decree).

With the approval of Legislative Decree 13/2023, the maximum time limit that the President of the Council of Ministers gives to the involved implementing party to act in cases of stalled efforts was reduced from within thirty to within only fifteen days. A resolution by the Council of Ministers also indicates identifying a person who is delegated to adopt the acts or measures needed to ensure the project schedule is met. In the face of persistent stalling or delay, the Council of Ministers may also authorise this designated person to waive any legal provisions other than criminal laws.

37 On desired changes to the PNRR, see the proposals by Franco Bassanini and Silvia Paparo, 'In tema di rimodulazione del PNRR: tre proposte in linea con gli obiettivi di Next Generation EU', (2023) 7 *Astrid Rassegna*.

38 According to data from the third implementation status report for the NRRP presented by the Minister for Regional Affairs to Parliament on 31 May 2023, Municipalities are the implementers of more than 53% of the projects linked to allocated measures, with 47% of all PNRR resources being allocated through them. Moreover, almost all municipal entities are involved in the plan's initiatives.

39 Legislative Decree of 24 February 2023, no. 13.

In the current phase, this need for refining substitution mechanisms appears far from being a discouraging factor. Rather, it suggests not ruling out the preparation of a procedure for this in the near future. Assuming this, it will be necessary to verify what has been the concrete impact of the overall reorientation of the PNRR governance envisaged under Decree-Law No.13 of 2023. This law has decisively strengthened the strategic guidance and coordination functions for plan implementation delegated to the Presidency of the Council of Ministers. This, in turn, has expanded the latter's support structures, including those aimed at activating substitution powers.[40]

3.5 The call for revising the PNRR: Towards a rethinking of the role of cities?

The transmitting of the third Ministerial Report on PNRR Implementation Status (dated 31 May 2023) to the Houses of Parliament on 7 June 2023, in fact, seems to have represented a turning point in the government's approach to managing its relationships with the cities. While acknowledging the impressive efforts of local administrations in plan implementation,[41] this recent report also presents a negative opinion on the fragmenting of planned measures due to the preponderant role of municipalities as implementing entities. While the strategic significance territorially spread initiatives may have for the entire country cannot be discounted, concern has been expressed for the first time over the scattering of resources and the particular difficulty local administrations have in realising planned investments and managing their dialogue with national and European-level monitoring bodies.

This impression is only heightened by reading the 27 July 2023 document in which the government made public the "Proposals for Revising the PNRR and the Integration of REPowerEU" which will be forwarded to the European Commission. In fact, the negative opinion about the fragmenting of measures is confirmed therein and even more doubt is expressed as to the appropriateness of focussing on municipalities as the main implementers. This

40 The role of the new mission structure set up in the Presidency of the Council of Ministers to verify the coherence of results achieved in implementing plan objectives and targets appears relevant in this regard. On this point, see Alberto Tabacchi, 'Le procedure per l'esercizio dei poteri sostitutivi e il superamento dei dissensi nell'attuazione del PNRR' (2023) 9 *Federalismi .it* 164.

41 In fact, the document states (112) that "*le amministrazioni locali hanno assicurato, su tutto il territorio nazionale, un intenso impegno nelle fasi di attuazione del piano, contribuendo in maniera significativa ai risultati sinora raggiunti*" (local administrations throughout the country have ensured their strong commitment during the plan's implementation phases, significantly contributing to the results achieved so far). This statement is supported by data on the number of tenders launched by municipalities, which more than doubled in the first half of 2023 (from approximately 24,000 in January 2023 to about 52,000 by mid-June 2023, according to data from the National Anti-corruption Authority – *Autorità Nazionale Anticorruzione*/ANAC).

doubt leads, in particular, to the proposed defunding of measures that were less critical during the last monitored trimester. These were noted especially in the case of the three main measures targeting municipalities and metropolitan cities (i.e. energy efficiency, urban regeneration, integrated urban plans). As previously indicated, these measures relate to objectives that are undoubtedly strategic ones for the entire country, such as preventing and mitigating risks linked to hydrogeological factors and securing built-up areas, managing flood and hydrogeological risk by maintaining and repurposing public areas and buildings and regenerating and enhancing underused or unused urban areas. Moreover, the aforementioned document reconstructs the path laid down for "fully sharing" the revision proposal content with all the involved actors. However, it remains silent about the fact that the document was transmitted to the steering committee the same day it was to be examined. This has provoked a critical reaction from the regions[42] who pointed out that it was unclear to what extent the proposed reprogramming would affect the regulatory obligation of allocating at least 40% of the applicable resources to the *Mezzogiorno* (Southern Italy). The municipalities and metropolitan cities, which had asked for more immediate guarantees, had an even more critical reaction over the refinancing of measures that are at risk of being removed from the plan. As with the small-scale works financed by the Ministry of the Interior, these measures have also already been implemented.[43] In addition to the lack of consultation regarding the change of perspective, vogue remained the reasons put forward by the Government to justify why specific measures were selected for defunding or content revision. Furthermore, while there was a view to finding refinancing for these measures, there was a failure to precisely identify refinancing sources[44] beyond noting a generic (and very problematic) recourse to European Cohesion or REPowerEU funds.

42 See the document of 2 August 2023 by the Conferenza delle Regioni/Conference of the Regions, *Valutazioni in ordine alla proposta di revisione del PNRR e REPowerEU presentata nell'ambito della Cabina di Regia PNRR del 27 luglio 2023*, which specifically challenges the failure to involve regions in the process of defining the proposal and recalls the provisions of Art. 28 of Regulation (EU) No. 2021/241. The latter refers to coordination and complementarity between EU-financed measures for strengthening technical coordination mechanisms between the Authorities responsible for PNRR implementation and those responsible for implementing EU-funded Programmes and the Unitary Cohesion Policy (*Politica Unitaria di Coesione*/UCP) with the aim of having more effective programme implementation in the 2021–2027 cycle.

43 According to SVIMEZ, more than 10 of the 15.9 billion the government proposes diverting away from the financed measures originally included in the PNRR, falls under projects that have already been financed and started up. These projects also variously concern urban enhancement and municipal redevelopment from which significant social benefits were expected.

44 The Dossier by the Chamber of Deputies Study Service *Le proposte del Governo per la revisione del PNRR e il capitolo REPower EU*, 31 July 2023, 24 notes "*rischi di rallentamenti o incertezze attuative che potrebbero conseguire al mutamento del regime giuridico e finanziario e del sistema di rendicontazione cui tali misure sarebbero sottoposte*" (the risks of implementa-

In this context, it seems that it may be precisely the role cities have earned at the European level which has finally convinced the European Commission to approve only a reduction of the so-called "fragmented" investments" (precisely the most "critical" ones, according to the Italian Government), whose cancellation could have negatively affected achieving the balanced territorial distribution of resources as well as the allocation of the cohesion funds in favour of Southern and disadvantaged areas in Italy. As a matter of fact, the latest monitoring data shows that it is precisely the urban regeneration projects included in the Integrated Urban Plans, and involving some 600 implementing local authorities, that comprise the vast majority of projects which have reached their planned deadlines. Given this situation, it is justified to assert, at least partly, that these projects need "a dose of reality" to ensure Italy is not blamed for failing to implement the PNRR.[45]

3.6 "Beyond" the PNRR: Reforms underway and their impact on cities

On 24 May 2023, the European Commission published its proposed Country-specific Recommendations for Italy for the current European Semester. These recommendations reiterated the importance of strengthening administrative capacity, particularly at the local level, in implementing the PNRR since its success closely depends on the effective involvement of regional and local administrations. It is significant here that the aforementioned Legislative Decree 13/2023, perhaps aware of the outright impossibility of a "large-scale" substitute measure and its likely ineffectiveness, has targeted a series of administrative capacity building measures towards local administrations. These measures include, for example, rules that allow local authorities already benefiting from funding to implement investments partly or entirely financed by PNRR resources, to increase the proportion of executives hired on fixed-term contracts and to provide additional compensation for staff involved in PNRR implementation (Art. 8). The law also suggests that administrations may enter into administrative agreements with each other to implement PNRR measures. There are also rules aimed at simplifying the fund dispersal procedure for the advances paid to entities executing PNRR project implementation measures. In summary, this decree combines state incentive and disincentive measures in relation to cities. Therefore, hope should focus on cities in correcting

tion slowdowns or uncertainties that could result from changes in the legal and financial regime and the reporting system to which these measures would be subject) and the need for determining new sources of financing "*al fine di verificare che dispongano di una adeguata dotazione di competenza e di cassa nell'ambito del bilancio dello Stato*" (in order to verify that they have adequate accrual and cash allocations within the state budget). ,

45 About the need of a realistic approach, and perhaps even a reflection on whether to forego some of the borrowed funds, Tito Boeri and Roberto Perotti, *PNRR. La grande abbuffata* (Feltrinelli 2023).

issues affecting Italian administrative system efficiency and preventing its full modernisation. Cities should also be a focus in sketching out a design for overall administrative reform which can then be better defined once the crisis has passed.

It is natural, however, to speculate whether these emergency measures will succeed in bridging the structural gaps in Italian local administrations or in overcoming the "administrative, institutional, social and economic weakness"[46] that now characterise Italy's suburban as well as metropolitan areas. It is about overcoming the inability to spend and the other shortcomings of administrations, especially local ones[47]. The doubt raised is legitimate. The minister in charge of the PNRR, himself, has been forced to note that the spending capacity of municipal administrations faces difficult-to-overcome short term obstacles due to a lack of human resources as well as a shortage of managerial and technical skills, further leading to planning and spending inefficiencies. Also, local government's procurement of qualified human resources faces the standard difficulties of recruitment processes and is additionally complicated by the temporary nature of the recruitment modes tied to the plan's time horizon and thus, potentially not alluring.[48]

In fact, the PNRR intervenes in a group of sectors that, in turn, demand a highly articulated, but (deliberately) constant framework of responsibility. Yet, the revision of local government systems was not included among the so-called enabling and horizontal reforms.[49] It was evidently not considered urgent enough to be integrated into the PNRR objectives, or, more likely, it was considered too complex to be approved within a certain time frame.

However, the uncertainty of the institutional framework can only weigh down the ability of cities to be major actors in PNRR implementation. The unequivocal link between the urban community and its representative institutions presupposes the latter are capable of entirely playing their role. In this case, one cannot fail to point out, firstly, that the institutions Italy has set up to specifically solve urban problems, that is metropolitan cities, have long suffered from ambiguity in terms of development conditions, forms of government, and comprehensive endowments. Cities are also affected by a series of

46 Marzia De Donno, 'La nuova Provincia' (2023) 5 *Astrid Rassegna* 1.

47 On the origins of these structural flaws, and the potential impact of the PNRR's administrative capacity-building measures, see Fabrizio Di Mascio and Alessandro Natalini, 'L'attuazione del PNRR dal governo Draghi al governo Meloni: le pubbliche amministrazioni sotto stress per eccesso di risorse', in Federica Genovese and Salvatore Vassallo (eds), *La Politica in Italia* (Il Mulino 2023), 185 ff.

48 See the third Ministerial Report on PNRR Implementation Status, 118, at www.italiadomani.gov.it.

49 On the (controversial) results of the enabling and horizontal reforms made so far in relation to PNRR implementation, see the analysis carried out by Giampaolo Galli, Federico Neri and Francesco Scinetti, 'Il PNRR e le riforme', *Osservatorio sui conti pubblici italiani*, 28 April 2023, at *https://osservatoriocpi.unicatt.it/*.

basic problems stemming from their very genesis via "universal succession" within their corresponding provinces. The trust the PNRR places in the ability of metropolitan authorities to implement plan objectives requires revising their territorial, organisational and institutional set-up. This will allow these authorities to more adequately reflect their general institutional aims as envisaged under Art. 1, paragraph 2 of Law 56/2014, and, in particular, to fulfil the "development mission" which is their hallmark.

In conclusion, then, one hope might be expressed. It is that the reform paths that have so far run along separate parallel tracks, that is, PNRR approval and implementation on one hand, and the adapting of local government administrations to structural reforms on the other, should merge into one.

Bibliography

Arban E., *Constitutional Law, Federalism and the city as a Unique Socio-economic and Political Space*, in Hirsch Ballin E., van der Schyff G., Stremler M. and De Visser M.(eds), *European Yearbook of Constitutional Law 2020.The City in Constitutional Law* (Springer 2021).

Auby J.-B., *Droit de la ville: Du fonctionnement juridique des villes au droit à la Ville* (LexisNexis 2013).

Bassanini F. and Paparo S., 'In tema di rimodulazione del PNRR: tre proposte in linea con gli obiettivi di Next Generation EU', (2023) 7 *Astrid Rassegna* 1.

Boeri T. and Perotti R., *PNRR. La grande abbuffata* (Feltrinelli 2023)

Carloni E. and Pineiro M., 'Le città intelligenti e l'Europa. Tendenze di fondo e nuove strategie di sviluppo urbano' (2015) 4 *Istituzioni del Federalismo* 865.

Cecchetti M., 'L'incidenza del PNRR sui livelli territoriali di governo e le conseguenze nei sistemi amministrativi' (2022) 3 *Rivista AIC* 13.

Cortese F., 'Il nuovo diritto delle città: alla ricerca di un legittimo spazio operativo', in Ferrari G.F. (ed), Smart city. L'evoluzione di un'idea (Mimesis 2020).

Cortese F., 'Gestione dei fondi "RRF" e diritto amministrativo: sguardo di sintesi e di contesto' (2022) 2 *Istituzioni del federalismo* 382.

De Donno M., 'La nuova Provincia' (2023) 5 *Astrid Rassegna* 1.

Di Mascio F. and Natalini A., 'L'attuazione del PNRR dal governo Draghi al governo Meloni: le pubbliche amministrazioni sotto stress per eccesso di risorse', in Genovese F. and Vassallo S. (eds), *La Politica in Italia* (Il Mulino 2023).

Dugato M., 'L'intervento pubblico per l'inclusione, la coesione, l'innovazione e la sostenibilità ed il ruolo del servizio pubblico locale nel piano nazionale di ripresa e resilienza' (2022) 1 *Munus* 1.

Fabbrini F., *Next Generation EU. Il futuro di Europa e Italia dopo la pandemia* (Il Mulino 2022).

Font T., 'De la autonomía local al poder de las ciudades' (2019) Special Issue *Istituzioni del Federalismo* 115.

Galli G., Neri F. and Scinetti F., 'Il PNRR e le riforme', *Osservatorio sui conti pubblici italiani* (28 April 2023).

Giglioni F., 'Consolidamento e futuro dell'amministrazione condivisa' (2022) 20 *Federalismi.it* 212.

Pavani G., Profeti S. and Tubertini C., *Le città collaborative ed eco-sostenibili* (Il Mulino 2023).
Profeti S. and Baldi B., 'Le regioni italiane e il PNRR: la (vana) ricerca di canali d'accesso all'agenda' (2021) 2 *Rivista Italiana di Politiche Pubbliche* 431.
Romeo A., 'Le misure amministrative per la ripresa e la resilienza economica. Il piano italiano' (2022) 2 *Istituzioni del federalismo* 400.
Sciortino A., 'PNRR e riflessi sulla forma di governo italiana. Un ritorno all'indirizzo politico "normativo"?' (2021) 18 *Federalismi.it* 235.
Tabacchi, A., 'Le procedure per l'esercizio dei poteri sostitutivi e il superamento dei dissensi nell'attuazione del PNRR' (2023) 9 *Federalismi.it* 164.
Viesti G., Chiapperini C. and Montenegro E., *Le Città italiane e il PNRR* (AmsActa Unibo 2022) 13 Working Papers – Urban@it.
Violini L., 'La predisposizione e la prima attuazione dei Piani Nazionali di Ripresa e Resilienza in alcuni Paesi europei: il ruolo delle Regioni' (2022) 6 *Le Regioni* 1159.
Zanardi A., 'Il ruolo degli enti territoriali nell'attuazione del PNRR' (2022) 3 *Rivista AIC* 240.

4 Law of the city, spatial justice and participatory democracy

Against the "*Hostile City*"

Marzia De Donno

4.1 Foreword: New paradigms countering the "*Hostile City*"

Numerous studies across different disciplines have seen cities as a central issue of concern for several decades now. These studies highlight, *inter alia*, the growing role cities play in ensuring an acceptable quality of life for their residents and thus guaranteeing people's rights as well.[1] Starting with the writings of Zygmunt Bauman and Saskia Sassen,[2] this recognition – that has been ever increasingly and vitally expressed in terms of both the "right *to* the city" and "the law *of* the city" – is imputed to the effects of globalisation and the European integration process, which have entailed a recognisable decrease in State sovereignty alongside a rediscovery of the local aspects of space, including the legal ones.

Given these trends, the crisis in state sovereignty is becoming increasingly more patent. It is evident in the crisis of the welfare state, characterised by the progressive retreat of state administrations from their role in guaranteeing fundamental rights. Consequently, a rediscovery of the territorial dimension of administrative activity, and the role of local administrations in protecting and caring for territories, might counteract this trend. Thus, during the so-called new "urban millennium", the city, according to some observers, may become "a new power centre, [even] replacing the State" and "the privileged place, whose point of view dominates the drafting, design and testing of current policies".[3]

This rediscovery of the "local", driven also by theoretical debate, might lead to a veritable "spatial breakthrough" in the law. This change may also

1 For a survey of this, see Giulia Maria Labriola, 'Città e diritto. Brevi note su un tema complesso' (2018) 1 *Istituzioni del Federalismo*, 5. On the converging theme of the so-called human rights cities, and for more extensive references, see Giorgia Pavani, Stefania Profeti and Claudia Tubertini, *Le città collaborative ed eco-sostenibili* (il Mulino 2023), especially 17–25.

2 Zygmunt Bauman, *Globalizzazione e glocalizzazione* (Armando Editore 2005) and Saskia Sassen, *Territorio, autorità, diritti. Assemblaggi dal Medioevo all'età globale* (Mondadori 2008).

3 Orsetta Giolo, 'I diritti contro la città. Spazio urbano, soggettività e sfera pubblica', in Maria Giulia Bernardini and Orsetta Giolo (eds), *Abitare i diritti. Per una critica dei rapporti tra giustizia e spazi urbani* (Pacini Giuridica 2021) 49.

DOI: 10.4324/9781032665184-9

trigger an epistemological trend towards more territorialising of certain legal categories, including citizenship and fundamental rights. The latter have been seen historically in a soley state-centric context or as belonging exclusively to the domain of state law. However, these theoretical insights would seem to support that people may no longer see their rights as legally protected expectations met by a political or state community and/or an international system. Rather, they may conceive of themselves, *above all*, as city dwellers and, concurrently, cities may then become the privileged *legal space* to exercise their rights.[4]

This statement alone would suffice to convey the deeper significance of the "century of cities", as it has been called. It also opens up room for thought around the actual concept of citizenship[5] and the operational dimension of fundamental rights. However, we would like to highlight another aspect we see as relevant. We draw immediate attention to the fact that the rediscovered role of cities has never been followed up, at least in Italy, by central authorities in fully recognising local autonomy, e.g. in terms of their strengthening of local capabilities and administrative capacities. Nor have financial or aid policies really shifted or changed pace to create solid territorial or local welfare systems and development policies. However, the intentional link between protecting rights and promoting local autonomy should be clearly recognised by now.[6] We are thus, witnessing a fundamental tension. At the transnational level, in particular, a series of public policies are flourishing which are specifically orientated towards growth and development in urban (as well as rural) contexts.[7] However, these efforts continue to be counteracted by state (and regional) resistances and centralisms. This situation has been adding to the overall impoverishment of local systems over the last fifteen years, a trend which shows no sign of stopping.

Recent changes and efforts have been made and we await the real benefits of the Recovery and Resilience Plan (RRP) implementation. Despite this, it seems these tendencies and the dramatic effects of the "latest crises" (linked to pandemic, climate changes and armed conflict in Ukraine and the related energy issues) have perpetuated a particular negative kind of urban model. This model can be markedly characterised and defined as that of the *hostile city*, to borrow a common expression from architecture.[8]

4 For more extensive references, see, among other, Giolo (n 3). On this point, see also Fabio Giglioni, 'La città come ordinamento giuridico' (2018) 1 *Istituzioni del Federalismo* 29.

5 Fulvio Cortese, 'Dentro il nuovo diritto della città' (2016) 2 *Munus* XI.

6 Filippo Pizzolato, 'Città e diritti fondamentali: le ambivalenze della politicità dei diritti' (2022) 1 *Istituzioni del federalismo* 155.

7 For a survey of urban policies developed at the European level, we refer to Marzia De Donno, 'La governance multilivello delle politiche pubbliche per le città: nuovi scenari e dinamiche inclusive per i territori ai margini', in Bernardini and Giolo (n 3) 173.

8 See, for example, Stefano Boeri, *L'Anticittà* (Laterza 2011); James Petty, 'The London spikes controversy: Homelessness, urban securitisation and the question of "hostile architecture"'

The hostile city is a city that denies its own self and reflects at an urban-level the crisis of fundamental rights. It crumbles the same universal concept of citizenship, reducing it to a kind of "differential citizenship". This is the result of the territorial compartmentalising of opportunity in relation to access to resources, housing/labour markets and local services both inside and outside urban areas. Last but not least, this compartmentalisation is affecting political and administrative participation in all its various forms.[9]

It seems useful to turn to a relevant classification scheme in order to better grasp these city crises, while connecting them to the above territorialising of legal categories. As scholars stated,[10] we can classify the contemporary city like a constitutional democracy, according to the four constitutionally determined categories of civil, freedom-related, political and social rights. Relatedly, several different animating centres of the city may all coexist, i.e. the *civil* and *free city*, *the political city* and, finally, the *social city*. Upon reflection, it seems these dimensions of the city have been under continual stress throughout the 2008 economic crisis, the 2020 health crisis, and more recently, during the 2022 military conflict as well as the recent effects of climate change.

The crisis affecting the civil and free city can be grasped, for example, in the light of the restrictions placed on gatherings and freedom of movement which we saw during the pandemic. The crisis of the political city is clearly evident in the continual decrease in opportunities for administrative participation which has led to various types of exclusion from local political life. Finally, the crisis of the social city is evident in the presence of urban areas that generate social marginalisation, poverty, housing emergencies, new forms of urban segregation and resulting conflict and insecurity. Taken together, these phenomena contribute to a significant deterioration in the quality of life for people living in *hostile cities*, creating conditions far from those implied by the *right to the city* and the paradigms of *spatial justice*. As a result, citizens have turned against this kind of city, claiming back their own rights.

Exactly for this reason, this chapter aims to make a foray into theories of so-called spatial justice. These theories, in fact, address precisely conditions of injustice in cities and highlight the need to construct a "just space" where

(2016) 5, 1 *International Journal for Crime, Justice and Social Democracy*, 67; Attilio Pizzigoni, *La città ostile. La realtà dell'architettura urbana nelle sue contraddizioni storiche* (Marinotti Edizioni 2017); and Santina Musolino and Emanuele Rossi, 'La città ostile: architetture e strategie dell'esclusione nelle metropoli contemporanee' (2021) 9, 1 *Fuori Luogo. Rivista di Sociologia del Territorio, Turismo, Tecnologia* 86. The hostile city should be contrasted with the *just city* model. For an Italian legal approach on this model, see Gianluca Gardini, 'Alla ricerca della città giusta. La rigenerazione come metodo di pianificazione urbana' (2020) 24 *federalismi.it* 44.

9 Alfredo Alietti, 'Giustizia spaziale, periferie e vulnerabilità sociale: un nesso problematico?', in Bernardini and Giolo (n 3) 19–20.

10 See Giolo (n 3), who recalls the four-dimensional model of constitutional democracy described by Luigi Ferrajoli, *Principia Juris. Teoria del diritto e della democrazia. 2. Teoria della democrazia* (Laterza 2007).

individuals can have a qualitatively acceptable existence (§ 2). Consequently, we consider the impact of these theories on the same development of institutes linked to participatory democracy (§ 3). Finally, we relate the theoretical views linked to the above to the climate changes. The latter, in fact, add to the complexity in exercising rights and in democratic coexistence itself. And not surprisingly, this has led cities to develop new forms of participation, which the state has not yet accepted (§ 4).

4.2 The contribution of spatial justice theories and the relevance of participatory democracy

Places and cities, as a whole:

> are thus, not simply settings in which personal and collective events unfold, but rather the raw material on which existence thrives. Connections are constructed within cities between the most diverse spheres and at the most varied scales. Therefore, justice and injustice are part of cites.[11]

This awareness, together with the *housing* and *territorial* dimension of human life and personal rights, provides the basis for one line of thinking on so-called *spatial justice* and this approach both parallels and converges with theorising on the right to the city.[12] As noted above, spatial justice is not a legal term. It is a geographical, urban planning, philosophical, economic and environmental term at most, but not (as yet) a legal one.[13] For this reason, we briefly look at some of the main features of its related theories, striving to translate these ideas into potential legal concepts.

An immediate definition of spatial justice might start with the observation that:

> it should not be understood as a type of justice between places, but as a spatial dimension of justice between men [and thus] ... spatial justice also consists in correcting spatial injustices, in bringing coherence to territorial organisation with the goal of a making a more just society. It means taking direct action on a place in order to indirectly take action on people.[14]

11 Carla Danani, 'Sulla giustizia spaziale', in Annette Hilt, Holger Zaborowski and Virgilio Cesarone (eds), *L'Europa e l'idea di Giustizia. Crisi e sfide*, (2016) *Itinerari. Annuario di scienze filosofiche*, 127.

12 This is a line of inquiry that, to the best of our knowledge, has not yet been particularly explored by scholars of Italian administrative law. However, initial applications have occurred linked to French legal principles, e.g. see the volume edited by Vincent Dussart and Florence Lerique (eds), *Justice spatiale et politiques publiques territoriales* (Mare & Martin 2022).

13 Jean Marie Pontier, 'Justice spatiale et décentralisation', in Dussart and Lerique (n 12) 58.

14 Bernard Bret, 'Notion à la une: justice spatiale' (2015) *Géoconfluences*. By the same author see *Pour une géographie du Juste. Lire les territoires à la lumière de la philosophie morale de*

The concept of spatial justice began to develop within the thinking of geographers and urban planners[15] during the 1980s and as part of a move to define it as distinct from social justice issues.[16] This effort was added to studies on *territorial justice* by Bleddyn Davies,[17] David Harvey[18] and Henri Lefebvre[19] and Edward Soja's[20] theories on spatial justice, in particular. Their ideas have all led to thinking about justice in a spatial context. The attempt has been to understand what situations of injustice mean in terms of cultural, social and economic, and thus, political and institutional processes when played out on a territorial scale. This, in turn, may afford a better understanding what is meant by the hostile city referred to above.

Within these theoretical approaches, the search for and description of a "just space" takes on a complex relational nature. It rests on territoriality and emphasises spatial and geographical aspects. It also aims to capture the territorial differences and inequalities that may exist in both the distribution of opportunities and exercising of rights. The above considerations have traditionally and specifically referred to urban contexts and cities. However, it may be particularly useful at present to mark out a wider scope, connecting cities

---

John Rawls (Presses Universitaires de Paris Ouest 2015) and Bernard Bret, Philippe Gervais-Lambony, Claire Hancock and Frédéric Landy (eds), *Justice et injustices spatiales* (Presses universitaires de Paris Ouest 2010).

15 According to the historical reconstructions of Carla Danani (n 11) taken up in this paper, the concept of spatial justice was first used by the geographers John O'Laughlin in *Spatial Justice and the Black American Voter: The Territorial Dimension of Urban Politics* (Pennsylvania State University 1973), Alain Reynaud in *Société, espace et justice: inégalités régionales et justice socio-spatiale* (PUF 1981) and Gordon H. Pirie in his essay 'On Spatial Justice', (1983) 15, 4 *Environment and Planning A: Economy and Space*, 465. However, the term only began to take root in the 2000s. In 2001, the urban planner Mustafa Dikeç wrote 'Justice and Spatial Imagination', (2001) 33, 10 *Environment and Planning A: Economy and Space* 1785. The following year the first international conference on spatial justice, 'Justice et Injustice Spatiales', was held at the University of Paris X-Nanterre. This resulted in the launching of the journal, *Justice Spatiale/Spatial Justice*, under the direction of the geographer Philippe Gervais-Lambony. For a survey of the spatial justice debate see also, Ali Madanipour, Mark Shucksmith and Elizabeth Brooks, 'The concept of spatial justice and the European Union's territorial cohesion', (2022) 30, 5 *European Planning Studies*, 807.

16 Andreas Philippopoulos-Mihalopoulos, 'Spatial justice: law and the geography of withdrawal' (2010) 6, 3 *International Journal of Law in Context*, 201. On this point, see also, Kurt Iveson, 'Social or spatial justice? Marcuse and Soja on the right to the city' (2011) 15, 2 *City*, 250.

17 Bleddyn Davies, *Local Services Social Needs and Resources: A Study of Variations in Provision of Social Services between Local Authority Areas (*Joseph Rowntree 1968).

18 David Harvey, *Social Justice and the City* (John Hopkins University Press 1973).

19 Henri Lefebvre, *La production de l'espace*, (Anthropos 1974) and Id., *Writings on Cities* (Blackwell 1996).

20 Edward Soja, *Seeking Spatial Justice* (University of Minnesota press 2010); Id, 'The city and spatial justice', in Bret, Gervais-Lambony, Hancock, Landy (n 14); Id, 'Response to Kurt Iveson: Social or spatial justice? Marcuse and Soja on the Right to the City' (2011) 15, 2 *City*, 260.

and the right to the city itself. According to the European view of territorial cohesion, in fact, this kind of approach would make it possible to include both urban and rural areas.[21] After all, as Soja himself states, "spatial justice is 'a struggle over geography'", and therefore, "the right to the city needs to be seen much more explicitly [...] as a struggle for spatial justice".[22] Thus, we might observe that spatial justice encompasses, but does not end in, the right to the city.

Having said that, initial thinking on the topic has seen territorial justice as the main key to measuring territorial inequalities and the differential allocation of resources. Space has been understood in a traditional geographical sense – that is, as a container for socio-economic, institutional, political and administrative drivers and facts. Thus, these elaborations were translated into indications to administrations themselves (especially public authorities with planning powers at regional and local level) with the aim of achieving an equitable distribution of resources and services on a territorial scale.

Later, since the early 1990s, the same public action needed to counteract poverty and social distress has led to a shifting emphasis from "people" to the "places" where degradation and spatial segregation are occurring.[23] Thus, more dynamically, the *administrative* organisation of space has been recognised as important: a necessary institutional solution to respond to the fundamental needs of the populations settled in the territories, especially the most disadvantaged ones, so as to trigger urban and regional development dynamics.

In this way, starting from the three ontological qualities of human existence – the social, temporal, and spatial – elaborated by Soja, an awareness definitively emerges regarding the need to overcome a conception of space as a mere environmental backdrop to social processes. The political and institutional dimension of geographical space refers, in fact, to the distribution of territory via its progressive lay out and division. This may be done through the use of private property, land registry maps, urban zoning and even establishing administrative boundaries. As such, it is highly evident that "lives are

21 "Whereas social justice is explicitly linked to the nation state and the national territory, and global justice refers to inequality across the national boundaries, the concept of spatial justice goes beyond both, referring to the demand for justice both within and across bounded territories. [...] Spatial justice, therefore, is a concern at all spatial scales and territorial levels, including the questions of regional inequality as well as social inequality and exclusion within localities and regions". In these terms Madanipour, Shucksmith, Brooks (n 15), 813, who also state: "Soja's definition of spatial justice is an explicit attempt at spatializing Rawls, adding a geographical dimension to distributive justice". As in fact Soja himself notes, spatial justice is "the fair and equitable distribution in space of socially valued resources and the opportunities to use them" (811).

22 Soja (2010) (n 20) 2 and 199.

23 Alietti (n 9) 18.

intertwined with the geographical areas they inhabit" and, at the same time, no "social process plays out uniformly in space".[24]

Human existence, as moreover Lefebvre already noted, is conditioned by conventional criteria, such as accessibility to services, and so by the relational dynamics that shape the actual distances between places and services themselves. Furthermore, urbanisation processes and the way cities are built and rebuilt (or *regenerated*, as we say today), contribute to generating types of ghettoization and pockets of injustice, primarily in the suburbs. According to Lefebvre, these areas are then dialectically opposed to urban centres, privileged places of service access. As such, spatiality ultimately also leads to a complex network of relationships of subjugation, which must necessarily be replaced by mechanisms of *solidarity* and *cooperation*, according to Doreen Massey.[25]

As can be seen, therefore, the conditions of justice and injustice concern "living in a place as an ontological form of the human existence". It follows that the theoretical paradigm of spatial justice targets both "the concern for the kind of life people would desire or are actually capable of leading" as well as, ultimately, the very "demand for *just* institutions, underlaying the social fabric".[26] The discourse thus shifts, thanks in particular to the contributions of Amartya Sen and then, among others, Martha C. Nussbaum and Kevin Lynch,[27] on the so-called capabilities. These can be understood as the capacities or opportunities available to individuals – also as a consequence of public decisions – necessary to ensure dignity to human life, especially in its development within the city.

Thus, the objective becomes the same construction of a *just urban form*. Whereby "just" is no longer meant only the fair territorial distribution of resources and services, including those on mobility, but now also the possibility of access to well-constructed places, be they work, study or green and recreational spaces, in which human personality develops.

The distinction between private spaces and public places takes on paramount and particular relevance. When in the cities private spaces predominate over public, there is a gradual transition from public and civic forms of life to what Evan McKenzie has called "privatopias": places that do not contemplate, but rather exclude any type of responsibility for the city and the lives that take place in it.[28] Thus, the actual extension of public versus private space

24 Danani (n 11) 133.
25 Doreen Massey, 'Politics and space' (1992) I/96 *New Left Review*, 65.
26 Danani (n 11) 136.
27 Amartya Sen, 'Well-being agency, and freedom: The Dewey lectures 1984' (1985) 82, 4 *The Journal of Philosophy*, 203; Id., *Commodities and Capabilities* (North Holland 1985) and Id., *The Standard of Living. The Tanner Lectures on Human Values* (Cambridge University Press 1987); Martha C. Nussbaum, *Sex and Social Justice* (Oxford University Press 1999); Kevin Lynch, *A Theory of Good City Form* (MIT Press 1981).
28 Evan McKenzie, *Private Privatopia. Homeowner Associations and the Rise of Residential Government* (Yale University Press 1994).

comes into question. Consequently, spatial justice theories also allow focussing attention on the enhancement of the local dimension as well as on the public decision-making processes themselves and, therefore, on the forms of civic participation, according to an overall democratic perspective that aims at social inclusion.[29]

As we note, it is precisely from the enhancement of the local dimension and the need to avoid forms of social exclusion and urban segregation that derives the recognition of the importance of participation, that is, of the possibility of creating "places" in which one can publicly discuss issues that affect territory, spaces, or, in a word, the city.

So, it seems interesting to note, especially for our purposes, that among the capabilities that must be ensured by public decision-makers there is the possibility for individuals to "be capable of justice" and, therefore, to "control their environment" at the political level as well. The first capability also implies, in turn, an ability to "protect institutions that establish and nurture forms of belonging"; the second, on the other hand, translates precisely into the ability "to be able to participate effectively in the political choices that govern one's life; to enjoy the right of political participation, the guarantees of freedom of speech and association".[30]

Clearly, these are statements that lend themselves to fruitful interdisciplinary analysis. Still outside the field of law, these topics have received attention within a long tradition of sociological studies addressing the so-called institution building. The latter precisely aims to change the organisational culture of local governments so they work better in implementing participatory democracy. The different dimensions of the right to the city are enhanced in this way. After all, the right to the city also implies and assumes there are demands for actively participating in urban life. This may allow coping with the loss of territorial control public institutions, themselves, have experienced. So, the ultimate goal is to enhance the capacity for collective action towards the common good, turning the same social complexity in a possibility for administrations to renew their urban policies.[31]

4.3 Participatory democracy, social complexity and the effectiveness of public decisions: Taking a cue from European climate law

Returning to the area of public law theory, it is no coincidence that scholars have highlighted how much the same processes triggered by globalisation – i.e. the crisis affecting nationally representative institutions and the administrative decentralisation, mentioned at the start, together with the increase in

29 Iris Marion Young, *Inclusion and Democracy* (Oxford University press 2000).
30 Danani (n 11) 142–143, takes up the list of *capabilities* defined by Nussbaum.
31 On this point, see Alietti (n 9), among others.

social complexity – have contributed to the development and flourishing of theories and institutes on participatory democracy.[32]

As known, in a comparative setting, participatory democracy notably entails referring to a "set of concrete participatory practices which citizens or, in any case, individuals interested in public decision making take part and they do so in an informed way, thus creating an 'interaction' between society and institutions".[33]

Practices traditionally included here are the Brazilian experience of participatory budgets, the German deliberative polls and planning units or the consensus conferences popular in the United States and Denmark. Last, but not least, some processes well known within the French system, such as consultation, debate and public enquiry, may be included. Each of these models is characterised by allowing for broad public participation, unencumbered by any need for formal legitimisation. Moreover, they recognise their capacity to influence the final decisions taken by public authorities, without this translating into any formal decision-making power.

In this way, therefore, the attempt to recompose the institutional knots, conflict and social disagreement finds in the same participatory method, of a procedural type, one of the possible solutions to ensure first and foremost legitimacy and trust in public institutions.

Moreover, according to the canons of procedural justice, these practices add substantial surplus value, which results in a more effective and higher quality public decision-making and ultimately greater acceptance of decisions as well.

The application of different options for exercising participatory democracy might be considered, especially at the current moment. This may be done as more than just a way of restating the (often unheard) demand for introducing individual, diffuse and common interests into public decision-making processes. It may serve, above all, as a tool for making administrations aware of the actual interests in play while concretely "verifying" these interests within administrative activity. This, in turn, ensures effective decision making.[34] On the other hand, the faint or disorganised interests of residents, *city users* or *city dwellers* may not be gathered via the normal procedural ways, which frequently involve the participation of only professional associations. There may be a risk, then, of blocking or not achieving full compliance with public decisions. This is especially the case with decisions of a general nature targeting *all* citizens.

32 For a broad survey of this area, including consideration of principles and the spread of deliberative and participatory democracy institutions, see Raffaele Bifulco, 'Democrazia deliberativa', (Enciclopedia del diritto Giuffrè 2011).

33 Bifulco (n 32) 275.

34 On the relationship between participation and the effectiveness of administrative decisions, see, most recently, Guido Corso, Maria De Benedetto and Nicoletta Rangone, *Diritto amministrativo effettivo. Una introduzione* (il Mulino 2022), especially 167 ff.

After all, the same theories on complexity have long shown that subjects, values and interests often coexist in conflict with each other within a fragmentary system encompassing a plurality of relationships.[35] Here, it is exactly the principles of unity, solidarity and collaboration that require "the members of society to behave in a necessarily constructive manner"[36] as this allows maintaining the same complexity in a "balanced state".[37] As noted, managing this complexity requires "synthesising", channelling and coordinating interests. This is possible also by using the appropriate participatory instruments, but always keeping in mind that, in the "public arena",[38] "complex reality can never allow democracy to be simplified into a single element".[39]

Concurrently, however, these efforts to reduce complexity in public action often also entail organisational and procedural choices that mean foregoing participatory methods. This may be done in order to follow a logic of administrative simplification, be cost-effective, or meet a procedural time frame. Eliminating the decision-making stages open to consultation, participation and input from interested parties may seem justifiable given the need for speed, timeliness and results-based administrative action. This may be the case particularly when an action presumably aims to meet the greater public interests.

The crisis around using participatory methods has also been linked more recently to the general difficulty public decision-makers have in managing administrative complexity. This has been even more evident with the use of emergency measures, exceptional legal regimes and administrative action in countering current crises. As a result, there has been a concurrent drastic reduction in opportunities for participation.[40]

35 In this sense, social complexity can be understood as the exponential growth within a given society of a plurality of interests. These interests, in turn, are a projection of the needs and demands people have for certain goods. People's needs tend to be hierarchical and ordered according to a scale of values that goes from basic interests at the bottom to social values on top. The tension around these needs is precisely captured by the flexible idea of "fighting for the right", as expressed in R. Von Jhering's famous work. This refers to the struggle by which only some of these hierarchical interests emerge and are legally recognised. On this, and for more principle-related references, we refer to Marzia De Donno, 'Imperfect polycentrism and 'loyal' coordination: From complication to the organisation of complexity', in Marzia De Donno and Francesca Di Lascio (eds), *Public Authorities and Complexity. An Italian Overview* (ESI 2022).

36 Francesco Manganaro, 'Politiche di coesione' (Enciclopedia del diritto Giuffrè 2022) 840.

37 Angelo Falzea, 'Complessità giuridica' (Enciclopedia del diritto Giuffrè 2007) 203.

38 In the sense expressed by Sabino Cassese, 'L'arena pubblica. Nuovi paradigmi per lo Stato' (2001) 3 *Rivista trimestrale di diritto pubblico* 601.

39 Umberto Allegretti, 'Democrazia partecipativa' (Enciclopedia del diritto Giuffrè 2011) 310.

40 This is, for example, what occurred at the local level while preparing project financing with RRP resources. The need to comply with the tight schedule of ministerial calls for proposals has sometimes forced cities to forego participatory approaches. This may have occurred e.g. in developing urban renewal projects linked to the Integrated Urban Programme funding. On the relationship between administrative complexity and participation, see Fabio Giglioni, 'Administrative complexity and participation: An inextricable knot', in De Donno and Di

This is a situation which requires additional reflection by scholars. And, in fact, not surprisingly, European law has recently shown itself to be particularly sensitive and attentive in this regard through Reg. EU 2018/1999 on the Governance of the Energy and Climate Action Union (adopted in line with the 2015 Paris Agreement on Climate Change).

From its first Recital, it has called for a joint, coherent and ambitious effort by the Union and Member States to achieve the long-term goals and targets set for 2030, exactly "while limiting administrative complexity". Indeed, limiting "complexity at the administrative level" should "ensure coherence and adequate EU and national-level policies, measures for transforming energy systems and transitioning to a sustainable low-carbon economy".[41] Notably, Member States must meet this objective when they "involve social partners in preparing integrated national energy and climate plans [... and/or] when fulfilling obligations related to public consultation"[42] as provided for in Article 10.[43]

The subsequent European Climate Act similarly works toward significantly strengthening public participation in the climate decision-making processes. In this respect, Reg. EU 2021/1119 seems to indicate even more clearly what approach is needed to address the "existential threat posed by climate change", "transform the Union into a *just* and prosperous society" and "protect the health and well-being of citizens from environmental hazards and their consequences".[44] According to this Regulation, public decision-makers now need three supports to this end. One is scientific knowledge, for carrying out rigorous objective assessments based on up-to-date, scientific, technical and socio-economic findings and represented by a wide range of independent expertise.[45] Secondly, there must be a multilevel dialogue with local authorities, civil society organisations, the business community, investors and other relevant stakeholders, and then, thirdly, civic participation itself.

The latter, in particular, is required under Art. 10, Reg. EU 2018/1999 which states the need to "to enable [the public] to participate and express their

Lascio (n 35), 3. According to him, in any case, "the statute of public action is incompatible with any assumption that seeks to reduce the complexity of the decision-making procedure to zero [...]. In this sense, it seems to trace in these knots a clear limitation to the application of the theory of new public management that has been widely diffused since the 1990s and that has perhaps now lost its impetus within the public sector" (18).

41 Recital 23, Reg. EU 2018/1999.

42 Recital 28 and Art. 10, Reg. EU 2018/1999.

43 This gives Member States the duty to "ensure that the public is given early and effective opportunities to participate in the preparation of the draft integrated national energy and climate plan" and "that the public is informed" in order to enable it "to participate and express its views". To this end, each Member State must limit "administrative complexity in implementing this Article".

44 Recital 1 and 2, Reg. EU 1119/2021.

45 Consider the provisions for establishing European and national scientific advisory committees on climate change; see Recital 37, and Art. 3 and 12, Reg. EU 1119/2021.

views" and "promote [...] the dissemination of scientifically based information about climate change and its social and gender aspects".[46] This must be promoted at all levels of government – national, regional and local – precisely to ensure achieving the EU's climate neutral goals.

As can be seen, the EU is evidently and expectedly taking a stance here on the ability of public participation itself, alongside traditional enforcement responses, to enable effective climate change measures and, hence, spontaneous compliance and implementation by citizens. As the Regulation goes on to say: "citizens and communities play a decisive role in advancing the transition to climate neutrality. Thus, a strong public and societal commitment to climate action at all levels (national, regional and local) should be encouraged and facilitated through an accessible inclusive process. The Commission should therefore involve all sections of society, including stakeholders representing the different sectors of the economy. It should give them the opportunity as well as responsibility of committing to a climate-neutral and climate-resilient society".[47]

Thus, we can understand well the serious delays accumulating within Italy's legal system given the current context and future scenario (including the time frame) which national administrations must move towards. Unlike other European and non-European states, Italy, in fact, does not yet have a general national regulation addressing public participation. This may still be prevented based on a formal interpretation of the provisions of Art. 13 of the Administrative Procedure Act, l. n. 241/1990. This article excludes the implementing of participatory instruments in so-called mass proceedings aimed at adopting regulatory, general administrative, planning and programming acts. However, over time the state legislature itself has introduced forms of public participation, i.e. public debates and inquiries on the locational procedures for public works,[48] but, despite this, Italy's legal system does not yet have a general regime regulating such instruments.[49] On the contrary, regional sectoral legislation, in particular urban planning legislation having significant environmental impacts, has been most open to popular participation. The case of Italy therefore tends to show that demands for participation have been heard and

46 Art. 9, Reg. EU 1119/2021.

47 Recital 38, Reg. EU 1119/2021. See also Recital 7 above: "In order to enhance involvement of all economic actors, the Commission should facilitate sector-specific climate dialogues and partnerships by bringing together key stakeholders in an inclusive and representative manner, so as to encourage sectors themselves to draw up indicative voluntary roadmaps and to plan their transition towards achieving the Union's climate-neutrality objective by 2050".

48 See, most recently, Art. 40 of Legislative Decree n. 36/2023 containing the "new" Public Contracts Code.

49 In relation to the need to overcome the provision in Article 13 of law n. 241/1990, in order to ensure broader participation in the regulatory proceedings aimed at defining the policies and measures to be adopted to implement the *Green Deal*, see Eugenio Bruti Liberati, 'Politiche di decarbonizzazione, costituzione economica europea e assetti di governance' (2021) 2 *Diritto pubblico* 432–440.

have a legally productive environment mainly at a territorial level: municipal first, and then regional.

4.4 The recent case of the Milan and Bologna climate assemblies

Against this backdrop, it is highly important to consider that new modes of participation, in the form of citizens' assemblies, have emerged in response to social conflicts linked to certain large public infrastructure projects (e.g. the well-known case of the Turin-Lyon high-speed train), and, more recently, in relation to the climate protection requests.

In addition, it is very important to consider that these new modes of participation have been legally recognised exclusively at the municipal level. The provisions for the citizens' assemblies, in fact, actually find their legal source (still) only in municipal regulations and statutes (e.g. as in the Municipality of Susa in 2020 and Milan and Bologna in 2021).[50] The unique exception to this is the law on citizen councils adopted by the Autonomous Province of Bolzano in 2018.[51]

On closer inspection, therefore, the cases considered here could also be read as a new manifestation of the 'law of the city'. That is, they specifically express an innovative kind of legal capacity of municipalities directly linked to their autonomy. Thus, under Articles 5 and 118, paragraph 4 of the Constitution itself, this new capacity has recognised novel types of participation and active citizenship geared towards safeguarding general interests.[52] In this sense, it is social complexity itself that takes on a "pre-legal" value, deriving from the power of social relations. This complexity strives to becomes a rule or *norm* in relation to local institutions and in an area still dominated by informality. As such, it has also influenced subsequent legal activity.

50 Notably, the idea of setting up a citizen's climate assembly had arisen previously in Milan and Bologna at the behest of their municipal institutions. The *Declaration of Climate and Environmental Emergencies* (*Dichiarazione di emergenza climatica e ambientale*) approved by their city councils in 2019 directly provided for such assemblies. Subsequently, both cities were admitted to the EU Mission linked to the 100 European Climate Neutral Cities by 2030 initiative. This foresees the Milan and Bologna civic assemblies becoming involved in commitments and actions under the so-called *Climate City Contract* signed with the European Commission.

51 Piera Vipiana, 'Gli istituti di partecipazione politica previsti dalla legge della Provincia autonoma di Bolzano n. 22/2018 a confronto con le discipline vigenti nella Provincia autonoma di Trento e in alcune regioni a statuto ordinario' (2019) 3 *Diritti regionali* 2.

52 As Labriola observes (n 1) in this context, "it may be true that the political and democratic nature of cities suggests, or almost imposes, that the lives playing out in them should be legally regulated. Given this, it is equally true that the law we speak of should have somewhat innovative characteristics (as it increasingly does, in practice), especially with regard to the political decision making process" (24). For the so-called shared administration model, see, most recently, Gregorio Arena and Marco Bombardelli, *L'amministrazione condivisa* (ES 2022).

The subject is wide-ranging and cannot be dealt with exhaustively here. Still, the issue should be kept in mind, particularly because of its current implications on the mechanisms driving the multilevel production of law. The latter occurs amidst the central and regional legislators' inertia and silence and the proactive role of local-authority regulatory autonomy. On the other hand, theorists of city law have expectedly discerned cases where a municipal regulatory power acknowledges the legal importance of spontaneous types of collaboration between administrations and the forces of civil society. This kind of collaboration may be a way of dealing with social complexity. It may also help create the new solutions needed to address the problems inherent in safeguarding the general interest.[53]

That being said, the local provisions mentioned here have nonetheless taken advantage of and benefited from a regional legal framework which legitimises such participatory practices. As noted previously, so-called second-generation urban planning regional laws have introduced various rules allowing "anyone who wants" to participate in public decision making, through debates, consultations and public inquiries, but also related institutions such as town or citizen meetings and other various participatory processes.[54] As noted previously, regional legislative activity may have advanced the general principle of popular participation in Italy. This is a sign of the "progressive acceptance [at least at a decentralised level] of the notion of active citizenship. Such citizenship is not linked to pertaining formally to a State, but rather a deep-seated existing link with the territory concerned".[55]

Moreover, on a transnational level, the *European Charter of Local Self-Government* adds to this basis of legitimacy. Article 3 of the *Charter* is dedicated to local self-government and mentions both elected and citizen assemblies. The latter represents an option, along with "referendums or any other form of direct citizen participation", for local authorities to exercise their "right and the ability [...] to regulate and manage a substantial share of public affairs under their own responsibility and in the interests of the local population".

53 On these aspects, also for broader reflections, see, most recently, Maria Vittoria Ferroni, Giovanni Ruocco (eds), *La città informale. Approcci teorici* (Castelvecchi 2021) and Fabio Giglioni, 'Verso un diritto delle città. Le città oltre il comune', in Enrico Carloni and Fulvio Cortese, *Diritto delle autonomie territoriali* (Wolters Kluwer 2020), especially 277 ff. and the doctrine cited therein. For additional reflections on this topic, see, Marco Bombardelli, 'L'organizzazione dell'amministrazione condivisa', in Arena and Bombardelli (n 52), 113.

54 See, among others, the laws in Tuscany, Emilia-Romagna, Marche and Apulia. For an analysis of this, see, Anna Simonati, 'La partecipazione dei privati al governo del territorio nella legislazione regionale: fra tradizione e sperimentazione, per una nuova urbanistica 'reticolare'', (2016) 3 *Rivista giuridica dell'edilizia*, 266, which also provides further references. Also see, more recently, by the same author, 'Rigenerazione urbana, politiche di sicurezza e governo del territorio: quale ruolo per la cittadinanza?' (2019) 1 *Rivista giuridica dell'edilizia*, 31.

55 Simonati (2016) (n 54) 270.

Thus, also in light of relevant experiences in other countries, e.g. the French *Convention Citoyenne pour le Climat*[56] and the German *Bürgerrat Klima*,[57] some of the largest cities in Italy (Milan and Bologna) have regulated assemblies to promote "citizen contributions in forming and implementing municipal policies and strengthening dialogue amongst citizens and with administrations".[58] These assemblies are qualified in the amended *Regulation on the Rights of Participation and Information* (*Regolamento sui diritti di partecipazione e di informazione*) in Bologna as a "temporary body of the municipality" of "high democratic value".[59] In Milan, they are seen as part of a permanent "participatory process"[60] under the city's *Regulation for the Implementation of Popular Participation Rights* (*Regolamento per l'attuazione dei diritti di partecipazione popolare*).

These citizen assemblies present specific features that differentiate them from the other participatory institutions mentioned above. This is because they aim to foster civic deliberation as part of the public decision-making processes, but at the same time they may be more appropriately seen as an expression of the so-called sphere of random democracy as in ancient Athens, or more recently, of the ***deliberative opinion polls***.[61] As such, they have no equivalent within the legislative context.

56 The so-called Citizens Convention for the Climate (*Convention citoyenne pour le climat / CCC*) was established at the national level in France at the behest of the President of the French Republic. The precise aim was to formulate proposals for reducing greenhouse gas emissions by 40% by 2030 (based on 1990 levels). The CCC is composed of 150 citizens chosen in a stratified and representative way from French society (based on various criteria of age, gender, background, profession, etc.). The Convention was involved in the legislative process that led to the entry into force of the so-called Climate and Resilience Law No. 2021-1104 of 22 August 2021 (*Loi Climat et Resilience*). Concurrently, the President of the French Republic, government and parliament formally committed themselves to negotiate and vote ("yes" or "no") on the CCC's proposals, potentially calling referendums as well. In the end, only 3 of the 149 proposals of the convention were rejected and 62 became law. For some comments on the law, see Jean-Charles Rotoullié, 'La loi n° 2021-1104 du 22 août 2021 portant lutte contre le dérèglement climatique et renforcement de la résilience face à ses effets' (2021) 5 *Revue Française de Droit Administratif* 949, and Dossiers no. 1 and 2 published in *Actualité Juridique des Collectivités Territoriales*, no. 12 December 2021 and no. 1 January 2022.

57 Other highly relevant experiences include: the Toronto Planning Review Panel; the Irish Citizens' Assembly; the climate assemblies in the cities of Berlin, Gdansk and Lublin; and the permanent citizen's council in eastern Belgium. For more details see Anja Röcke and Yves Sintomer, 'Estrazione a sorte e democrazia partecipativa: riflessioni sugli esiti delle giurie civiche berlinesi' (2006) 3 *Democracy and Law*, 87; and the OECD 2020 report, *Innovative Citizen Participation and New Democratic Institutions – Catching the deliberative wave* and the bibliography referred to therein.

58 Art. 6-a of the Statute of the Municipality of Bologna.

59 Art. 45 of the Regulation.

60 Art. 14 of the Regulation. See also Art. 6 on the participation pact, which further regulates the relationship between the municipal administration and the permanent assembly at the start of work.

61 On this topic, see Yves Sintomer, *Le pouvoir au peuple. Jurys citoyens, tirage au sort et démocratie participative* (La Découverte 2007).

A special feature of this type of assembly is that it is based on a random sample of citizens or city users, representing the larger reference population. The assembly is called upon to propose agendas and formulate opinions, observations and proposals to then present to their democratically elected governing bodies. Such an assembly has the powers to put issues forward, holds proper consultative and proposal-related functions and works within a specific time frame. The assembly may also be entrusted with a wide range of objectives that fall within the scope of municipal responsibility. The assembly in the Municipality of Bologna was recently called upon to develop proposals on the energy transition, emissions reductions, climate justice and anti-poverty and marginalisation measures. On the other hand, the permanent citizen's climate assembly in Milan is currently supervising the implementation and enforcement phases of the Air and Climate Plan.

In the Bologna assembly, the deliberative process and subsequent monitoring is guided by a number of required bodies (e.g. coordination, support, guarantee and monitoring committees).[62] Distinct phases of activity characterise both city assemblies and these range from informing and training assembly members to discussing, deliberating and final decision making. A simple majority is deemed sufficient for this in Milan. The so-called consensus method is required in Bologna so that deliberations do not become a mere expression of the majority of members.[63] Once a decision has been made by the citizen assemblies, the municipal governing bodies then have a duty to deliberate and give a reasoned opinion on it within a set time frame. The Rules of Procedure in Bologna stipulate that, when calling a meeting, the municipal council may make an enhanced political-administrative commitment to accept any proposals that the citizen assembly approves unanimously, by consensus or with a certain qualified majority.

62 The coordinating committee is comprised of two spokespersons from the assembly (randomly drawn during the first meeting), several technical municipal representatives and/or third parties. The latter are responsible for participatory processes and the assembly topic and are appointed by the mayor. The support and the guarantee committees, on the other hand, are elected by the municipal council after consulting with the mayor. They are comprised of three to five persons, chosen, respectively, from experts on the assembly topic and from patently independent persons who have proven capabilities in participatory processes. Finally, the monitoring committee is comprised of a limited number of representatives elected from the assembly at the end of its work period. The governance of the Milan assembly, in contrast, appears more flexible. It outlines a (potential) role for an assembly spokesperson, elected during the first meeting together with two alternates. It also relies on the municipal technical bodies responsible for the assembly topic. They have the right to participate in meetings and advise on and evaluate the feasibility and sustainability of proposals. On the other hand, substantial aspects are entrusted to a scientific committee identified via public selection.

63 If the set methods do not work, the Rules of Procedure allow for proceeding by vote, but only to ensure a decision by the meeting's end. In this way, proposals and recommendations are considered approved if a qualified majority of two-thirds of the members support them. A simple majority is, on the other hand, only allowed in exceptional cases or when it is impossible to proceed otherwise within a reasonable time.

4.5 Some concluding remarks

As can be seen, there are several necessary and steadfast conditions for ensuring the legitimacy of these civic assemblies and thus, strengthening their role before governing bodies. These include the presence of objective experts, a balanced governance system and a structured deliberative process. We briefly summarise below the most significant further characteristics of the various types of assembly experiences currently underway:

i) They generally have about a hundred members on average, randomly drawn using advanced statistical procedures;
ii) Their governance systems are (sometimes) complex, but the involvement of municipal policy-making and administrative bodies/offices guarantee their orderly functioning;
iii) In terms of knowledge and information, they are supported by independent technicians and researchers selected (sometimes) through public tenders;
iv) All their operations must be inspired by transparency, from the initial through deliberation phases;
v) They produce suggestions, proposals and recommendations that may add to and influence discussions on environmental and climate issues in particular, without having a binding effect on public choices;
vi) They flank rather than replace elected bodies, who are obliged to keep up transparent dialogues and faithful, continual and appropriate exchanges with assemblies' members.

Thus, if well regulated, civic assemblies may represent a democratic and innovative method of involving citizens in public action, especially in the current phase of climate change. However, we would like to conclude this paper by pointing out some potentially critical concerns. In fact, our personal conviction is that the use of assemblies may lend itself to potential distortion. It is, therefore, worth specifically distancing ourselves from some new and recent trends (that may be open to rebuke). One is the trend in responding to a crisis in democratic institutions using randomisation. The aim here is to replace political with statistical representations of society.[64] With this, there is a risk of "nobilisation" or creating further differences between those who participate in deliberative processes and those who look on as mere bystanders. Equally open to criticism is the somewhat mirror intention which surreptitiously views opportunities for random bottom-up participation as a way of removing responsibility from those who have an institutional duty to make decisions in the common interest. Worse still, this may be used to give difficult or unpopular political and administrative options some legitimacy.

64 For a reflection on the pros and cons of random selection, see Nadia Urbinati, Luciano Vandelli, *La democrazia del sorteggio* (Einaudi 2020).

In the face of climate risks, in particular, public institutions are required to strive to adapt, revise and innovate in terms of their decision-making systems and this can no longer be neglected.[65] In order to concretely address the environmental threats facing people, the role of citizens is certainly in play. This is the case in terms of their acquiring new behaviours and lifestyles and, more generally, in being actively involved in defining policies to combat climate change. However, what is mainly at stake is the role of public decision-makers and the responsibilities – political or otherwise – they are called on to assume vis-à-vis their own citizens. In other words, climate change will mean new adaptation processes. These will require involving stakeholders and communities, but they can only be steered and guided by the government democratically elected bodies, especially by those closest to citizens.

What, therefore, must be grasped about this new participatory practice is the very sophisticated nature of the selective mechanism and deliberative procedure. Citizens' assemblies, especially if well devised also at the legal level, can concretely open up new and balanced forms of collaboration and dialogue between civil society and local administrations. This may improve the quality of life in the face of all the challenges any complexity poses. Ultimately, citizen assemblies are a last useful important instrument developed by the *law of the city* for counteracting the *hostile city* itself. But, there is an intimate link between changing private behaviour and institutional representativeness and this entails paying attention to both democracy at the local level and spatial justice.

Bibliography

Alietti A., 'Giustizia spaziale, periferie e vulnerabilità sociale: un nesso problematico?', in Bernardini M.G. and Giolo O. (eds), *Abitare i diritti. Per una critica dei rapporti tra giustizia e spazi urbani* (Pacini Giuridica 2021).

Allegretti U., *Democrazia partecipativa* (Enciclopedia del diritto Giuffrè 2011).

Arena G. and Bombardelli M., *L'amministrazione condivisa* (ES 2022).

Auby J.-B., 'La decisione pubblica tra scienza e crisi' (2021) 4 *Istituzioni del federalismo* 920.

Barbati C., 'La decisione pubblica al cospetto della complessità: il cambiamento necessario' (2021) 1 *Diritto pubblico* 15.

Bauman Z., *Globalizzazione e glocalizzazione* (Armando Editore 2005).

Bernardini M.G. and Giolo O. (eds), *Abitare i diritti. Per una critica dei rapporti tra giustizia e spazi urbani* (Pacini Giuridica 2021).

Bifulco R., 'Democrazia deliberativa' (Enciclopedia del diritto Giuffrè 2011).

Boeri S., *L'Anticittà* (Laterza 2011).

65 On this topic, see Jean-Bernard Auby, 'La decisione pubblica tra scienza e crisi' (2021) 4 *Istituzioni del federalismo* 920 and Carla Barbati, 'La decisione pubblica al cospetto della complessità: il cambiamento necessario' (2021) 1 *Diritto pubblico* 15.

Bombardelli, 'L'organizzazione dell'amministrazione condivisa', in Arena G. and Bombardelli M., *L'amministrazione condivisa* (ES 2022).
Bret B., 'Notion à la une: justice spatiale' (2015) *Géoconfluences.*
Bret B., Gervais-Lambony P., Hancock C. and Landy F. (eds), *Justice et injustices spatiales* (Presses universitaires de Paris Ouest 2010).
Bret B., *Pour une géographie du Juste. Lire les territoires à la lumière de la philosophie morale de John Rawls* (Presses Universitaires de Paris Ouest 2015)
Bruti Liberati E., 'Politiche di decarbonizzazione, costituzione economica europea e assetti di governance' (2021) 2 *Diritto pubblico* 415.
Cassese S., 'L'arena pubblica. Nuovi paradigmi per lo Stato' (2001) 3 *Rivista trimestrale di diritto pubblico* 601.
Corso G., De Benedetto M. and Rangone N., *Diritto amministrativo effettivo. Una introduzione* (il Mulino 2022)
Cortese F., 'Dentro il nuovo diritto della città' (2016) 2 *Munus* V.
Danani C., 'Sulla giustizia spaziale', in Annette Hilt, Holger Zaborowski and Virgilio Cesarone (eds), *L'Europa e l'idea di Giustizia. Crisi e sfide*, (Itinerari. Annuario di scienze filosofiche 2016) 127.
Davies B., *Local Services Social Needs and Resources: A Study of Variations in Provision of Social Services between Local Authority Areas (*Joseph Rowntree 1968).
De Donno M. and Di Lascio F. (eds), *Public Authorities and Complexity. An Italian Overview* (ESI 2022).
De Donno M., 'Imperfect polycentrism and 'loyal' coordination: From complication to the organisation of complexity', in De Donno M. and Di Lascio F. (eds), *Public Authorities and Complexity. An Italian Overview* (ESI 2022) 101.
De Donno M., 'La governance multilivello delle politiche pubbliche per le città: nuovi scenari e dinamiche inclusive per i territori ai margini', in Bernardini M.G. and Giolo O. (eds), *Abitare i diritti. Per una critica dei rapporti tra giustizia e spazi urbani* (Pacini Giuridica 2021).
Dikeç M., 'Justice and the Spatial Imagination', (2001) 33, 10 *Environment and Planning A: Economy and Space* 1785.
Dussart V. and Lerique F. (eds), *Justice spatiale et politiques publiques territoriales* (Mare & Martin 2022).
Falzea A., *Complessità giuridica* (Enciclopedia del diritto Giuffrè 2007).
Ferrajoli L., *Principia Juris. Teoria del diritto e della democrazia. 2. Teoria della democrazia* (Laterza 2007).
Ferroni M.V. and Ruocco G. (eds), *La città informale. Approcci teorici* (Castelvecchi 2021).
Gardini G., 'Alla ricerca della città giusta. La rigenerazione come metodo di pianificazione urbana' (2020) 24 *federalismi.it* 44.
Giglioni F., 'Administrative complexity and participation: An inextricable knot', in De Donno M. and Di Lascio F. (eds), *Public Authorities and Complexity. An Italian Overview* (ESI 2022).
Giglioni F., 'La città come ordinamento giuridico' (2018) 1 *Istituzioni del Federalismo* 29.
Giglioni F., 'Verso un diritto delle città. Le città oltre il comune', in Carloni E. and Cortese F. (eds), *Diritto delle autonomie territoriali* (Wolters Kluwer 2020).
Giolo O., 'I diritti contro la città. Spazio urbano, soggettività e sfera pubblica', in Bernardini M.G. and Giolo O. (eds), *Abitare i diritti. Per una critica dei rapporti tra giustizia e spazi urbani* (Pacini Giuridica 2021).

Harvey D., *Social Justice and the City* (John Hopkins University Press 1973).

Iveson K., 'Social or Spatial Justice? Marcuse and Soja on the Right to the City' (2011) 15, 2 *City* 250

Labriola G.M., 'Città e diritto. Brevi note su un tema complesso', (2018) 1 *Istituzioni del Federalismo* 5.

Lefebvre H., *La production de l'espace* (Anthropos 1974).

Lefebvre H., *Writings on Cities* (Blackwell 1996).

Lynch K., *A Theory of Good City Form* (MIT Press 1981).

Manganaro F., *Politiche di coesione* (Enciclopedia del diritto Giuffrè 2022).

Madanipour A., Shucksmith M. and Brooks E., 'The concept of spatial justice and the European Union's territorial cohesion', (2022) 30, 5 *European Planning Studies* 807.

Massey D., 'Politics and space' (1992) I, 96 *New Left Review* 65.

McKenzie E., *Private Privatopia. Homeowner Associations and the Rise of Residential Government* (Yale University Press 1994).

Musolino S. and Rossi E., 'La città ostile: architetture e strategie dell'esclusione nelle metropoli contemporanee' (2021) 9, 1 *Fuori Luogo. Rivista di Sociologia del Territorio, Turismo, Tecnologia* 86.

Nussbaum M.C., *Sex and Social Justice* (Oxford University Press 1999).

O'Laughlin J., *Spatial Justice and the Black American Voter: The Territorial Dimension of Urban Politics* (Pennsylvania State University 1973).

OECD 2020 Report, *Innovative Citizen Participation and New Democratic Institutions – Catching the Deliberative Wave.*

Pavani G., Profeti S. and Tubertini C., *Le città collaborative ed eco-sostenibili* (il Mulino 2023).

Petty J., 'The London spikes controversy: Homelessness, urban securitisation and the question of 'hostile architecture'' (2016) 5, 1 *International Journal for Crime, Justice and Social Democracy*, 67.

Philippopoulos-Mihalopoulos A., 'Spatial justice: law and the geography of withdrawal' (2010) 6, 3 *International Journal of Law in Context* 201.

Pirie G.H., 'On Spatial Justice', (1983) 15, 4 *Environment and Planning A: Economy and Space*, 465.

Pizzigoni A., *La città ostile. La realtà dell'architettura urbana nelle sue contraddizioni storiche* (Marinotti Edizioni 2017).

Pizzolato F., 'Città e diritti fondamentali: le ambivalenze della politicità dei diritti' (2022) 1 *Istituzioni del federalismo* 155.

Pontier J.M., 'Justice spatiale et décentralisation', in Dussart V. and Lerique F. (eds), *Justice spatiale et politiques publiques territoriales* (Mare & Martin 2022).

Reynaud A., *Société, espace et justice: inégalités régionales et justice socio-spatiale* (PUF 1981).

Röcke A. and Sintomer Y., 'Estrazione a sorte e democrazia partecipativa: riflessioni sugli esiti delle giurie civiche berlinesi' (2006) 3 *Democracy and Law* 87.

Rotoullié J.-C., 'La loi n° 2021–1104 du 22 août 2021 portant lutte contre le dérèglement climatique et renforcement de la résilience face à ses effets' (2021) 5 *Revue Française de Droit Administratif* 949.

Sassen S., *Territorio, autorità, diritti. Assemblaggi dal Medioevo all'età globale* (Mondadori 2008).

Sen A., 'Well-being Agency, and Freedom: The Dewey Lectures 1984' (1985) 82, 4 *The Journal of Philosophy* 203.

Sen A., *Commodities and Capabilities* (North Holland 1985).
Sen A., *The Standard of Living. The Tanner Lectures on Human Values* (Cambridge University Press 1987).
Simonati A., 'La partecipazione dei privati al governo del territorio nella legislazione regionale: fra tradizione e sperimentazione, per una nuova urbanistica 'reticolare'' (2016) 3 *Rivista giuridica dell'edilizia* 266.
Simonati A., 'Rigenerazione urbana, politiche di sicurezza e governo del territorio: quale ruolo per la cittadinanza?' (2019) 1 *Rivista giuridica dell'edilizia* 31.
Sintomer Y., *Le pouvoir au peuple. Jurys citoyens, tirage au sort et démocratie participative* (La Découverte 2007).
Soja E., *Seeking Spatial Justice* (University of Minnesota press 2010).
Soja E., 'The city and spatial justice', in Bret B., Gervais-Lambony P., Hancock C. and Landy F. (eds), *Justice et injustices spatiales* (Presses universitaires de Paris Ouest 2010).
Soja E., 'Response to Kurt Iveson: Social or spatial justice? Marcuse and Soja on the right to the city' (2011) 15, 2 *City* 260.
Urbinati N. and Vandelli L., *La democrazia del sorteggio* (Einaudi 2020).
Vipiana P., 'Gli istituti di partecipazione politica previsti dalla legge della Provincia autonoma di Bolzano n. 22/2018 a confronto con le discipline vigenti nella Provincia autonoma di Trento e in alcune regioni a statuto ordinario' (2019) 3 *Diritti regionali* 1.
Young I.M., *Inclusion and Democracy* (Oxford University press 2000).

Part III

European green and climate-neutral cities

Case studies

1 The role of the University of Bologna in contributing to the Climate City Contract process for Bologna

Angela Santangelo, Simona Tondelli, Gian Luca Morini and Giacomo Bergamini

1.1 Introduction

Although cities were initially ignored by most climate-change scientists,[1] nowadays scholars[2] and policy-makers[3] acknowledge that urban areas play a crucial role in mitigating the effects of climate change. Cities concentrate people and activities that are responsible for high levels of energy consumption, generating about 70% of the global greenhouse gas (GHG) emissions.[4] At the same time, urban density allows for more efficient infrastructure, as people use less space per capita for utilities, transportation, and living.[5] The latestIntergovernmental Panel on Climate Change (IPCC)'s report on Mitigation of Climate Change highlights in Chapter 8 "Urban systems and other settlements"[6] that, although the global share of emissions that can be attributed to urban areas is increasing, these areas can create opportunities through systematic transition pathways towards net zero emissions. Cities are required to act as living laboratories[7] to test new development models to enhance inclusive and sustainable

1 Cynthia Rosenzweig et al., 'Cities Lead the Way in Climate–Change Action' (2010) 467 *Nature* 909–911.

2 Mahendra Sethi et al., 'Climate Change Mitigation in Cities: A Systematic Scoping of Case Studies' (2020) 15, 9 *Environmental Research Letters*.

3 United Nations, *Cities and Climate Change*. Available online at: https://www.unep.org/explore-topics/resource-efficiency/what-we-do/cities/cities-and-climate-change (accessed August 3, 2023).

4 European Commission, *The Future of Cities*. Available online at: https://urban.jrc.ec.europa.eu/thefutureofcities/climate-action#the-chapter (accessed August 3, 2023).

5 Christopher A. Kennedy, Nadine Ibrahim, and Dan Hoornweg, 'Low-Carbon Infrastructure Strategies for Cities' (2014) 4 *Nature Climate Change* 343–346.

6 IPCC, *AR6 Climate Change 2022: Mitigation of Climate Change* (Cambridge University Press 2022).

7 Monica Salvia et al., 'Key Dimensions of Cities' Engagement in the Transition to Climate Neutrality' (2023) 344 *Journal of Environmental Management* 118519.

DOI: 10.4324/9781032665184-11

urbanisation and capacity for participatory planning and management of urban settlements, as required by the Sustainable Development Goal (SDG) 11.[8]

At present, the first priority on the EU agenda is the so-called European Green Deal,[9] a set of policy initiatives with the overarching aim of making Europe climate neutral by 2050. In November 2019, the European Parliament declared a climate emergency asking the European Commission to adapt all its proposals in line with a 1.5°C target for limiting global warming and ensure that greenhouse gas emissions are significantly reduced. In response, the European Commission formulated the European Green Deal. Parliament adopted the EU Climate Law in June 2021, which makes legally binding a target of reducing emissions 55% by 2030 and climate neutrality by 2050.

The European Commission has identified key missions to guide the Horizon Europe research and innovation framework programme running from 2021 to 2027.[10] Indeed, Horizon Europe aims to deliver on five main missions by providing concrete solutions to address some of the most significant challenges of our time: adapting to climate change to become climate resilient by 2030, restoring oceans and water, fighting cancer, creating climate-neutral and smart cities by 2030, and leading the transition towards healthy soils by 2030. Altogether, these missions support the European Commission priorities.[11]

According to the EU Mission Climate-Neutral and Smart Cities[12] (also called Cities Mission), cities play a pivotal role in achieving climate neutrality by 2050, the goal of the European Green Deal. Urban areas take up only 4% of the EU's land area,[13] but they are hosting 75% of EU citizens.[14] Since climate mitigation is heavily dependent on urban actions, there is an urgent need to support cities in accelerating their green and digital transformation. In particular, European cities are believed to be able to substantially contribute to the Green Deal target of reducing emissions by 55% by 2030 and, in more

8 Target 11.3 of the Sustainable Development Goal (SDG) 11 promoted by the United Nations, https://sdgs.un.org/goals/goal11
9 The European Green Deal COM/2019/640.
10 European Commission (2023) *Missions in Horizon Europe*. Available online at: https https://research-and-innovation.ec.europa.eu/funding/funding-opportunities/funding-programmes-and-open-calls/horizon-europe/eu-missions-horizon-europe_en (accessed August 3, 2023).
11 European Commission, *A Union that strives for more. My agenda for Europe by candidate for President of the European Commission Ursula von der Leyen. Political Guidelines For The Next European Commission 2019–2024*. Available online at: https://commission.europa.eu/system/files/2020-04/political-guidelines-next-commission_en_0.pdf (accessed August 3, 2023).
12 European Commission, *EU Mission: Climate-Neutral and Smart Cities (2023)*. Available online at: https://research-and-innovation.ec.europa.eu/funding/funding-opportunities/funding-programmes-and-open-calls/horizon-europe/eu-missions-horizon-europe/climate-neutral-and-smart-cities_en (accessed August 3, 2023).
13 According to World Bank data.
14 Eurostat data refers to 2021 and considers both EU population living in cities (38.9%) and living in towns and suburbs (35.9%).

practical terms, to offer cleaner air, safer transport and less congestion and noise to their citizens.

Many cities in Europe and beyond have engaged in climate action for decades, while several initiatives have tried to set the conditions to allow them to take actions towards a carbon neutral reality and EU priorities. A number of city networks have provided frameworks for peer-to-peer collaborations and city-level actions on climate change and sustainable development, and Transnational Municipal Networks (TMNs) related to climate change have been born to support cooperation between cities for improving their climate change mitigation and adaptation policies and tools.[15]

The Cities Mission is the latest initiative launched in this context, and it has already been analysed by some research.[16] By investigating TMNs and assessing their impacts, scholars advocate for harmonised, transparent and open reporting framework by cities' initiatives.[17] Furthermore, there is a need to link on-the-ground scientific expertise to the needs and requirements of local city decision-makers.[18]

The aim of this chapter is to contribute to the discourse about the importance for cities to engage and collaborate with academia, key stakeholders and citizens to deliver EU ambitious goals on climate neutrality. It describes the collaborative process which sees the Municipality closely collaborating with the Alma Mater Studiorum – University of Bologna (UNIBO), from the Expressions of Interest of the Municipality of Bologna in the Mission on 100 Climate-Neutral and Smart Cities by 2030, to the commitment of UNIBO to an active role in contributing to the city's climate neutrality by 2030. At first, the main characteristics of the Cities Mission are presented, together with the key concepts of climate neutrality and Climate City Contract (CCC). In the following section, the relationship between the city of Bologna and the Alma Mater Studiorum – University of Bologna is presented, followed by the description of the key features of the Bologna expression of interest, jointly

15 Milja Heikkinen et al., 'Transnational Municipal Networks and Climate Change Adaptation: A Study of 377 Cities' (2020) 257 *Journal of Cleaner Production* 120474.

16 Katherine Shabb et al., 'Launching the Mission for 100 Climate Neutral Cities in Europe: Characteristics, Critiques, and Challenges' (2022) 3 *Frontiers in Sustainable Cities* 1–6; Katherine Shabb and Kes McCormick, 'Achieving 100 Climate Neutral Cities in Europe: Investigating Climate City Contracts in Sweden' (2023) 2 *NPJ Climate Action* 6; Giulia Ulpiani et al., 'Towards the First Cohort of Climate-Neutral Cities: Expected Impact, Current Gaps, and Next Steps to Take to Establish Evidence-Based Zero-Emission Urban Futures' (2023) 95 *Sustainable Cities and Society* 104572; Monica Salvia et al. (n 7).

17 Jennifer S. Bansard et al., 'Cities to the Rescue? Assessing the Performance of Transnational Municipal Networks in Global Climate Governance' (2017) 17 *International Environmental Agreements: Politics, Law and Economics* 229–246; Paolo Bertoldi et al., *Energy Consumption and Energy Efficiency Trends in the EU 28 2000 2015. European Commission* (JRC Science for Policy Report 2018); Mahendra Sethi et al. (n 2).

18 Cynthia Rosenzweig et al. (n 1).

developed in partnership with UNIBO. Lastly, conclusions and next steps are drawn.

1.2 Climate neutrality, the EU 100 Climate-Neutral and Smart Cities Mission and the Climate City Contract

In brief, "climate neutrality is about emitting less and absorbing more".[19] It refers to the idea of reducing emissions through climate action. It consists of achieving net zero greenhouse gas emissions by balancing those emissions with the emissions that are removed through natural absorption in "sinks" such as forests and oceans. While carbon neutrality refers to zero CO_2 emissions, climate neutrality extends the concept to anthropogenic emission of greenhouse gases (GHG).

The introduction of the climate neutrality concept into the climate change-related policies goes back to 2015, when the UN Climate Change launched the "Climate Neutral Now" initiative[20] to encourage stakeholders around the world to take immediate action to reach the target of net zero emissions by 2050.

Focusing on the EU, the main elements of the climate neutrality definition provided by the Cities Mission, included in the Info Kit for cities and quoted by Ulpiani et al.[21] regard reducing the city emissions: i) in 5 sectors: stationary energy (i.e., buildings, facilities, equipment, and public lighting), transport, waste/wastewater, Industrial Processes and Product Use (IPPU), and Agriculture, Forestry and Other Land Use (AFOLU); ii) across 3 scopes: direct GHG emissions (Scope 1) and indirect GHG emissions (Scope 2) within the city boundary as well as out of boundary GHG emissions (Scope 3) due to the disposal and treatment of waste/wastewater generated within the city boundary; iii) of 7 GHG gases,[22] which should be included in terms of carbon dioxide equivalent (CO_2e). Both absolute-zero and net-zero GHG emissions are in line with the definition of climate neutrality applied for the Cities Mission. The former considers avoiding 100% of greenhouse gas emissions (absolute-zero), while the latter foresees the possibility of balancing direct reduction

19 European Council, *Five facts about the EU's goal of climate neutrality*. Available online at: https://www.consilium.europa.eu/en/5-facts-eu-climate-neutrality/ (accessed August 3, 2023).

20 The Climate Neutral Now Initiative is one of several initiatives launched by the United Nations Framework Convention on Climate Change (UNFCCC) secretariat to increase climate action by engaging non-party stakeholders (sub-national governments, companies, organisations, individuals). More information is available online at: https://unfccc.int/climate-neutral-now (accessed August 3, 2023).

21 The Info Kit for cities, published in October 2021, is not available anymore online. However, the key elements of the climate neutrality definition provided by the Cities Mission have been included in: Giulia Ulpiani et al. (n 16).

22 The 7 GHG gases are: carbon dioxide (CO_2), methane (CH_4), nitrous oxide (N_2O), F-gases (PFCs), sulphur hexafluoride (SF_6) and nitrogen trifluoride (NF_3).

with offsetting of residual emissions (net-zero) through carbon sinks and/or carbon credits.

Between 25 November 2021 and 31 January 2022, the European Commission launched the Call for Expression of Interest addressed to cities to allow them to state their interest in becoming climate-neutral by 2030 as part of the Mission and to submit information on their current situation, ongoing work, and future plans with regard to climate neutrality. The expression of interest consisted of an online survey with more than 350 questions divided according to 2 mandatory sections (1. Eligibility; 2. Additional information) followed by 7 thematic sections, covering all the critical aspects to determine the state of the art (3. Current emissions; 4. Current policies), the ambition and the capacity to deliver results (5. Ambition for climate neutrality; 6. Partnerships; 7. Capital needs and investment strategies; 8. Governance) and the awareness about the challenges and barriers (9. Barriers, risks and assistance needs).

377 cities from all EU member states, as well as nine associated countries, and countries negotiating association submitted an expression of interest. The possibility to apply was limited to cities with at least 50,000 inhabitants, with the exception of EU countries with few larger cities,[23] for which this threshold was lowered to 10,000 inhabitants. After an evaluation of the submissions, in April 2022 the Commission announced the 100 cities that are participating in the Cities Mission; they represent 12% of the EU population and come from all 27 Member States, with 12 additional cities coming from countries associated or in the process of being associated to Horizon Europe. 24 are capital cities and only 15 have a population of less than 100,000 inhabitants. It is worth noting that 8 applications were submitted jointly by two or more small cities, highlighting the importance of inter-municipal alliances to catalyse the interests of public and private parties to pursuit common environmental and climate objectives.

In total, 112 selected cities have been invited to develop their Climate City Contract (CCC), a governance innovation tool to help cities collaboratively address their barriers to reaching climate neutrality by 2030.[24] Led by cities, this process should involve multiple stakeholders at various governance levels, as well as the wider ecosystem of private and civic stakeholders. Together, they will identify all the key actions to achieve 2030 climate neutrality, and the ways and means to implement them, with the support of a Mission Platform.[25] The CCC is one process with three interlinked components: Commitments,

23 Namely: Croatia, Cyprus, Estonia, Ireland, Latvia, Lithuania, Luxembourg, Malta, Slovenia, and Slovakia.

24 Net Zero Cities, Climate City Contract. Available online at: https://netzerocities.app/QR-CCC (accessed August 3, 2023).

25 NetZeroCities is developing the Mission Platform, a one-stop for cities providing access to online resources and tools. Available at: https://netzerocities.app

Actions, and Investments. Firstly, the commitments capture the outcomes of a co-creation process with local, regional, and national stakeholders to establish new ways of working together to achieve climate neutrality faster. It is the core contract, and it includes a shared ambition and a strategy to achieve it, as well as the specific commitment(s) to action from stakeholders in the contract. Afterwards, the action plan identifies the strengths and gaps of existing strategies, policies, and plans, establishing a coordinated portfolio of interventions to achieve the ambition. Lastly, the investments plan strategically mobilises and organises public resources and addresses how to attract private capital for funding and financing cities pathways to climate neutrality.

As investigated by Salvia et al.[26] who have analysed five dimensions (i.e., local climate plans, transnational municipal networks and initiatives, climate emergency declarations, international projects, international competitions and city awards) to capture the level of "activism" of the candidates to the Cities Missions in pursuing smart and climate projects and initiatives, 17 cities out of 18 which have declared experiences that fall into all the five dimensions have been selected among the 100 EU cities, meaning that leveraging on previous and current experiences resulted to be a winning approach.

Another recent study by the European Commission Joint Research Centre,[27] which carried out an in-depth analysis of the 362 eligible cities (out of 377 submissions received) which expressed their interest in the Cities Mission, assessed the credibility and estimated the effects of their mitigation commitments in terms of GHG emissions reduction. It found that the Cities Mission represents a unique opportunity for rapid transition, workforce development, increased climate resilience and leadership, but it also requires facing political, technical and financial challenges as never before. Therefore, cities need support to develop and assess their actions, to integrate creative and innovative approaches and must collaborate with all relevant stakeholders at all governance levels.

1.3 The University of Bologna and the city: A long-lasting partnership

In history, the university has often been conceptualised as a city in itself, an area where different values and rules applied.[28] The historical autonomy of the university was, however, replaced in the early modern period by a more important role that universities gained, especially at the national level as nation building, and the separation between the university and city was also gradually

26 Monica Salvia et al. (n 7).
27 Giulia Ulpiani et al. (n 16).
28 Clare Melhuish et al. (eds), *Co-curating the City: Universities and urban heritage past and future* (UCL Press 2022).

erased, giving birth to a seamless interaction and integration between the university and the society.[29]

As investigated by Caldenby, understanding the material infrastructure of the University of Gothenburg,[30] universities struggle to "balance between two important aims of university location, ever since its beginning in medieval times: a search for autonomy, or identity, and a search for integration in the surrounding city".

Founded in 1088, the Alma Mater Studiorum – University of Bologna (UNIBO) represents one of the largest public universities in Italy, having more than 88,000 students, 3,176 faculty members, and 3,153 technical and administrative staff. It counts 31 departments, 7 interdepartmental research centres for industrial research, 17 Centres for Education and Research, and 303 degree and master courses, as well as specialisation courses, research doctorate courses, and vocational training courses.[31]

Bologna was born as a university spread out in the city. Since its foundation, classes were taught wherever space was available, such as churches and professors' homes. The university was not meant as a physical space but consisted of a spontaneous and informal initiative of a few students. In the following centuries, the University of Bologna developed by maintaining its spread character and establishing the different faculties before within and then outside the historical city walls. While the idea of a "city university" gradually spread in the 1990s, and cities were seen as creative environments, where universities and student life were an asset,[32] the University of Bologna was ready for enforcing its diffused character even more. Since 2000, UNIBO has adopted a multicampus structure, supporting the diffusion of the educational offering and the activation of a stable research activity in the eastern part of the Emilia-Romagna Region, establishing four campuses in the cities of Cesena, Ravenna, Forlì, and Rimini that offer interdisciplinary study programmes on different subjects. In each of the campuses, the spread nature of the University is confirmed, with courses that are taught in different buildings across the cities.

Nowadays, UNIBO activities are carried out in 256 buildings, for a total of about 1 million square meters. The greatest part of these buildings (161) is located in the metropolitan city of Bologna, where 176 out of 303 courses are held, involving a total of over 68,000 students, about half of whom are coming from other regions or from abroad and, thus, moving temporarily to Bologna. Considering that the total inhabitants of the city of Bologna is about

29 Ibid.

30 Claes Caldenby 'From Dispersed Multi-Site to Cluster and Campus: Understanding the Material Infrastructure of University of Gothenburg as Urban Heritage', in Melhuish C. et al. (n 28).

31 Data refer to 2022 and they have been published in the UNIBO Sustainability Report. Available online at: https://www.unibo.it/en/university/who-we-are/sustainability-report/sustainability-report (accessed August 3, 2023)..

32 Claes Caldenby (n 30).

393,000, the incidence of the university community on the city is considerable, comprising almost one-fifth of the entire residential population.

This makes the city of Bologna an outstanding example of "university city" and the partnership towards sustainability between city and university essential.

Indeed, even beyond numbers, urban sustainability transformations require deep and durable partnerships between cities and universities.[33] There is an opportunity to accelerate positive sustainability transformations within urban systems by bringing universities and cities together so as to leverage their collective strengths.[34] University researchers may contribute by providing valuable and trusted expertise that practitioners can use to inform sustainability policy and practices. At the same time, collaboration offers practitioners opportunities to guide research efforts toward the development of practically relevant sustainability solutions.[35] Partnerships and collaborations with a wide range of outside entities and organisations provide cities with the opportunity to expand their reach, analyse problems from multiple angles, and make the coordinated sweeping changes necessary to achieve sustainability and resilience.[36]

The central role of education in each country's development, highlighted by the United Nations 2030 Agenda as a fundamental sustainable development goal (SDG4 Quality education), is a value that each university shares with the society. According to UNIBO Performance Report 2022,[37] priority tasks of the University are the training of students in highly professional figures required by the labour market, the production of new knowledge through world-class scientific research, and the transfer of knowledge to society. The university has two specific target groups to deal with: on the one hand, the students, on the other hand, the society as a whole. Students represent the primary category of stakeholders of the university institution being at the same time direct users and co-participants of the education process. It is to them, therefore, that actions are directed to ensure services that promote the right to study and learn what is needed to realise themselves in work and civil society. In 2021, almost 60% of the graduates at the University of Bologna were employed in the Emilia-Romagna region three years after graduation. Today

33 Gregory Trencher et al., 'University partnerships for co-designing and co-producing urban sustainability' (2014) 28 *Global Environmental Change* 153–165.

34 Lauren Withycombe Keeler et al., 'Building Transformative City-University Sustainability Partnerships: The Audacious Partnerships Process' (2023) 5 *Urban Transformations* 1.

35 Stefan U. Pauer, Angelique Pilon, and Brad Badelt, 'Strengthening City–University Partnerships to Advance Sustainability Solutions: A Study of Research Collaborations between the University of British Columbia and City of Vancouver' (2020) 21 *International Journal of Sustainability in Higher Education* 1189–1208.

36 Liliana Caughman, Fletcher Beaudoin, and Lauren Withycombe Keeler, 'The Project - Partnership Cycle : Managing City - University Partnerships for Urban Sustainability and Resilience Transformations' (2023) 5, 10 *Urban Transformations.*

37 Alma Mater Studiorum – University of Bologna, Performance Report 2022, available online at: https://www.unibo.it/it/ateneo/amministrazione-trasparente/performance/relazione-sulla-performance/relazione-sulla-performance (accessed August 3, 2023).

students are the citizens of tomorrow rather than temporary city-users only. This explains the close relationship that UNIBO has with both its students and the rest of the local society.

Today, many urban universities are engaged in processes of expanding and opening their physical and institutional borders to facilitate greater engagement with the cities in which they are situated. University cities in turn are home to increasingly mixed, multicultural populations. Urban universities are indeed focussing increasingly on internationalisation, contributing to global development on the one hand, while promoting place-based community outreach and engagement with a variety of urban stakeholders on the other, including direct participation in urban development initiatives.[38]

The current mission and vision of the University of Bologna are stated in the Strategic Plan 2022–2027.[39] It envisages 4 areas of actions: teaching and students' community, research, people and society, underling the need to work in partnership with and for the local society; 3 goals out of 50 focus specifically on energy transition – and climate neutrality – related topics (i.e., Goal 48: Reduce energy consumption and improve the energy efficiency of buildings; Goal 49: Facilitate low environmental impact mobility; Goal 50: Adopt an efficient environmental management model, also in the framework of circular economy). The wide building asset, the commitment to contribute to the city energy and climate transition towards neutrality through the University Strategic Plan, and the ongoing collaboration on several projects and initiatives from local to international levels made the University of Bologna a key partner for jointly conceptualising and developing the climate city process of the Municipality of Bologna within the Cities Mission.

1.4 The application of the Municipality of Bologna to the EU Mission as a joint commitment

1.4.1 Engaging the community of Bologna towards climate neutrality

Apart from being home to the University of Bologna, the eldest in Europe, attracting young talents and providing the economic system with skills and opportunities, Bologna can also count on a vibrant socio-economic environment, and it is growing in terms of resident population as well as people who visit the city daily (e.g., tourists and commuters). Bologna's typical feature is an ever-increasing attractiveness, confirmed by tourist flow data, where cultural heritage plays a major role. On the one hand, the historical city, one of the widest among similar cities in Europe, is the backdrop for a diverse cultural offer. The portico system, UNESCO World Heritage Site since 2021, is a

38 Clare Melhuish et al. (n 28).

39 Alma Mater Studiorum – University of Bologna, *Strategic Plan 2022–2027*. Available online at: https://www.unibo.it/en/university/who-we-are/strategic-plan (accessed August 3, 2023).

model of active social life every day, regardless of the weather conditions. In addition, Bologna relies on its rich natural capital as the green/blue infrastructure, made of agricultural/hilly areas, river strips, private and public urban green areas, which covers about 65% of the territory.

The historical centre represents one of the hardest challenges for reaching neutrality, due to the very high number of historical buildings, monuments, and preserved sites, which makes it extremely ambitious and challenging to carry out radical energy retrofit and to introduce renewable energy plants.

Stakeholders are covering the quadruple helix, encompassing citizens, academia, and research, business, and local institutions.

The Municipality of Bologna and UNIBO carry out many joint studies and research projects on sustainable local development both at the local and international levels. This strategic partnership has also beenconfirmed for the application to the Cities Mission, where the University of Bologna provided a letter of support, and the two institutions have closely collaborated since the conceptual phase. The symbiotic relationship between the city and the University led to a strong collaboration towards an innovative, digital, and ecological city based on science and knowledge.

Also, a strong partnership with the Metropolitan Institution (led by Bologna's Mayor) and the Emilia-Romagna Region is an asset to the mission. In addition, the Municipality of Bologna has activated partnerships with other relevant organisations and environmental research institutes for analysis and monitoring, to define its own plans and strategies, and to carry out pilots and experimental projects. In particular, the Regional Agency for Environmental Protection & Energy (ARPAE), the National Agency for New Technologies, Energy & Sustainable Economic Development (ENEA), and the Euro-Mediterranean Centre for Climate Change (CMCC) have collaborated with the Municipality of Bologna in the realisation of the inventories of climate-altering emissions and in the study of the climatic profile of the city at the base of the Sustainable Energy and Climate Action Plan and the Urban Plan.

The Municipality of Bologna has been working on all sectors for long to improve the environmental balance, while managing and transforming the city. It has taken up the climate change mitigation and adaptation challenge, and it is well aware of its serious impacts at the local and global scales, adopting Kyoto Protocol's targets in 2007, joining the first generation Covenant of Mayors in 2008, through to Mayor's adapt in 2014 and the most recent targets, until the Declaration of Climate Emergency in 2019 and introduction of neutrality as a strategic goal in the Municipal Statutes in 2021. To enable the city to step forward, in 2021, the Municipality of Bologna approved the new Urban Plan, conceived as the main tool to push both public and private sectors to turn pilot climate-neutral projects into stable and replicable measures. Therefore, by embracing the Climate Neutral Cities Mission, the Municipality of Bologna intended to continue the path to reduce greenhouse gas emissions within a broader strategy for sustainability, nature, and ecosystems protection, health and well-being for all.

Bologna can also rely on an active citizenship and on a strong third sector that shares the ambition towards climate neutrality and set the basis for developing a citizen science ecosystem.[40] A Citizen Assembly on Climate has been established to increase democratic participation and citizens' engagement in the transition to climate neutrality. This new participatory tool has been recently introduced in the Statute of the Municipality in accordance with the Declaration of Climate Emergency requested by a wide number of environmental and social movements and associations. The Assembly is made up of 100 members. Eighty of these are people over 16 years old, residents in the Municipality of Bologna, randomly selected, ensuring that the sample represents the socio-demographic characteristics of the city (i.e., the sampling was carried out proportionally to the age groups, neighbourhoods, and gender). The Assembly also welcomes 20 "city users" intended as people who usually frequent the city although they are not residents: 10 are students from the University of Bologna, while the others are commuters holding a season ticket for public transport.

1.4.2 The University of Bologna Action Plan towards climate neutrality

The University of Bologna's energy consumption is about 14,000 tonnes of oil equivalent per year (toe/year), for a total cost of about €15 million in 2021 and €21 millionin 2022, and a production of about 32,000 tons of CO_2 emissions, which corresponds to about 1.5% of the total emissions in the city of Bologna.

The University of Bologna is highly committed to reducing its energy consumption. To this aim, UNIBO approved in October 2023 the first University Energy Plan[41], that provides an innovative framework of actions to be adopted towards climate neutrality. The plan encompasses actions referring to different sectors: improved management and digitalisation of the energy system, buildings (i.e., new developments and refurbishment of existing buildings), relamping, heating plants replacement, self-production of energy from renewable sources. The University has already approved an impressive construction plan that will lead to the realisation of 100,000 sqm, that even if constructed with up-to-date techniques (i.e., one of the new buildings will be nearly Zero Energy Building – nZEB), with an increase of 13% of the total energy consumption. This makes it necessary to act immediately with a set of measures able to tackle the energy consumption issue, both for environmental and economic reasons.

40 Aelita Skarzauskiene et al., 'Developing Citizen Science Ecosystem: Critical Factors for Quadruple Helix Stakeholders Engagement' (2023) *Journal of Enterprising Communities.*

41 Alma Mater Studiorum – University of Bologna, University Energy Plan. Available online at: https://www.unibo.it/en/university/who-we-are/university-energy-plan (accessed May 16, 2024).

First, the actions to be put in place refer to the adoption of a deeply innovative energy management system, compliant with the international standard created by the International Organisation for Standardisation (ISO) 50001 Energy management systems - Requirements with guidance for use. By the digitalisation of the entire UNIBO building asset and the heating and cooling plants, it will be possible to monitor continuously the energy consumption and quickly detect malfunctions and anomalies, thus allowing a prompt intervention and benchmarking of the plants' performance. The innovative energy management system includes a communication campaign towards the university community, including both students and staff, to promote awareness of the impact of an individual's behaviours, that are estimated to be responsible for 7% of the total energy consumption. The users will also be invited to actively contribute to monitoring the systems' efficiency through a QR code installed in each room of the university buildings that will allow users to point out malfunctions.

Second, a series of retrofitting interventions will be carried out, allowing the energy performance of 8 building complexes in Bologna to be improved.

Third, interventions on the heating and cooling plants are foreseen, with massive substitution of old and non-efficient heating boilers and the connection of more buildings to the district heating network. The replacement programmes include the need to remove all the oil boilers still present in some ancient buildings and the progressive replacement of gas boilers with heat pumps. A further intervention refers to the increase of the rate of self-produced solar energy, from the current 3% up to 9% of the total consumed energy in the Bologna campus.

Finally, an investment in relamping is foreseen, thus tackling the electric consumption that is estimated to be about the 33% of the total energy consumption. It consists of the replacement of the incandescent light bulbs and neon lamps with LED lighting and, where possible, the adoption of a smart lighting system allowing the remote control and supervision.

The mix of actions that has been defined will allow the university to reduce its CO_2 emissions to about 8300 tons/year.[42]

In addition to the interventions to the building asset, a set of initiatives recently adopted by UNIBO refers to the enhancement of sustainable mobility among students and staff. On the one hand, the University of Bologna has signed an agreement with the public transport provider to reduce the cost of the annual pass. Thanks to this, the number of annual passes has increased from around 9,000 in 2021 to 16,000 in 2022. On the other hand, UNIBO has promoted cycling mobility by providing university bicycles and agreements with the Municipality of Bologna for the development of the cycling network.

42 Total emissions for all the campuses, also beyond the city of Bologna.

1.5 Conclusions and next steps

Launched in 2021 by the European Commission to accelerate the way cities are moving towards climate neutrality, the Cities Mission has created a powerful community of ambitious cities, where they exchange best practices, link up and work together with other ambitious cities in their country and beyond to address shared challenges related to accelerating climate-neutral solutions. As Europe faces multiple and unprecedented geopolitical, environmental, post-pandemic and energy challenges, initiatives in cities able to bring together different stakeholders – policymakers, business, academia, citizens and non-profit organisations – for common goals and the common good are considered extremely needed.[43]

Urban transformations are of paramount importance for the long-term sustainability of societies, and cities in partnership with universities are key institutions that can play a role in envisioning and implementing the climate transition.[44] At local level, as this paper presented for the city of Bologna, the Cities Mission has reinforced existing collaborations – such as the long-lasting one between the Municipality of Bologna and the Alma Mater Studiorum – University of Bologna – and brought stakeholders together. It also enabled strategic collaborative approaches across departments and engaged citizens and the university community represented by the university students in the design and implementation of urban transitions through the establishment of the Citizen Assembly on Climate, bringing them closer to the aims and actions foreseen by the European Green Deal.

Beside supporting the application of the Municipality of Bologna to the Cities Mission, the University of Bologna has identified specific actions to be included in the Climate City Contract to contribute to accelerating the green transition, acting on building retrofitting, heating and lighting plants, self-production of renewable energy, and adoption of cleaner energy sources, with district heating included. Moreover, the University has launched a massive communication campaign to both increase users' awareness about their behaviour and engage users to monitor the systems' efficiency. Finally, more actions address sustainable mobility, both by promoting the use of public transport and by enhancing cycling mobility.

Nevertheless, looking at the near future where the CCC will be in force, and the forthcoming steps to implement it, a number of open issues need to be addressed to ensure the success of the initiative. Firstly, collaborating across

43 The Mission Board for Climate-Neutral and Smart Cities, Letter to the Executive Vice-President Vestager and Commissioner Gabriel, 21 May 2023. Available online at: https://research-and-innovation.ec.europa.eu/document/download/f5226bd5-c40e-4b41-b4a4-4c23afe3d55b_en?filename=Letter%20to%20EVP%20Vestager%20Commissioner%20Gabriel_Cities%20Mission%20Board_21%2003%202023.pdf (accessed August 3, 2023).

44 Lauren Withycombe Keeler et al., 'Building Actor-Centric Transformative Capacity through City-University Partnerships' (2019) 5 *Ambio* 48, 529–38.

Municipality departments and sectors might not be enough for achieving the Cities Mission goal. Breaking silos and reorganising the way city administrations work to properly reflect the cross-cutting nature of the climate action seems to be essential to foster local cross-sectoral solutions to accelerate the green transition. Secondly, how to leverage investments from regional and national funds, attracting and blending private investments is a common concern that the Cities Mission has shared through the Mission Board,[45] since facilitating the access of cities to EU and national funding is considered to be key to the success of the Cities Mission, alongside the mobilisation of private sector investment, but it is still unclear to what extent the Cities Mission will provide a financing framework that interlinks available funds at different territorial scales. Finally, at this stage, there is a lack of clarity about the resources to the NetZeroCities Mission Platform to properly support the climate-neutral transition in cities. Therefore, its effectiveness in supporting mutual learning and upscaling of proven solutions is currently difficult to evaluate..

In conclusion, although the Cities Mission approach embeds some limitations and provides a one-size-fits-all solution that does not appear to recognise that societal challenges can be different in type, nature, and size,[46] it is considered to be an initiative that might have an unprecedented impact on urban transformations towards climate-neutrality.

Bibliography

Alma Mater Studiorum – University of Bologna, *Performance Report 2022*. Available online at: https://www.unibo.it/it/ateneo/amministrazione-trasparente/performance/relazione-sulla-performance/relazione-sulla-performance (accessed August 3, 2023).

Alma Mater Studiorum – University of Bologna, *Strategic Plan 2022–2027*. Available online at: https://www.unibo.it/en/university/who-we-are/strategic-plan (accessed August 3, 2023).

Alma Mater Studiorum – University of Bologna, *Sustainability Report 2022*. Available online at: https://www.unibo.it/en/university/who-we-are/sustainability-report/ (accessed August 3, 2023).

Alma Mater Studiorum – University of Bologna, *University Energy Plan*. Available online at: https://www.unibo.it/en/university/who-we-are/university-energy-plan (accessed May 16, 2024).

Bansard J.S., Pattberg P.H. and Widerberg O. 'Cities to the Rescue? Assessing the Performance of Transnational Municipal Networks in Global Climate Governance'

45 The Mission Board for Climate-Neutral and Smart Cities, Letter to the Executive Vice-President Vestager and Commissioner Gabriel, 21 May 2023. Available online at: https://research-and-innovation.ec.europa.eu/document/download/f5226bd5-c40e-4b41-b4a4-4c23afe3d55b_en?filename=Letter%20to%20EVP%20Vestager%20Commissioner%20Gabriel_Cities%20Mission%20Board_21%2003%202023.pdf (accessed August 3, 2023).

46 Katherine Shabb et al. (n 16).

(2017) 17 *International Environmental Agreements: Politics, Law and Economics* 229.

Bertoldi P., Diluiso F., Castellazzi L., Labanca N. and Serrenho T. *Energy Consumption and Energy Efficiency Trends in the EU-28 2000–2015. European Commission* (JRC Science for Policy Report 2018).

Claes C. 'From Dispersed Multi-site to Cluster and Campus: Understanding the Material Infrastructure of University of Gothenburg as Urban Heritage', in Melhuish C., Benesch H., Martins Holmberg I. and Sully D. (eds), *Co-Curating the City: Universities and Urban Heritage Past and Future* (UCL Press 2022).

Caughman L., Beaudoin F. and Withycombe Keeler L. 'The Project - Partnership Cycle: Managing City - University Partnerships for Urban Sustainability and Resilience Transformations' (2023) 5, *Urban Transformations* 10.

European Commission, *The Future of Cities*. Available online at: https://urban.jrc.ec.europa.eu/thefutureofcities/climate-action#the-chapter (accessed August 3, 2023).

European Commission (2023). Missions in Horizon Europe. Available online at: https https://research-and-innovation.ec.europa.eu/funding/funding-opportunities/funding-programmes-and-open-calls/horizon-europe/eu-missions-horizon-europe_en (accessed August 3, 2023).

European Commission, A Union that strives for more. My agenda for Europe by candidate for President of the European Commission Ursula von der Leyen. Political Guidelines For The Next European Commission 2019–2024. Available online at: https://commission.europa.eu/system/files/2020-04/political-guidelines-next-commission_en_0.pdf (accessed August 3, 2023).

European Commission, *EU Mission: Climate-Neutral and Smart Cities* (2023). Available online at: https://research-and-innovation.ec.europa.eu/funding/funding-opportunities/funding-programmes-and-open-calls/horizon-europe/eu-missions-horizon-europe/climate-neutral-and-smart-cities_en (accessed August 3, 2023).

European Council, *Five Facts about the EU's Goal of Climate Neutrality*. Available online at: https://www.consilium.europa.eu/en/5-facts-eu-climate-neutrality/ (accessed August 3, 2023).

Heikkinen M., Karimo A., Klein J., Juhola S. and Ylä-Anttila T. 'Transnational Municipal Networks and Climate Change Adaptation: A Study of 377 Cities' (2020) 257 *Journal of Cleaner Production* 120474.

IPCC, *AR6 Climate Change 2022: Mitigation of Climate Change* (Cambridge University Press 2022).

Kennedy, C.A., Ibrahim N. and Hoornweg D. 'Low-Carbon Infrastructure Strategies for Cities' (2014) 4 *Nature Climate Change* 343.

Melhuish C., Benesch H., Holmberg I.M. and Sully, D. (eds) *Co-Curating the City: Universities and Urban Heritage Past and Future* (UCL Press 2022).

Pauer S.U., Pilon A. and Badelt B. 'Strengthening City–University Partnerships to Advance Sustainability Solutions: A Study of Research Collaborations between the University of British Columbia and City of Vancouver' (2020) 21 *International Journal of Sustainability in Higher Education* 1189.

Rosenzweig C., Solecki W., Hammer S.A. and Mehrotra S., 'Cities Lead the Way in Climate–Change Action' (2010) 467 *Nature* 909.

Salvia M., Pietrapertosa F., D'Alonzo V., Clerici Maestosi P., Simoes S.G. and Reckien D. 'Key Dimensions of Cities' Engagement in the Transition to Climate Neutrality' (2023) 344 *Journal of Environmental Management* 118519.

Sethi M., Lamb W., Minx J. and Creutzig F. 'Climate Change Mitigation in Cities: A Systematic Scoping of Case Studies' (2020) 15 *Environmental Research Letters* 093008.

Shabb K., McCormick K., Mujkic S., Anderberg S., Palm J. and Carlsson A. 'Launching the Mission for 100 Climate Neutral Cities in Europe: Characteristics, Critiques, and Challenges' (2022) 3 *Frontiers in Sustainable Cities* 817804.

Shabb, K. and McCormick K., 'Achieving 100 Climate Neutral Cities in Europe: Investigating Climate City Contracts in Sweden' (2023) 2 *NPJ Climate Action* 6.

Skarzauskiene A., Maciuliene M., Wildevuur S., van den Berg M., Bakratsas T., Psaltoglou A., Stylianidis E., Tavantzis I. and Karatzas K. 'Developing Citizen Science Ecosystem: Critical Factors for Quadruple Helix Stakeholders Engagement' (2023) *Journal of Enterprising Communities: People and Places in the Global EconomyVol. ahead-of-print No. ahead-of-print.*

Trencher G., Bai X., Evans J., McCormick K. and Yarime M., 'University Partnerships for Co-Designing and Co-Producing Urban Sustainability' (2014) 28 *Global Environmental Change* 153.

Ulpiani G., Vetters N., Melica G. and Bertoldi P. 'Towards the First Cohort of Climate-Neutral Cities: Expected Impact, Current Gaps, and Next Steps to Take to Establish Evidence-Based Zero-Emission Urban Futures' (2023) 95 *Sustainable Cities and Society* 104572.

United Nations, *Cities and Climate Change*. Available online at: https://www.unep.org/explore-topics/resource-efficiency/what-we-do/cities/cities-and-climate-change (accessed August 3, 2023).

Withycombe Keeler L., Beaudoin F., Cid A., Cowley R., Fahy S., Lerner A., Moran C. and Torney D. 'Building Transformative City-University Sustainability Partnerships: The Audacious Partnerships Process' (2023) 5 *Urban Transformations* 1.

Withycombe Keeler, L., Beaudoin F., Wiek A., John B., Lerner A.M., Beecroft R., Tamm K., et al. 'Building Actor-Centric Transformative Capacity through City-University Partnerships' (2019) 5 *Ambio* 48, 529.

2 Climate governance and climate planning

The case of Paris

Camille Mialot

2.1 Introduction

What are Paris climate governance and climate planning, and how are they developed and coordinated across the multiple levels of Paris governance?

Before answering this question in the following developments, two sets of methodological observations appear to be necessary. Lawyers must take IPCC reports seriously. In addition, an approach based on physical or terrestrial constraints explains more about the stakes involved in dealing with climate than the classic institutional-based approach.

In my opinion, when dealing with climate, legal research cannot be limited to describing the legal tools adopted and implemented. This descriptive approach, which is no doubt necessary, is not sufficient. I believe it is necessary to add a dimension of criticism. The work of the International Panel on Climate Change (IPCC), the very purpose of which is to provide policy makers with studies and means to take actions for the climate, constitutes reference data for evaluating the climate strategies and policies developed by local authorities. Cities are the subject of a specific chapter in the Assessment Reports (AR WGII and AR WGIII) which are published every eight years. Furthermore, a specific research group was set up and met in March 2018 to work on a special report focusing on cities and climate change science.[1]

Assessing the climate action of cities in the light of the IPCC's works also means admitting that the law is probably not a system that produces in itself its own truths. It is not a system that is not questioned by other sciences.[2] In my opinion, the analysis of the capacity of the legal tools deployed by cities for the climate must be usefully enriched by a critical approach, and even more so if

1 Intergovernmental Panel on Climate Change Cities and Climate Change Science Conference, 'Progress Report – International Conference on Climate Change and Cities' (2018) https://www.ipcc.ch/event/cities-and-climate-change-science-conference/.

2 Bruno Latour, 'Entretiens avec Bruno Laotur' (2021) https://www.arte.tv/fr/videos/106738-008-A/entretiens-avec-bruno-latour-.

DOI: 10.4324/9781032665184-12

we place the climate at the summit of the law.[3] Knowledge about the climate, how it changes, and how to adapt and mitigate greenhouse gases continues to grow, particularly through the IPCC. Lawyers cannot ignore the ongoing research on climate, as the latest AR6 general reports demonstrate a strong interaction between climate and biodiversity that was not apparent in previous reports. When approaching climate, lawyers cannot continue to treat climate and biodiversity separately as per usual legal categories. This is unlikely.

As the IPCC reminds us in its sixth report on mitigation:[4] on established cities, urban planning is not very effective in terms of mitigating GHG emissions because once a city is built, it is very difficult to change the orientation of buildings, the configuration of public spaces, to establish a green and blue grid and to change mobility. Urban functions are engraved for a long time in the stone and in the subsoil. Paris is essentially an established and very dense city, probably one of the densest capitals in Europe since the second half of the 19th century. The vast destruction-reconstruction of Paris led by Prefect Haussmann from 1850 onwards was carried out according to a very specific model driven by administrative police motives: hygiene, safety, traffic and aesthetics. The main characteristics of which are still evident today. Haussmann's reconstruction of modern Paris on medieval Paris through a vast operation of expropriation differentiates the French capital very significantly from other large European cities. For example, Barcelona was built in extension[5] following an urban plan over a period of 60 years from 1860. The urban development was obeying motives much broader than the administrative police, in application of comprehensive urban planning.[6] The high density of Paris resulting from the works of the 19th century is coupled with a strong historical heritage. These two characteristics, density and heritage, determine a very limited margin of maneuver in terms of urban climate planning, as the IPCC indicates.

On the contrary, according to the IPCC,[7] in established cities, energy renovation operations on a building scale can have a much greater impact on reducing greenhouse gas emissions and adapting to heat waves. However, this thermal renovation must not itself be blocked by the historical heritage of the

3 Jean-Bernard Auby, 'La lutte contre le changement climatique comme impératif juridique catégorique' (2021) https://www.chemins-publics.org/articles/la-lutte-contre-le-changement-climatique-comme-imperatif-juridique-categorique.

4 Intergovernmental Panel on Climate Change 'Climate Change 2022. Mitigation of Climate Change, Working Group III contribution to the Sixth Assessment Report of the Intergovernmental Panel on Climate Change' (2022); Chapter 8, fig. 8.20, 8.21, 8.87, and 8.8.

5 With the exception of Via Laietana, for example, which is a Haussmannian breakthrough in Roman and medieval Barcelona.

6 Marta Lora-Tamayo Vallvé, *Urbanismo de obra Pública y derecho a urbanizar. Análisis comparado desde las aportaciones de G. E. Haussmann y la doctrina de Ildefonso Cerdá* (Marcial Pons 2002).

7 Intergovernmental Panel on Climate Change (n 4).

buildings concerned. Here again, Paris is a city with a strong heritage and the renovation of buildings has structural and heritage limitations.[8]

Dealing with climate and urban planning, the IPCC reports provide a critical apparatus that, I think, is useful to develop a critical approach to the strategies from two angles: the conciliation of mitigation and adaptation, and the capacity of the different levels of governance to work together.

The need for coupling mitigation and adaptation in climate strategies is highlighted by the IPCC in its latest report:[9]

> There are numerous synergies that come from coupling urban adaptation and mitigation. A number of studies have developed methods to assess the synergies between mitigation and adaptation strategies, as well as their co-benefits (Solecki et al. 2015; Buonocore et al. 2016; Chang et al. 2017; Helgenberger and Jänicke 2017). Co-benefits occur when implementing mitigation (or adaptation) measures that have positive effects on adaptation (or mitigation) (Sharifi 2021). In contrast, the trade-offs emerge when measures aimed at improving mitigation (adaptation) undermine the ability to pursue adaptation (mitigation) targets (Sharifi 2020). The magnitude of such co-benefits and trade-offs may vary depending on various factors. To illustrate this approach, we could for example consider how the Seine, the river that runs through Paris, could be used more for logistics and passenger transport to reduce greenhouse gas emissions from road transport and make transport infrastructures located in flood-prone areas more resilient to flood risk.
>
> The ability of different levels of governance to "govern together" the climate is crucial; whether between different levels of public governance or non-state actors. The ability of different levels to collaborate in the development and implementation of climate policies leads to greater efficiency: "Further, regional, national, and international climate goals are most impactful when local governments are involved alongside higher levels, rendering urban areas key foci of climate governance more broadly (high confidence)" (Fuhr et al. 2018; Kern 2019; Hsu et al. 2020b). Since AR5, multilevel governance has grown in influence within the literature and has been defined as a framework to understanding the complex interaction of the many players involved in GHG generation and mitigation across geographic scales-the "vertical" levels of governance from neighbourhoods to the national and international levels, and those "horizontal" networks of non-state and subnational actors at various scales (…) A multilevel, multi-player framework highlights both the opportunities and constraints on local autonomy to engage in urban mitigation

8 Julien Bigorne and Stéphanie Jankel, 'Le Patrimoine Bâti Parisien – Premier repérage pour des réhabilitations thermiques' (2016) 105 *Atelier Parisien D'Urbanisme* 1.

9 Intergovernmental Panel on Climate Change (n 4) 8.2.3.

> efforts (Castán Broto 2017b; Fuhr et al. 2018; Vedeld et al. 44 2021). When multiple actors-national, regional, and urban policymakers, as well as non-state actors work together to exploit the opportunities, it leads to the most impactful mitigation gains (Melica et al. 2018). This framework also highlights the multiple paths and potential synergies available to actors who wish to pursue mitigation policies despite not having a full slate of enabling conditions (Castán Broto 2017b; Keller 2017; Fuhr et al. 2018; Hsu et al. 2020b, a; Seto et al. 2021).[10]

When considering the case of Paris in the face of climate change, there are several scales: Paris city center (2,165,000 inhabitants, 105 km^2), Paris metropolitan area (7 million inhabitants, 815 km^2) and the Paris region known as the "Île de France" (12 million inhabitants, surface area 12,000 km^2) (Institut Paris Région 2022).[11] Beyond the administrative districts, there are physical determinants: for example, when the hazard of overflowing of the Seine, the river which crosses Paris, is evoked: the relevant scale is the Seine Normandy basin, which is certainly not the administrative districts mentioned above. Presenting the few elements relating to the city of Paris in what it has of visible and invisible,[12] seems to us more relevant than a classic institutional approach in administrative law. For classically, administrative law is concerned with institutions and laws. In our opinion, the issue of the city in the face of climate change requires us to change our usual reflexes as lawyers. It is useful to understand that competences in the field of urban planning are shared between the various institutions, namely the municipality of Paris, which draws up the local urban plan, the metropolis of greater Paris, which draws up the strategic plan, and the Ile-de-France region, which draws up the master plan at a much larger scale. Furthermore, the competence for mobility is shared between the state (Réseau Autonomme de Transports de Paris), the region, the Société National des Chemins de Fer, the metropolis and the city. However, it is probably more important to understand the physical constraints: human, spatial, infrastructure and networks, and also the hazards to which the city is exposed. All of which determine the adoption of a climate plan or strategy and its real possibility of implementation in the territory concerned.[13]

Several climate studies on Paris provide an adequately precise description of the current and anticipated impacts of climate change on the city in the coming decades. Despite the availability of detailed climate studies, the public authorities do not utilize them in establishing sensible climate strategies for Paris. As I see it, climate actions across all dimensions of Paris are currently limited to

10 Intergovernmental Panel on Climate Change (n 4) 8.5.1.
11 Institut Paris Région, 'Chiffres-clés 20220' (2022) https://www.institutparisregion.fr/nos-travaux/publications/chiffres-cles-2022/.
12 Bruno Latour, Émile Hermant, *Ville invisible* (B42 2021).
13 Camille Mialot, 'Local Policies on Climate Change in a Centralized State: The French Example' (forthcoming) 1 *French Yearbook of Public Law (FYPL)*.

singular components. Taken together, these elements create an impression of a city in transition. What follows is based on a differentiation between climate plans or strategies, and the action means for addressing climate issues, which could take the form of plans such as urban planning or risk management but are not exclusively focused on climate issues.[14] I would like to additionally emphasize that the means for taking action are progressively becoming related to climate, as seen in the "bioclimatic" urban planning approach in Paris. In this regard, the distinction between climate strategies and broader "urban" actions and planning is becoming less clear.

2.2 Comprehensive climate studies have not yet facilitated sufficient climate plans

The abundance of studies and data makes it possible to sketch a fairly accurate climatic portrait of the city of Paris (8.2.1). However, this mass of knowledge on Paris and the climate does not lead to the development of coherent climate strategies (8.2.2). To sum up, on the scale of Paris as well as on the global scale: we already know a lot about climate and its impact, but we do not yet really know how to handle it, we are at the beginning of attempts to "govern" climate change in Paris.

2.2.1 Sketching a climatic portrait of Paris

2.2.1.1 Context

The Parisian urban planning workshop (APUR)[15] has been producing numerous thematic and general studies on Paris and the climate for the past twenty years, as has the Paris Region Institute at the regional level.[16] The municipality of Paris produces in-depth climate studies. For instance, the study "Paris face au changement climatique" updated in 2021, analyzes the robustness and vulnerabilities of the city of Paris in seven thematic sections,[17] or the recent "Paris at 50°C" report[18] sets out policy options and proposes actions to be taken in the event of a heat dome in Paris.

14 Camille Mialot, *La ville face au changement climatique, nouveaux instruments juridiques* (Berger Levrault 2020).

15 https://www.apur.org, created by the City of Paris in 1967.

16 Institut Paris Région, 'Vunérabilité de la Région au changement climatique' (2022) https://www.institutparisregion.fr.

17 Ville de Paris, 'Étude Paris face au changement climatique 2021, étude de robustesse et de vulnérabilité de la Ville de Paris' (2022) https://www.paris.fr/pages/paris-s-adapte-au-changement-climatique-18541#:~:text=Ainsi%2C%20la%20majorit%C3%A9%20des%20risques,tendent%20%C3%A0%20survenir%20d%C3%A8s%202030.&text=Les%20d%C3%A9fis%20climatiques%20auxquels%20devra,des%20risques%20li%C3%A9s%20aux%20inondations.

18 Ville de Paris, 'Paris à 50°C. Rapport de la Mission d'Information et d'Évaluation du Conseil de Paris' (2023) https://www.paris50degres.fr/.

The city of Paris practices open data, and this abundant database contains numerous data that can be used for climate purposes, particularly on mobility, nature in the city, the state of buildings, energy consumption, etc.[19] The smart city, before being a governance, is first and foremost a vast source of data.[20]

The participation of the city of Paris in international networks of cities for the climate, such as the C40 cities, contributes to a comparative approach to studies. This comparative approach is all the more relevant as climate change affects all cities in the world, even if they are impacted in very different ways. The city of Paris, a member of the international 100 Resilient Cities network, justifies its own proposals for action in its resilience strategy by explicitly referring to the experiences of foreign cities.[21]

The following is some general and non-exhaustive information from the above-mentioned studies.

2.2.1.2 Human vulnerability

Concerning the human vulnerability of the Parisian territory,[22] Paris, as a central city, is the densest in Europe with 202 inhabitants/hectare compared to 150 for Barcelona, only 100 for Berlin and 85 for London. Paris is also the densest city in Europe on a metropolitan scale and is second only to Barcelona on a regional scale. This very high population density determines a higher vulnerability, i.e. a large population exposed to climatic hazards in a small area.

2.2.1.3 Green and blue infrastructure

On the scale of Paris, nature represents only about 20% of the Parisian territory, including the Bois de Vincennes to the east and the Bois Boulogne to the west; the city of Paris is therefore a particularly artificial city.[23] Concerning the potential for planting trees in the open air, there is no mapping to determine the subsurface consistency and even less planning of the Parisian subsoil and particularly its networks, unlike, for example, Helsinki, which has had an underground master plan since 2021.[24] Subsurface data are indeed crucial in a strategy of renaturation of public spaces because they determine the open spaces likely to accommodate trees, as we shall see below.

19 https://opendata.paris.fr.
20 Jean-Bernard Auby and Vicenzo De Gregorio, *Données urbaines et smart city* (Berger Levrault 2017).
21 Ville de Paris, 'Stratégie de résilience de Paris 2017' (2022) https://www.paris.fr/pages/paris-resiliente-4264.
22 APUR, 'Déplacements dans les villes européennes' (2004) https://50ans.apur.org/data/b4s3_home/fiche/91/04_deplac_villes_europeennes_2004_broapu244_41289.pdf.
23 APUR, 'Evolution de la Nature à Paris de 1730 à nos jours' (2018) https://www.apur.org/fr/nos-travaux/evolution-nature-paris-1730-nos-jours.
24 https://hri.fi/en_gb/.

The blue network of Paris is determined by the Seine and the existing open canals. The project to take the Bièvre, a river that flowed into the Seine in the 19th century, out of the south of Paris at the level of Notre Dame Cathedral, is underway in order to restore the Parisian blue network.[25] The drinking water network is very varied in its supply, but it is very vulnerable to flooding because of the location of the treatment plants on the banks of the Seine in flood-prone areas. The drinking water network is also very vulnerable to the drought hazard and very vulnerable to the heat wave hazard.[26]

2.2.1.4 Housing

Limiting ourselves to housing alone (without mentioning other land uses), it should be noted that on the scale of the city of Paris 75% of housing was built before 1914.[27] This has a double climatic effect: on the one hand, greenhouse gas emissions linked to heating and cooling are significant (15% of the territory's greenhouse gas emissions are caused by housing[28] this figure is almost identical to the level of the Paris metropolitan area as indicated in the Climate Air Energy Plan of the greater paris Metropolis).[29] On the other hand, the historical heritage protections of Paris are a definite brake on the energy renovation of buildings, notably through insulation from the outside or the installation of air circulation systems.[30] Housing is particularly vulnerable to heat waves and floods.[31]

2.2.1.5 Mobilities

Public mobility infrastructures and services are particularly developed in Paris. They have developed significantly since the end of the 19th century with the development of the metro, before individual motorized mobility. In this respect, Paris is in a similar situation to London.[32] Mobility has been changing rapidly since the beginning of the 21st century at the scale of the metropolitan

25 Agence Eau Seine Normandie, 'Signature du contrat Bièvre Eau Climat Trame Verte et Bleue 2020–2024' (2020) https://www.eau-seine-normandie.fr/node/3605.
26 Ville de Paris (n 17).
27 APUR, 'Consommation d'énergie et émissions de gaz à effet de serre des logements à usage de résidence principale' (2007) https://www.apur.org/fr/nos-travaux/consommations-energie-emissions-gaz-effet-serre-liees-chauffage-residences-principales-parisiennes.
28 APUR, 'Patrimoine Bâti parisien premiers repérages pour des réhabilitations thermiques' (2016) https://www.apur.org/fr/nos-travaux/patrimoine-bati-parisien-premier-reperage-rehabilitations-thermiques.
29 Métropole du Grand Paris, 'Plan Climat Air Energie Territorial de la Métropole du Grand Paris' (2018) https://www.metropolegrandparis.fr/fr/plan-climat-air-energie-metropolitain-76; p. 85.
30 APUR (2016).
31 Ville de Paris (n 17) 66.
32 APUR (n 22).

area with the development of intermodality and the new public transport lines of the Grand Paris Express which aim to the transport lines that converge on Paris by doubling the current concentric system with a radial system linking the centers located outside the city of Paris.[33]

The average number of trips per inhabitant (all modes combined) is twice as high in Paris compared to other major European cities and up to four times higher than in London.[34] At the beginning of the 21st century, the Paris metropolitan area is still very much marked by spatial specialization: business districts are far from residential areas, which in turn are far from cultural, leisure or shopping areas, which explains this high level of mobility. The development of the "Grand Paris Express" public transport network mentioned above has not been accompanied by a global redefinition of the way of living in Paris and its region, despite the ambitious studies carried out in the 2010s by the Atelier internationale du Grand Paris[35]. Like the Paris of the 19th century, the greater Paris of the 21st century is primarily conceived in terms of traffic and not in terms of ways of living.

At the scale of the metropolitan area, the carbon footprint of road transport[36] and air transport combined represents more than 40% of the total carbon footprint of the metropolitan area.[37]

Public transport systems are highly exposed to the risk of flooding, with almost 100% paralysis in the event of a 100-year flood of the Seine.[38]

2.2.1.6 Energy infrastructure

From an energy point of view, the city's energy mix is only composed of 18.4% renewable and recovered energy in 2019, a level roughly equivalent to the overall French level. The city is 93% dependent on energy imported from outside its territory.[39] Projections for 2050 call for a 50% reduction in energy consumption compared to 2012 and a 100% renewable supply, of which 20% is locally produced. Electricity infrastructures and networks, which are in a current state of the vulnerability, according with a study carried out by the city of Paris in 2021 highly exposed to flood and heat wave hazards.[40]

33 APUR 'Évolution des mobilités dans le grand Paris tendances historiques Évolutions en cours et émergentes' (2021) https://www.apur.org/fr/nos-travaux/evolution-mobilites-grand-paris-tendances-historiques-evolutions-cours-emergentes.
34 APUR (n 22) 30.
35 Atelier International du Grand Paris, *Habiter le Grand Paris* (Archibooks / Bookstorming 2013); and see, in this sense, the work of the Atelier International du Grand Paris (AIGP) carried out between 2010 and 2017, when it was dissolved.
36 APUR (n 33).
37 Métropole du Grand Paris (n 29) 85.
38 Ville de Paris (n 17) 101.
39 Ibid. 11–12.
40 Ibid. 10.

2.2.1.7 Climatic risks: The risk of flooding and heat waves

The main climatic hazard to which the city of Paris and its metropolitan area is exposed is the risk of flooding, the probability of occurrence of which increases by 40% by 2050.[41]

It would undoubtedly be necessary to mention the heat wave and urban heat island hazards, which are very significant on the scale of the metropolitan area (APUR EPICEA study 2012 and five Urban Heat Island APUR 2020 booklets)[42] or forest fires, which were an issue particularly in France in the summer of 2022 Paris is surrounded by forests within a radius of less than 50km: Fontainebleau, Rambouillet, Meudon, Chantilly, etc., which have not experienced mega fires but which are exposed to this hazard, while Paris suffered air pollution from fires in the south-west of France in the summer of 2022).

The public report of the Cour des Comptes of November 2022,[43] entitled "La prévention insuffisante du Risque Inondation en Ile-de-France" underlines that the state planning of flood risk since the beginning of the 2000s has not succeeded in containing the increasing number of people exposed to the hazard, and the transfer to local authorities of competences in the field of flood development and prevention has not been sufficiently implemented. The Cour des Comptes points out in particular an under-use of financial allocations intended for the restoration and creation of structures, dykes, etc., allowing for the mitigation of the effects of a 100-year flood by overflow or flooding by rising water tables and runoff.

2.2.2 Paris climate planning

Ironically, the studies mentioned above do not significantly contribute to Paris' climate strategies. Although they are present and cited in strategic documents as part of the diagnostics, no significant actions have been taken based on their findings.

2.2.2.1 Lack of coordination of climate strategies between the different levels

Contrary to what the IPCC indicates as a necessity, "governing the climate together", the different layers of legislation creating local climate plans have not achieved strong coordination between the different levels, and the different

41 Ibid. 6.

42 APUR 'Ilôts de chaleur urbain – Project EPICEA' (2012) https://www.apur.org/fr/recherche?keyword=ilots+of+heat&sort_bef_combine=score+DESC.

43 Cour des Comptes, 'La prévention insuffisante du Risque Inondation en Ile-de-France' (2022) https://www.ccomptes.fr/fr/publications/la-prevention-insuffisante-du-risque-dinondation-en-ile-de-france.

levels of territorial administration have not created real coordination between the different territorial climate strategies.

This lack of coordination between the different levels of administration is explained in part by the fact that many local authorities have been engaged in a scattered approach since the end of the 1990s, integrating the objectives of sustainable development, the local Agenda 21s, which were initiated by the Aalborg Charter in 1994. This voluntary approach was carried out in a scattered manner, without a binding legal framework. It is similar to the current efforts to integrate the 2030 sustainable development goals initiated by the UN into local policies. These purely local initiatives did not fall within any legal framework, but they benefited from the support of state agencies such as ADEME (the French Environment and Energy Management Agency). These local initiatives have led to the recognition of a legal status for climate plans, but have not yet led to their general coordination, except in the cases described below.

Law 2010-788 of 12 July 2010 on National Commitment to Environment created regional (Regional Climate Air Energy Scheme – SRCAE) and local (territorial climate energy plans) climate plans without any state strategies being defined in a coordinated manner with the territorial level. The National Climate Change Adaptation Plan (PNACC) adopted in 2011 is the first and only national climate strategy resulting from the 2010 law on National Commitment to Environment, but it is presented as a simple guide plan with merely informative content and no normative force for local and regional authorities.

At the time of the adoption of the Paris Agreement, the 2015 Law on Ecological Transition and Green Growth[44] defined two new state climate plans: the National Low Carbon Strategy (SNBC) and the Multiannual Energy Programme (PPE). The SNBC is presented as a fairly general catalog of objectives and decreasing carbon budgets by emission sector (transport, building, agriculture, waste, etc.). The PPE, whose main content and objectives are set by law every five years[45] sets a trajectory for energy transition towards renewable energies. Incidentally, it should be noted that the various state plans have been judged insufficient by the administrative judge to achieve the objectives of reducing greenhouse gas emissions in 2030. In the case initiated by the city of Grande Synthe against the central state, the Council of State ruled in its decision of 1 July 2021 that the state, in the current state of its efforts to combat climate change, was not in a position to achieve the European targets for 2030.[46] Part of the recent campaign for the 2022 presidential election has

44 Loi n° 2015-992 of 17 August 2015 on the energy transition for green growth.
45 Since the Loi n° 2019-1147 du 8 novembre 2019 related to energy and climate issues is a law defining the objectives and priorities of the energy policy, it must be adopted every five years.
46 Conseil d'État, 1 July 2021 Ville de Grande Synthe req n°427301 abstract: "the need to step up efforts to achieve the objectives set for 2030 and the impossibility, with the measures

been the creation of a real ecological planning at the state level, which will consist of unifying the different state plans and probably giving them more legal force. In order to draw up this new national strategy, a general secretary for ecological planning was created, attached to the Prime Minister's office in order to facilitate the coordination and transversality of the central government's climate strategy.

The 2015 Law on Ecological Transition and Green Growth attempted to bring order to local climate planning by making territorial climate plans compulsory for all intermunicipalities with more than 20,000 inhabitants with their own tax status. Regional climate planning was strengthened in the same year with the creation of the Schémas Régionaux de Développement Durable et d'Égalité des Territoires (SRADDET) created by the Law of 7 August 2015 on the new territorial organization of the Republic. Those regional climate plans constitute the integration of numerous previously separate regional climate plans: regional plan for sustainable development, the aforementioned regional air-climate-energy plan, regional intermodality plan, regional transport infrastructure plan, regional ecological coherence plan and the regional waste prevention and management plan etc. However, the Paris region has kept a system in which climate planning, biodiversity planning, energy planning, waste planning and town and country planning remain separate. The above-mentioned law has excluded the Paris region from the new system of integration of the different plans at the regional level.

The three laws mentioned above did not establish legally binding links between the different climate plans, nor did they establish an obligation to update them when higher-ranking climate strategies are adopted. Nor has the law defined common evaluation criteria for comparing the expected results of strategies and actions. The legal links between the different levels of planning have been reduced to a simple relationship of "compatibility" or, even more weakly, of "taking into account", which is far from a full compliance legal relationship.

To address the insufficient coordination between different levels of governance, the Climate and Resilience Act (hereafter, "the Act") passed on August 22, 2021, introduced mandatory territorial targets in two domains: 1) The first area concerns the development of renewable energy sources, which must comply with the objectives of the national multiannual energy programme (PPE) established by decree and be implemented at the regional and local

adopted to date, of achieving them is not seriously contested by the Minister for Ecological Transition, who, in the briefs produced in the context of the supplemental investigation ordered on 19 November, highlights the various measures provided for in the bill [law of Aaugust 22 2021] to combat climate change and strengthen resilience to its effects, tabled last February and currently under discussion in Parliament, as well as in the regulatory measures that should be taken, in due course, for its application, in order to maintain that they will make it possible, in total, with the measures already in force, to achieve a reduction in emissions of the order of 38% in 2030."

levels; and 2) The second area targets the cessation of land-use conversion processes. It should be noted, however, that the legislative body opted to incorporate the second target into urban plans rather than climate plans. This decision was taken to avoid relying on strategic climate planning tools that were deemed too limited in their normative scope.

2.2.2.2 Strategic climate planning in Paris

The three main levels of administration, the region, metropolis of greater Paris, and the municipality have adopted separate climate plans.

Strategic climate planning in the Paris region: At the level of the Paris region, there is a large number of strategic climate plans, as they have not been unified by the 2015 Law on Ecological Transition and Green Growth.[47] They were adopted in different time frames. Following the aforementioned Law of 12 July 2010 on National Commitment to Environment, the Paris region adopted its regional climate air energy plan (SRCAE) at the end of 2012.[48] It should be noted that the regional climate plan was adopted by the region and by the state representative, which could lead to a certain coordination between the region and the state, but in 2012 there was no national climate strategy. The 2012 regional plan set fairly ambitious targets for the development of renewable energies, reduction of pollutants in the air, energy renovation of buildings, reduction of greenhouse gas emissions by 20%, etc., for the year 2020. However, I have not found any official evaluation of the Ile-de-France SRCAE, despite the existence of indicators in the plan that would underpin an evaluation after its adoption. An independent study from 2020 concerning only the energy component[49] notes an insufficient territorialisation of the renewable energy development objectives, which more generally reflects the inability to translate a climate policy territorially. However, it should be noted that the region had a regional wind energy development plan, but this plan, adopted by the state representative, was canceled on 14 November 2014, due to the lack of an environmental impact assessment as required by European Directive 2001/42.[50]

Noting the failure of its 2012 climate plan, the region, outside the legal framework determined by the aforementioned 2010 Law on National Commitment to Environment, adopted a new climate and energy strategy in June 2018,[51] which does not include the air issue, as this matter is dealt with

47 Loi n° 2015-992 of 17 August 2015 on the energy transition for green growth.

48 www.srcae-idf.fr/.

49 Régis Briday, 'Le SRCAE d'Île-de-France. L'épineuse territorialisation des objectifs nationaux de transition énergétique' (2020) *20-18 Document de travail du LATTS – Working Paper* 1, 45 https://enpc.hal.science/hal-02922745/document.

50 http://paris.tribunal-administratif.fr/Actualites-du-Tribunal/Selection-de-decisions-Acces-aux-jugements/Schema-regional-eolien-d-Ile-de-France.

51 https://www.iledefrance.fr/strategie-energie-climat-de-la-region-ile-de-france.

in another plan adopted by the state representative in the region.[52] This 2018 climate strategy was therefore produced without the state, which is normally the co-author of the regional climate and energy plan (SRCAE). The 2018 strategy has no legal value and is presented as a partnership to be established with the local authorities of Ile-de-France, but in the absence of monitoring of its implementation, it is very difficult to count the authorities that have signed up to the strategy. In September 2022, and again outside any legislative framework, the region adopted a regional climate change adaptation plan[53] which is presented as a list of actions in response, no doubt, to the severe heat wave experienced in the summer of 2022. This adaptation plan mentions the creation of climate shelters, fountains and tree planting. A budget of 1 billion euros is allocated, although no precise details are given, and the deadline for implementation is set for 2030. The 2022 adaptation plan does not mention the flood risks presented in the above developments, which are nevertheless an essential element of adaptation at the regional and Seine-Normandy basin level.

The regional planning concerning the green and blue infrastructure is, for the Paris region, the Schéma Régional de cohérence écologique (SRCE), adopted in 2013. Unlike other climate plans, the regional scheme is linked to the national level through the adoption of a national green and blue infrastructure, by decree,[54] in application of the aforementioned 2010 law on National Commitment to Environment. In the other metropolitan regions (except Corsica), it is incorporated into the regional plan for sustainable development and territorial equality. It should be noted that the Île de France SRCE is very weakly prescriptive and that its recent assessment carried out in June 2022 for the period 2013–2019 shows a decline in biodiversity mainly due to the land artificialisation.[55] The lack of normative power of the SRCE over urban planning is one of the explanations for the failure of the Ile-de-France SRCE.

Strategic climate planning at the level of the metropolitan area: The Greater Paris Climate Air and Energy Plan (PCAEM) was adopted on 12 November 2018.[56] It is the only strategic climate planning document on a metropolitan scale, which differentiates it from the multiple climate strategies on a regional or municipal scale (see below). The plan is divided into three parts: diagnosis, strategy and action plan, according to the typology imposed by the aforementioned 2015 law. The main part of the plan, which is very voluminous, is made up of a territorial diagnosis that takes up half of the document and an environmental assessment that takes up 1/5 of this document of over 500 pages. The

52 https://www.drieat.ile-de-france.developpement-durable.gouv.fr/IMG/pdf/2018-_arrete_ppa3_vsigne.pdf.
53 https://www.iledefrance.fr/environnement-lancement-du-plan-regional-dadaptation-au-changement-climatique.
54 https://www.legifrance.gouv.fr/jorf/id/JORFTEXT000039645239.
55 https://www.iledefrance.fr/le-schema-regional-de-coherence-ecologique.
56 Métropole du Grand Paris (n 29).

strategy provides for the reduction of greenhouse gas emissions, but it is presented simply as a descending curve[57] like the above-mentioned state SNBC. The natural carbon sink functions of forests are mentioned, but no specific strategy and actions are described to increase the capacity of natural carbon sinks. The issue of adaptation on a metropolitan scale is only addressed in a fragmentary and secondary manner. Actions to reduce greenhouse gas emissions are described in terms of cross-cutting and sectoral actions. Under the heading of cross-cutting actions,[58] the plan only presents elements of awareness-raising, the setting up of platforms or the inclusion of objectives in other documents, including the future metropolitan climate territorial coherence plan, which I will discuss below. The sectoral actions are limited, for example, to the inclusion of objectives in the local housing program, the creation of an observatory or a fund, but the amount is not quantified.

Similar to the regional level, the metropolitan climate plan appears to defer the description of precise metropolitan choices to other documents. One of such documents is the metropolitan territorial coherence plan that is currently being approved.

Strategic climate planning at the level of the city of Paris: The Paris Climate and Energy Plan adopted in 2018[59] is similar to the regional and metropolitan strategies. Shorter, about 100 pages, it presents an assessment of the territory's carbon footprint and greenhouse gas emission reduction trajectories similar to the previously mentioned strategies, with very ambitious projections such as moving from 17% renewable energy sources in 2018 to 25% in 2020. However, unlike the regional and metropolitan levels of Paris, many more concrete actions are included, such as mobility with the use of bicycles, energy renovation of buildings with existing measures initiated by the Paris City Council, such as free diagnosis of energy renovation of buildings, conversion of the ring road surrounding the city into a zone no longer exclusively dedicated to the use of cars, etc. In 2022, some of these actions were effectively implemented, as we will see in (8.3). However, the multiplicity of actions hides a lack of a clearly defined strategy and very unclear funding. The multiplicity of state actors involved in the territory of the city of Paris, which is also the capital of France, in the fields of transport, major cultural public services, etc. are not really associated with this plan. Finally, this document does not present any evaluation and monitoring indicators, which is a major shortcoming in terms of monitoring its implementation and ensuring that the public is properly informed.

Moreover, the city of Paris has developed a large number of climate-related plans: bicycle plan, resilience strategy, rain plan, zero waste strategy, food

57 Ibid. 273–274.
58 Ibid. 307–308.
59 https://www.apc-paris.com/Plan-climat

waste strategy, climate change adaptation strategy, etc., which are non-normative documents that are essentially informative.[60]

Like the region and the metropolis, the city of Paris is moving towards transposing its climate strategy into its urban planning document: the bioclimatic urban plan, which we will discuss in (8.3).

According to the two criteria extracted from the latest IPCC report, there is no real multi-level climate governance in Paris. The climate plans adopted have different timeframes and, especially when these plans describe actions, there is no real designated person in charge of these actions, no timeframes, no funding and no evaluation and monitoring methods. Evaluation and monitoring methods are indeed crucial: they really determine coordination. To ensure real multi-level coordination of climate plans, these monitoring and evaluation indicators should be unified and common to the different levels. However, this is not the case. In our opinion, this is an important task that must be carried out. In addition, there is a total lack of approach to reconciling adaptation and mitigation in each of the plans studied: adaptation and mitigation issues are addressed in different plans without any legal or temporal coordination. Generally speaking, the issue of adaptation to climate change is largely ignored in Parisian public climate policies.[61]

The strategies we have mentioned were likely affected by mistakes made during their early stages of development. They belong to a tradition of strategic climate planning that has been in place for a decade, implemented in accordance with the 2010 National Commitment to the Environment law. There are various possible explanations for the shortcomings of these strategies, including the fact that they were often hastily drafted with limited hindsight, as well as the challenge of formulating global and national issues at the local level. Addressing local issues requires a shift away from the accounting logic that prevails at the international and national levels, towards a logic of coordinated and evaluated territorial actions. Despite the wealth of information produced by studies over the last twenty years, the strategies exhibit significant shortcomings in terms of precision, coordination, and joint evaluation.

2.3 From climate strategies to climate actions

To tackle this multidimensional problem, I will adopt the methodology introduced by Jean-Bernard Auby,[62] which focuses on the city and its various dimensions. According to Auby, the city has four dimensions: urban public spaces, urban infrastructure, public services, and governance. In addition to these four

60 These plans and strategies are mentioned in the Paris Resilience Strategy 2017, https://www.paris.fr/pages/paris-resiliente-4264, 36.

61 Franck Lirzin, *Paris face au changement climatique* (L'aube 2022).

62 Jean-Bernard Auby, 'La Ville nouvelle frontière du droit administratif' (2017) 853 *AJDA*; Jean-Bernard Auby, 'L'espace public comme notion émergente du droit administratif' (2021) 2565 *AJDA*.

dimensions, I propose the existence of a fifth dimension,[63] which is intangible or indistinct. This dimension might be framed as the question, "How do people live and inhabit the city of Paris?" Although the phrasing might be imperfect. This dimension links with the other four dimensions mentioned above. The "living in Paris" dimension encompasses themes like gender and the city, tourism, tangible cultural heritage, and primarily accounts for intangible cultural facilities such as Paris's two opera houses, its theaters or concert halls, the Louvre Museum, Notre-Dame, the National Library of France, among others. The fifth dimension also encompasses the social question, which extends beyond social housing to include access to the city's amenities. This can be classified as the "Right to the City". This fifth dimension will be discussed in the conclusion.

The four dimensions of the city mentioned above have undoubtedly been modified by the general laws that have been passed in the last ten years. In this sense, Paris is not legally in a fundamentally different situation from other French cities, but in some cases the city of Paris has been a precursor of measures that have subsequently been included in the law.

2.3.1 Land use and climate governance

2.3.1.1 Urban climate planning and tourism regulation

Acknowledging that their climate strategies are not very operational or that there is a gap between these strategies and their actual implementation, the region, the metropolis and the city have simultaneously or concurrently embarked on a process of adopting urban climate plans.

The aforementioned Climate Resilience Law also requires that urban planning at regional, inter-municipal and local levels should stop artificialising land (article 194). This Copernican change in urban planning, previously conceived as a tool for building and extending the city, requires that urban plans be rethought and recast from a climate perspective. On the scale of the city of Paris, this new principle of net zero artificialisation has little impact because the city is already artificialised, but on the scale of the metropolis or the region, this principle will impose a significant modification of urban strategies.

In November 2021, the Paris region initiated the adoption of its new Île-de-France Environmental Master Plan (SDRIF-E). According to the public consultation notice prior to the drafting of the document "The new master plan, the SDRIF-Environmental, established for the year 2040, will have to follow paths towards 'zero net artificialisation' (ZAN), 'zero net emissions'' (ZEN) and 'zero waste'".[64]

63 Latour, Hermant (n 12).
64 https://www.iledefrance.fr/la-concertation-prealable-lelaboration-du-sdrif-e-est-lancee.

At the same time, the greater Paris metropolis has initiated its strategic plan (SCOT), which is at the formulation stage, with a first draft adopted in January 2022.[65] Among the major orientations, the plan aims to achieve greater functional diversity in order to attain the "quarter-hour city", to transform public spaces dedicated to cars, to commit the metropolis to the circular economy and the energy transition, and, in terms of adaptation, to fight urban heat islands, to develop nature in the city, and to integrate flood risk. It should be noted, however, that this plan did not wish to apply the legislative order of 17 June 2020[66] relating to the modernization of territorial coherence plans. This ordinance makes it possible to merge climate plans and territorial coherence schemes and thus to combine urban planning in the broad sense with climate planning.

The city of Paris has initiated the adoption of its "bioclimatic" Local Urban Plan (PLU) in December 2020, according to the deliberation of launching

> The bioclimatic character of the future Local Urban Plan will be one of the major levers of (the) municipal action and refers to a mode of architectural design that relies on the site and the environment of the project to obtain optimal conditions of quality of life and comfort, in respect of the environment, biodiversity and the biosphere. In the face of the climate and health emergency, this is a profound paradigm shift.[67]

After two years of consultation and development, some elements are available in the form of a project.[68] The project proposes six development and programming guidelines (OAP) relating to the climate. The OAPs are imposed on the building licences in a relationship of compatibility, i.e. not full compliance. These guidelines include a biodiversity adaptation guideline, a quarter-hour city guideline, proximity to services, transformation and rehabilitation of Parisian buildings, etc. Among the rules envisaged, which are imposed in a full compliance report, applicable to new constructions and heavy building rehabilitation, a supply of renewable energy, a high level of thermal performance, and high waste management level will be imposed.

Although the bioclimatic PLU has its limitations, it is the first of its kind in France. While many PLUs in France consider the climate, Paris was the first to make it the centerpiece of its urban planning.

Nevertheless, it is worth remembering that the IPCC emphasizes that urban planning is a very weak climate lever for established cities,[69] and even

65 Métropole du Grand Paris, 'Schéma Métropolitain de Cohérence Territoriale (ScoT)' (2018) https://www.metropolegrandparis.fr/fr/schema-de-coherence-territoriale-scot-metropolitain-un-vote-historique-pour-la-metropole-du-grand.

66 Ordinance No. 2020-744 of 17 June 2020 on the modernization of territorial coherence schemes.

67 https://cdn.paris.fr/paris/2021/04/09/eb3d51cee7a49dc55167bdd082d39932.pdf.

68 https://plubioclimatique.paris.fr/projet/.

69 Intergovernmental Panel on Climate Change (n 4) Chapter 8 fig 8.20, 8.21, 8.87, 8.8.

more so for cities like Paris which are both established and heritage cities, and therefore doubly constrained.

In addition, by a municipal regulation of 15 December 2021,[70] the city of Paris has made the conversion of commercial buildings into furnished tourist accommodation subject to authorisation in order to kerb the massive development of furnished tourist accommodation in Paris, which is the world's leading destination for Airbnb.[71] This legislation obviously will have an effect on the reduction of mass tourism and greenhouse gas emissions from transport, particularly air transport. It will also have an effect on the way the city is inhabited, which we will discuss in conclusion.

2.3.1.2 Climate governance

To be exhaustive, we should deal in this section with all the elements relating to climate governance, such as the carbon footprint of the municipality of Paris as an administrative institution and the low-carbon strategy of the Parisian administration.[72] Indeed, the aforementioned 2010 law on National Commitment to Environment required local authorities with more than 50,000 inhabitants to draw up their carbon footprint, and Law n°2019–1147 of 8 November 2019 on energy and the climate required them to adopt a strategy to reduce their carbon emissions. In addition, the 2021 Climate Law imposed the life cycle and environmental criteria in public procurement from 2026, and the implementing decree has already been issued to prepare public authorities and companies for a major change in public procurement.[73]

Climate agencies: Since 2011, the city of Paris has had a climate agency: the Paris Climate Agency[74] organised in the form of a private law association whose members include public, semi-public, and private actors. The agency has three distinct missions: a mission to assist the city of Paris in the development of its climate air energy plan studied above, a mission to provide information to residents and studies and partnerships with other actors in climate change, and a mission to support and assist in the energy renovation of buildings according to a personalised assistance system for the energy renovation of condominiums.

This agency, which was created outside of any legal framework, was given a legal existence by the 2021 Climate Resilience Act, which gave legal status to

70 Règlement municipal fixant les conditions de délivrance des autorisations visant la location de locaux à usage commercial en meublés de tourisme en application de l'article L. 324-1-1 du code du tourisme, adopté le 15/12/2021 par le Conseil de Paris et publié au Bulletin Officiel de la Ville de Paris le 18/01/2022 (délibération 2021 DLH 460).

71 Clément Guillou, 'Paris et la France, bastions d'Airbnb face à la diminution du tourisme' *Le Monde 26-06-2021.*

72 https://www.paris.fr/pages/le-bilan-carbone-de-paris-2018-7479.

73 Décret n° 2022-767 du 2 mai 2022 portant diverses modifications du code de la commande publique.

74 https://www.apc-paris.com/.

energy and climate agencies responsible for assisting local authorities in drawing up their climate and energy plans and for monitoring and providing information on energy consumption.[75] The Climate Resilience Act also created a public service for the energy performance of housing responsible for informing and supporting homeowners in the energy renovation of their homes.

At the level of the Paris region, the regional energy and climate agency[76] is a branch of the Paris Region Institute with the mission of assisting in the elaboration of the region's climate plans and informing the public.

It should be noted that the choice of the municipality and the region of Paris to create a climate agency, an external body, has not yet been accompanied by an internal administrative reform. The environment and climate issues are therefore still dealt with internally by specific administrative departments and not in a transversal logic. The state government has tried to remedy the isolation of climate policies within the Ministry of Ecology by creating a general secretariat for ecological planning attached to the Prime Minister with a cross-cutting vocation.

Citizen participation: The participatory budget: As part of public participation in the city of Paris, a participatory budget has been in place since 2014. The participatory budget is open to all residents, regardless of age or nationality. From now on, arrondissement or central town halls can submit projects within their remit to the participatory budget, such as the renovation of schools or gymnasiums, churches or even studies.[77] The implementation of projects can be followed online. The participation rate is very low at the city level, as the projects with the most votes hardly exceed 10,000 voters out of 2 million inhabitants.[78] The participatory budget as implemented in Paris is therefore very far from the Brazilian model of shared and citizen administration of the city in Porto Alegre.

I would like to add that the Paris region has had a participatory ecological budget since 2018. This participatory budget, which is more specific in its purpose, is carried out in a similar way to the municipality's participatory budget.

2.3.2 Public spaces, infrastructure, and urban public services for climate

2.3.2.1 Public spaces for climate

The notion of public space is emerging in French public law,[79] and it is relevant in a climatic approach to the city of Paris. I will use it in these developments to refer to public spaces as physical public spaces, although, in Paris more than

75 Articles 164 and 165 of the Climate Resilience Act.

76 https://www.arec-idf.fr/larec-ile-de-france.html.

77 https://budgetparticipatif.paris.fr/bp/jsp/site/Portal.jsp?page=idee&campagne=G&idee=1422.

78 https://opendata.paris.fr.

79 Auby (n 3).

elsewhere, physical public spaces are also places of public expression, spaces of public debate, since not a week goes by without demonstrators "pounding the pavement".

Over the last twenty years, Parisian public spaces have undergone major changes to reduce the presence of cars, in the image of the main European capitals or other French cities such as Bordeaux, Nantes, Lyon, Grenoble etc. The banks of the Seine have been pedestrianized at the cost of numerous disputes between the city and the region of Paris.[80] Although progress has been made, through the redevelopment of large squares such as Place de la République, Place de la Bastille or Place de la Nation, or the creation of vast bicycle paths, notably on Rue de Rivoli during the Covid-19 epidemic, the city of Paris is still marked by the extreme abundance of roadways dedicated to road traffic. In 2004, the road network represented[81] 25% of the territory of the city of Paris, far ahead of Brussels Capital 15% and Barcelona 17%. The progress made since 2004 has not, however, represented a major reversal of the trend. Despite announcements by the Paris City Council to pedestrianize large areas of the center of Paris (the center of Paris is a tourist area and not very densely populated), which have not yet been carried out, no large-scale strategy on the scale of Barcelona's *super-cities* to pedestrianize entire neighborhoods constituting living units has been implemented. The "city of a quarter of an hour" mentioned in the climate plans and urban plans being drawn up, which we mentioned above, has not been implemented in the public space in Paris.

The reclamation of public spaces for the benefit of non-motorized users, which constitutes a strategy for mitigating emissions, has not, however, been accompanied by an approach to adapting new developments to climate change: the new developments have not been carried out with the aim of combating urban heat islands or creating green and blue infrastructure. In this sense, in terms of action on public spaces, there has been no conciliation between mitigation and adaptation as recommended by the IPCC.[82]

In addition, the speed limit has been lowered to 30 km/h in 2020 on the entire Parisian road network, and a low emission zone has been instituted under the 2019 Law on Mobility following the 2015 Law on Ecological Transition and Green Growth. The application of the low emission zone has been postponed, however, for reasons relating to the social inequalities generated by the exclusion of the most polluting vehicles, which generally belong to the poorest households. The fight against air pollution in Paris remains very weak due to the lack of implementation of the texts.[83]

80 CAA Paris, 22 October 2018, n 18PA01325, n 18PA01326 and n 18PA01649.
81 APUR (n 22).
82 Intergovernmental Panel on Climate Change (n 4) 8.2.3.
83 Mialot (n 13).

In 2015, the municipality of Paris instituted a greening permit for the public space. The greening permit is presented as an occupation authorization free of charge, with an obligation to plant and to maintain at the expense of the beneficiary of the authorization. The beneficiary of the greening permit can be a resident or an association. The greening permit is therefore close to the notion of common good and shared administration, since it allows individuals or neighborhood associations to maintain plants for the benefit of the public on part of the public space. The 2021 Climate Law authorized vegetation permits on the public domain, which constitutes a free occupation of the public domain normally subject to a fee. Consultation of the city of Paris' open data shows that the greening permits mainly concern planters or trees planted in the ground. Two thousand five hundred greening permits have been issued since 2015, even if a careful reading of the data reveals that a large proportion of the permits were filed and obtained by the city of Paris services and not by inhabitants.

Urban forest projects intended to create green infrastructure and combat urban heat islands in Paris have been abandoned due to difficulties in finding undeveloped areas underground, due to the lack of prior mapping and planning of the subsurface mentioned above.[84]

For the sake of completeness, let's add that the 2021 Climate Resilience Law has banned all heating and cooling devices in the public domain, including café and restaurant terraces, a provision that was previously adopted in 2019 by the city of Rennes itself inspired by the city of Barcelona.

2.3.2.2 Urban infrastructure and public services

I will quickly mention three urban public services: transport, waste treatment, and energy renovation of housing.

We have already mentioned the studies giving an overview of the significant development of urban transport services and their saturation due to the very large number of trips per inhabitant. Let us add the development since 2007 in Paris of a vast network of bicycle rental representing more than 1,500 stations in more than 60 municipalities of the metropolis and covering 450 km^2 of service.[85] This service is currently used more than 150,000 times a day.

The public waste treatment service is strongly impacted by the 2020 law on the fight against waste and the circular economy, which imposes major restrictions on the use of plastic in catering, the reduction of household waste, recycling, and composting. Composting is developing rapidly in Paris with the free distribution of individual and collective composting devices in condominiums and on a neighborhood scale since 2016 with the adoption of the

84 https://parissecret.com/nature-les-forets-urbaines-en-projet-par-la-ville-de-paris-vont-elles-voir-le-jour/.

85 https://opendata.paris.fr.

compost plan.[86] Composts created at the neighborhood level are sometimes managed by neighborhood associations and residents in a shared administration approach.

The energy renovation of housing is a public service that has been developed for eight years on the initiative of the municipality of Paris through the Paris Climate Agency described above. This service is now shared with the metropolis of greater Paris and is an example of two levels of administration working together. The financing of the energy renovation audit is provided by the city and financial aid for renovation is granted by the city, the metropolis, and the state; this aid is subject to income conditions. On the scale of the greater Paris metropolis, 81,630 homes out of a total of 3.5 million have benefited from at least one energy renovation service. The scheme is therefore clearly not being deployed on a massive scale. However, the 2021 Climate Resilience Law imposes important obligations in terms of energy renovation of housing. A new classification of dwellings according to their energy performance has led to a freeze on rents for the least efficient dwellings since 22 August 2022, and from 2025 onward, the least efficient dwellings will be considered non-decent, opening up the possibility for tenants to impose energy renovation work and rent reductions on landlords. By 2028, more than half of Parisian housing will be affected by the obligation to renovate energy efficiency due to their classification when they are rented. In addition, the Climate Resilience Law requires an energy performance audit detailing the work to be carried out when buildings are sold.

Combined with the legal obligations, the initiatives of the city and the metropolis in terms of energy renovation of housing will probably lead to a massive energy renovation of housing in Paris in the coming decade.

2.4 Conclusion: Living in Paris in transition

Bruno Latour wrote about Paris at the end of the 1990s: "For the first time in its long existence, the City of Light is aging for good, preserved intact in an illusion of the past, lit only by the spotlights of the tourist boats that pass on the Seine".[87] However, at the beginning of the 21st century, the city of Paris is no longer exactly characterized by immobility when faced with climate change. To describe the strategies and actions carried out today in Paris in terms of climate, the word climate transition in that it signifies the beginning of a slow, scattered and not very operational process gives a fairly accurate picture of Parisian attempts to "govern the climate". Transition is not mutation, i.e. the complete change of the city to cope with climate change. The

86 Ibid.
87 Latour, Hermant (n 12) 169.

mutation is above all a question of policy and choices to be made.[88] These political choices are not currently being implemented, as the study of the legal tools deployed reveals, but they are in the making, such as the "quarter-hour city" or the energy renovation of buildings.

The dimension of "living in Paris" that we have highlighted in our developments is undeniably affected by climate change. This is particularly evident during the major heatwave episodes that occurred in the summer of 2022, which rendered the city of Paris nearly uninhabitable. Similarly, in the event of a 100-year flood, which is likely to occur more frequently by 2050, the situation will be no different. The aspect of "living in Paris" that we have referred to has not yet experienced any favorable impact from the city of Paris' climate policies. Although there has been a decline in car use and an increase in mobility, there has been no corresponding decrease in the level of urbanization along the roads affected, such as the banks of the Seine or the Rue de Rivoli, which still remain largely artificial. Despite the reduction in the use of cars, there has not yet been a significant decrease in air pollution. Public spaces are more than ever affected by numerous conflicts of use. Pedestrians, bicycles, electric scooters, motorbikes, cars, along with greenery resulting from the issuance of vegetation permits and café terraces, are attempting to coexist within the same limited public spaces. The physical characteristics of Paris both limit and strongly influence public policy decisions, which results in choices that are yet to be made.

Bibliography

Agence Eau Seine Normandie, 'Signature du contrat Bièvre Eau Climat Trame Verte et Bleue 2020–2024' (2020) https://www.eau-seine-normandie.fr/node/3605.

APUR, 'Déplacements dans les villes européennes' (2004) https://50ans.apur.org/data/b4s3_home/fiche/91/04_deplac_villes_europeennes_2004_broapu244_41289.pdf.

APUR, 'Consommation d'énergie et émissions de gaz à effet de serre des logements à usage de résidence principale' (2007) https://www.apur.org/fr/nos-travaux/consommations-energie-emissions-gaz-effet-serre-liees-chauffage-residences-principales-parisiennes.

APUR 'Ilôts de chaleur urbain – Project EPICEA' (2012) https://www.apur.org/fr/recherche?keyword=ilots+of+heat&sort_bef_combine=score+DESC.

APUR, 'Patrimoine Bâti parisien premiers repérages pour des réhabilitations thermiques' (2016) https://www.apur.org/fr/nos-travaux/patrimoine-bati-parisien-premier-reperage-rehabilitations-thermiques.

APUR, 'Evolution de la Nature à Paris de 1730 à nos jours' (2018) https://www.apur.org/fr/nos-travaux/evolution-nature-paris-1730-nos-jours.

88 Christophe Bonneuil and Jean-Baptiste Fressoz, *L'évènement anthropocène, la terre l'histoire et nous* (Seuil 2016).

APUR 'Évolution des mobilités dans le grand Paris tendances historiques Évolutions en cours et émergentes' (2021) https://www.apur.org/fr/nos-travaux/evolution-mobilites-grand-paris-tendances-historiques-evolutions-cours-emergentes.

Atelier International du Grand Paris, *Habiter le Grand Paris* (Archibooks/Bookstorming 2013).

Auby J-B and Gregorio V., *Données urbaines et smart city* (Berger Levrault 2017).

Auby J-B., 'La Ville nouvelle frontière du droit administratif' (2017) *AJDA* 853.

Auby J-B., 'L'espace public comme notion émergente du droit administratif' (2021a) *AJDA* 2565.

Auby J-B., 'La lutte contre le changement climatique comme impératif juridique catégorique' (2021b) https://www.chemins-publics.org/articles/la-lutte-contre-le-changement-climatique-comme-imperatif-juridique-categorique.

Aykut S., and Dahan A., *Gouverner le climat ? Vingt ans de négociations internationales* (Presses de SciencesPo 2014).

Bigorne J. and Jankel S., 'Le Patrimoine Bâti Parisien – Premier repérage pour des réhabilitations thermiques' (2016) 105 *Atelier Parisien D'Urbanisme* 1.

Bonneuil C., and Fressoz J-B., *L'évènement anthropocène, la terre l'histoire et nous* (Seuil 2016).

Briday R., 'Le SRCAE d'Île-de-France. L'épineuse territorialisation des objectifs nationaux de transition énergétique' (2020) *20–18 Document de travail du LATTS – Working Paper* 1, 45 https://enpc.hal.science/hal-02922745/document.

Cour des Comptes, 'La prévention insuffisante du Risque Inondation en Ile-de-France' (2022) https://www.ccomptes.fr/fr/publications/la-prevention-insuffisante-du-risque-dinondation-en-ile-de-france.

Institut Paris Région, *Chiffres-clés 20220* (2022a) https://www.institutparisregion.fr/nos-travaux/publications/chiffres-cles-2022/.

Institut Paris Région, 'Vunérabilité de la Région au changement climatique' (2022b) https://www.institutparisregion.fr.

Intergovermental Panel on Climate Change Cities and Climate Change Science Conference, 'Progress Report – International Conference on Climate Change and Cities' (2018) https://www.ipcc.ch/event/cities-and-climate-change-science-conference/.

Intergovermental Panel on Climate Change, 'Climate Change 2022. Mitigation of Climate Change, Working Group III contribution to the Sixth Assessment Report of the Intergovernmental Panel on Climate Change' (2022).

Latour B., 'Entretiens avec Bruno Laotur' (2021) https://www.arte.tv/fr/videos/106738-008-A/entretiens-avec-bruno-latour-.

Latour B. and Hermant É., *Ville invisible* (B42 2021).

Lirzin F., *Paris face au changement climatique* (L'aube 2022).

Lora-Tamayo Vallvé, M., *Urbanismo de obra Pública y derecho a urbanizar. Análisis comparado desde las aportaciones de G. E. Haussmann y la doctrina de Ildefonso Cerdá* (Marcial Pons 2002).

Métropole du Grand Paris, 'Plan Climat Air Energie Territorial de la Métropole du Grand Paris' (2018a) https://www.metropolegrandparis.fr/fr/plan-climat-air-energie-metropolitain-76.

Métropole du Grand Paris, 'Schéma Métropolitain de Cohérence Territoriale (ScoT)' (2018b) https://www.metropolegrandparis.fr/fr/schema-de-coherence-territoriale-scot-metropolitain-un-vote-historique-pour-la-metropole-du-grand.

Mialot C., 'Local Policies on Climate Change in a Centralized State: The French Example' (forthcoming) 1 *French Yearbook of Public Law (FYPL)*.

Mialot C., *La ville face au changement climatique, nouveaux instruments juridiques* (Berger Levrault 2020).

Ville de Paris, 'Étude Paris face au changement climatique 2021, étude de robustesse et de vulnérabilité de la Ville de Paris' (2022) https://www.paris.fr/pages/paris-s-adapte-au-changement-climatique-18541#:~:text=Ainsi%2C%20la%20majorit%C3%A9%20des%20risques,tendent%20%C3%A0%20survenir%20d%C3%A8s%202030.&text=Les%20d%C3%A9fis%20climatiques%20auxquels%20devra,des%20risques%20li%C3%A9s%20aux%20inondations.

Ville de Paris, 'Stratégie de résilience de Paris 2017' (2022b) https://www.paris.fr/pages/paris-resiliente-4264.

Ville de Paris, 'Paris à 50°C. Rapport de la Mission d'Information et d'Évaluation du Conseil de Paris' (2023) https://www.paris50degres.fr/.

3 Toward a new model of the city

The superblock program in Barcelona

Marc Vilalta Reixach

3.1 Introduction

The global phenomenon of increased urbanization has persisted over recent decades, as is well known. Subsequently, there has been a trend toward the growth of large urban areas in Spain as in many other countries in our region. These areas concentrate a large percentage of the population and play an essential role in the economic activity of various States.

A report by the Spanish Ministry of Transport, Mobility and the Urban Agenda in November 2022 indicated that more than 69% of the country's population lives in large urban areas which account for 76% of employment.[1] These new territorial entities undoubtedly offer multiple opportunities to their residents. At the same time, they also pose important challenges in the social, political, cultural, economic and environmental spheres.

Much specific emphasis has been placed on the environmental impact that large cities have on the individual and collective well-being of their inhabitants as well as sustainable territorial development overall. Hence, one of the 2015 Sustainable Development Goals (SDGs) set by the United Nations General Assembly focuses on cities. This goal aims to reduce negative environmental impacts in urban areas, increase sustainable urbanization and provide universal access to green spaces and safe, inclusive, accessible public spaces in cities.

The discussion below specifically addresses this environmental dimension of large cities. Given the importance of the issue, we examine it mainly from a legal point of view. We do this by considering some transformative measures the Spanish city of Barcelona has adopted to promote an energy and ecological transition within its large urban area. We specifically look at the so-called "superblock" (*superilla/supermanzana*) model. This aims to limit the number of vehicles in certain parts of the city and make better use of public spaces. The idea is to have many more green areas, adding to the health and well-being of residents and creating more sustainable mobility patterns.

1 Ministerio de Transportes, Movilidad y Agenda Urbana (2022) *Áreas urbanas en España 2022* 4.

DOI: 10.4324/9781032665184-13

Before continuing, we should mention that this initiative is part of the political commitment Barcelona has shown in recent decades to enhancing environmental protection and sustainability. Thus, related municipal policies have emerged across very different areas. Multiple units, programs, services and council departments have been created which are specifically dedicated to the environment and environmental sustainability. These have been created pursuant to the city's joining the *Aalborg Charter* in 1995 and approving *Agenda 21*, which defined various objectives and actions to achieve a better city environment.[2]

More recently, Barcelona has been included in the EU program, "100 Climate-neutral cities in Europe By 2030 – by and for citizens", along with several other Spanish cities (e.g. Madrid, Seville and Valencia). Under this activity, Barcelona's city council (*Ayuntamiento de Barcelona*) has committed itself to promoting various transformative energy and urban renewal projects.[3]

Given our topic, we should also mention the Climate Emergency Declaration (*Declaración de Emergencia Climática*) approved by the Barcelona City Council in January 2020. This document is based on the premise that large urban areas offer enormous potential in fighting climate change. It particularly focuses on Barcelona's urban model, which includes increasing urban green areas, transforming public spaces and thereby improving environmental and health conditions for citizens.

Among many other actions, this declaration foresees reclaiming areas for social use that were previously allocated to private vehicles. It also advances sustainable and collective transport means, which is precisely the main goal of the city council's superblock model as we will see below.[4]

3.2 Barcelona's superblock model

To better understand what the superblock initiative consists of, we must start from the fact that Barcelona is a compact city like many other large European urban areas. It has a high population density, a lack of green spaces and a transport system that is over-dependent on motorized vehicles. In fact, Barcelona is one of the European cities with the highest density of automobiles, encompassing 5,844 of them per km^2. This is the case despite the city having a good public transport network. According to data from the Work Day Mobility Survey (published in 2021 by the Barcelona City Council's Department of Statistics and Data Dissemination), 47% of motorized journeys during work

2 Barcelona City Council (2015) *Compromís ciutadà per la sostenibilitat.*

3 The commitments made by the city are found in their Institutional Declaration, *Ciudades climáticamente neutrales en 2030*, signed in September 2021 and accessible at: https://ajuntament.barcelona.cat/premsa/wp-content/uploads/2021/09/Declaracion_institucional-def-.pdf [Last accessed 17 February 2023].

4 Ayuntamiento de Barcelona (2020): *Declaración de emergencia climática* (2020) 13–17.

days are still made using private transport (e.g. an automobile, motorbike or lorry).[5]

These factors negatively affect environmental conditions in the city, increase air, noise and vehicle pollution and, as a result, worsen the health and well-being of inhabitants. Hence, the main challenges facing different government teams in recent years have been to improve urban mobility and promote public policies that make it more sustainable, thereby reducing congestion and fossil fuel consumption.

Once again, Barcelona's increased attention to environmental and sustainable mobility policies is by no means unique. On the contrary, it is part of a growing global concern over the issue. The European land transport directives and European climate legislation (e.g. Regulation EU 2021/1119 of 30 June 2021 establishing a framework for achieving climate neutrality) are good examples of this concern at the European level. This legislation notes the importance of sustainable and intelligent mobility systems in helping EU Member States achieve the goal of climate neutrality. This concern is also noted in the European Commission Communication COM (2021) 811 on "The New EU Urban Mobility Framework".

Looking beyond the EU level, the 2015 Sustainable Development Goals (SDGs) set by the United Nations also encompass the need to transform the way citizens move around cities by providing universal access to green spaces and safe, inclusive and accessible public spaces (SDG 11). The 2016 New Urban Agenda adopted by the United Nations General Assembly also highlights the essential value of mobility as a fundamental characteristic and condition determining urban quality of life. Most public policies evolving from the New Urban Agenda's innovative paradigm arguably require gradually, but significantly, reducing the space cities allocate to private automobile traffic.[6]

As far as the Spanish legal system is concerned, it contains various regulations that aim to promote sustainable mobility at the local level, *inter alia*. Law 2/2011, of 4 March, on the Sustainable Economy (*Ley de Economía Sostenible*/LES) is a particular example of this. It introduces, among other things, so-called state-level sustainable mobility plans. These plans are defined as a set of actions establishing more sustainable forms of travel and prioritizing collective transport systems over individual ones. These plans also promote other non-motorized modes of transport and developing options compatible with economic growth, social cohesion, road safety and environmental

5 Ayuntamiento de Barcelona (2021) *Encuesta de movilidad en un día laborable*. Available at: https://ajuntament.barcelona.cat/estadistica/catala/Estadistiques_per_temes/Transport_i_mobilitat/Mobilitat/Enquesta_mobilitat_dia_feiner/index.htm [Last accessed 17 February 2023].

6 Andrés Boix Palop, 'Los desafíos internacionales de la regulación de la movilidad urbana y la nueva agenda urbana', in Antonio Fortes Martín (ed.), *Movilidad urbana sostenible y acción administrativa* (Thomson Reuters – Aranzadi 2019) 96.

protection. The end result of this activity is to guarantee citizens a better quality of life (Art. 101 LES).

Despite the fact that the LES sees sustainable urban mobility plans as purely voluntary, they have become widespread in many Spanish municipalities, especially in large cities. This has undoubtedly been helped by the fact that the LES also introduced important economic incentives to act accordingly. For example, Article 102 of the LES made obtaining state subsidies for public transport conditional on the public entity involved making related mobility plans.

In the Autonomous Community of Catalonia, concern over sustainable urban mobility arose even earlier. The mobility law passed by the Parliament of Catalonia, Law 9/2003 on 13 June 2003 (*Ley del Parlamento de Catalunya de movilidad*/LMCat) regulated urban mobility plans and was influenced by European law. These mobility plans were to be basic documents setting out sustainable municipal strategies for the Autonomous Community.

More recently, Law 7/2021 of 20 May on climate change and the energy transition (*Ley de cambio climático y transición energética*/LCCTE) aims to ensure Spain's compliance with the 2015 Paris Agreement objectives and also includes measures promoting sustainable mobility. Unlike previous regulations, Article 14 of the LCCTE requires municipalities with more than 50,000 inhabitants to adopt sustainable urban mobility plans and introduce mobility-related emission reduction measures by 2023. Such measures may include, for example, setting up low-emission zones (LEZs), measures to facilitate walking, cycling or other active modes of transport and linking these activities to healthy lifestyles. They may also involve creating intra-urban green corridors and connecting green spaces with larger peri-urban green areas.

As discussed further below, these sustainable mobility plans are of interest since they have been used as legal tools in implementing Barcelona's superblock model. While the spread of superblocks in Barcelona has been seen as a recent phenomenon, in fact, their origin goes back quite far. For this reason, we briefly take a look at their history.

3.2.1 History of the superblock model

Barcelona's current superblocks are inevitably indebted to the model established under the 1860 *Cerdà Plan* for the city's reform and expansion.[7] This plan proposed urbanizing the large land area made available after the city walls were demolished. It did this by introducing a continuous grid of building blocks, 113.3 meters long, with rectangular private green areas allotted for community use within them.

The superblock initiative can be linked, above all perhaps, to another great urban planning project during the first half of the 20th century. This was the

7 Salvador Rueda Palenzuela, 'Les superilles per al disseny de noves ciutats i la renovació de les existents. El cas de Barcelona' (2017) 59 *Papers. Regió Metropolitana de Barcelona* 82–83.

so-called *Plan Macià*, drawn up in 1932 by two architects, Le Corbusier and Josep Lluís Sert. They aimed to organize Barcelona's growth and internally reorder the city.[8] Although this Plan was never implemented, it envisaged the possibility of creating 400 x 400 meter units made up of large residential areas and urban greenery within the as yet "undeveloped" areas of the city's urban fabric.

As a result of a 1987 noise pollution study in the city, Salvador Rueda, then director of the Urban Ecology Agency of the Barcelona City Council, resurrected the idea of these 400 x 400 meter urban units and proposed reorganizing the city into these so-called superblocks.[9] In fact, the city's first superblock was created in 1993. This involved reconverting the inner perimeter of several streets in Barcelona's Ribera neighborhood into pedestrian zones.

However, it was not until 2004 that the term "superblock" (*supermanzana*) was actually used in an official Barcelona City Council project, the 2004 Mobility Plan for the District of Gràcia. This plan specifically mentioned superblocks as a tool for reorganizing internal mobility in that area. The plan consisted of creating 400 x 400 meter units within the neighborhood in which space for pedestrians was prioritized over motorised traffic. Later, the concept and term "superblock" was used again in the 2006 Strategic Plan for the District of Sants-Montjuïc. In 2013, there was also a proposal for implementing superblocks in the Maternitat and Sant Ramon neighborhoods in the district of Les Corts.

Going beyond this history, the spread of superblocks in Barcelona has been given a decisive boost in recent years by other events, especially the approval of the city's Urban Mobility Plan for 2013–2018 (*Plan de movilidad urbana de Barcelona 2013 2018*/PMU 2013 2018), whose main objective was reducing private automobile use.[10]

3.2.2 The development of the superblock model: Barcelona's Urban Mobility Plan 2013–2018

In terms of the development of Barcelona's superblock system, the city's Urban Mobility Plan 2013–2018 was certainly an important milestone. Intensive motor vehicle use has had considerable social, economic, and environmental impacts in the city. This type of transport takes up the most land area, consumes the most fuel, and generates significant externalities (accidents, pollution, noise, congestion, etc.). Thus, this mobility plan sought to reduce the number of private motorized vehicles on Barcelona's streets to an absolute

8 Rueda Palenzuela (n 7) 83–84 and Beatriz Guijarro Turégano, *Repensar los cruces: la implementación del modelo Superilles: el caso de la Superilla del Poblenou de Barcelona (2016 2021)* (Universitat de Barcelona 2022) 102–104.

9 Guijarro Turégano (n 8) 105.

10 Barcelona City Council (2015) *Pla de Mobilitat Urbana de Barcelona. PMU 2013–2018*, 41.

minimum. It also sought, if necessary, to make them more environmentally friendly too.

In order to achieve these objectives, the Urban Mobility Plan revolved around four main strategic axes:

A) Firstly, it involved safe mobility, with the aim of reducing accidents, protecting pedestrians, bicycles, and motorbikes and promoting respect amongst the users of different transport means.
B) Secondly, it advanced equitable mobility and ensured the right of all citizens to move around the city in a safe, healthy and sustainable way. This meant, among other things, guaranteeing access to the transport system, promoting alternative uses for public ways and increasing public spaces for pedestrians.
C) Thirdly, efficient mobility was seen as involving improved logistical management in terms of infrastructure, lighting, noise control systems, street furniture, intelligent signage and mobile digital apps for updating citizens. The aim was to achieve smoother traffic flows, optimize public transport and reduce the environmental, social and economic costs of mobility.
D) Fourthly, the plan also emphasized sustainable mobility. In order to comply with European Union standards on suspended particle pollution, the Plan also envisaged introducing measures for shifting toward more efficient types of mobility (e.g. from private motor vehicles to public or non-motorized transport). It also sought to increase the use of renewable energy sources.

In order to implement these four strategic axes, Barcelona's City Council had to undertake action on numerous fronts. It meant creating a new octagonal bus network to reduce waiting times by half, increasing the number of cycle lanes and improving access to metro stations. For the purpose of this discussion, what is of greatest interest is that implementing the Mobility Plan also involved reorganizing Barcelona's urban fabric into superblocks.

The plan defined superblocks as a basic urban unit of 16/20 hectares, or about 400 × 400 meters. These contained several dense, multifunctional city blocks and had an optimal population of 7,000–8,000 people. Most importantly, each of these superblocks significantly limited internal traffic, giving priority to pedestrians and cyclists. Thus, the basic traffic flows in a superblock are mainly external ones. In these, public transport circulates much more efficiently than private motor vehicles along frequently used routes.

According to the Plan, 503 superblocks were to be created throughout the city. Traffic was to be reduced by 21%, freeing up more than 60–70% of the city's internal space for public redevelopment as shared or pedestrian areas. These new urban spaces would therefore offer a higher quality of life, comfort and liveability. They would also be more noise-free and have better air quality and safety.

The Barcelona superblocks model is based on a new way of organizing a city. It revolves around reversing the amount of public space dedicated to vehicles versus people, prioritizing the citizen and improving environmental conditions and quality of life.

In any case, the effective implementation of this initiative has apparently gained momentum since 2016, especially since Ada Colau won the 2015 local elections. In fact, one of the first government measures taken by the new municipal officer was to commit to creating the superblocks.[11] From this moment on, several of the measures envisaged under the plan swung into action, including creating superblocks in the Poblenou (2016), Sant Antoni (2018) and Horta (2018) neighborhoods.

3.2.3 Current situation: From superblocks to green axes

The health crisis resulting from the COVID-19 pandemic, and the 2020 Climate Emergency Declaration, enhanced the importance of public spaces and the need for a healthier city. As a result, the Barcelona City Council presented the Barcelona Superblock Program (*Programa Superilla Barcelona*) in 2021, taking this model to a new level (Barcelona City Council, 2021). The aim is to no longer act in isolation within certain units or closed areas (such as the Sant Antoni or Poblenou neighborhood superblocks), but to focus on more generally transforming all the city's streets.

Among the different initiatives envisaged under this Program, the creation of new green axes in the Ensanche district of Barcelona stands out. Different spaces will be turned into "peaceful streets, which have areas to rest and more greenery, allowing people to move around by foot in comfort, convenience, and safety".[12] In addition, intersections in these green axes will be transformed into new squares, each recuperating about 2,000 m^2 of urban space.

As in the previous case, all these planned measures have been included in the new five-year Urban Mobility Plan for 2024, which was finally approved by the Barcelona City Council in January 2023. This recent Plan aims to achieve an even more sustainable mobility model that improves the quality of life for citizens by creating these new "Green Axes" in the city.

3.3 Some legal issues raised by the Barcelona superblock model

Having generally presented Barcelona's superblock model, we now turn to consider several of the main legal issues that have arisen with its implementation. We do not undertake a complete and exhaustive analysis of the legality of

11 Comisión de Ecología, Urbanismo y Movilidad, *Omplim de vida els carrers. La implantació de les Superilles a Barcelona* (Ayuntamiento de Barcelona 2016).

12 Ayuntamiento de Barcelona (2022) *Supermanzanas crece en el Eixample.* Available at: https://ajuntament.barcelona.cat/superilles/es/superilla/eixample#

all the measures, but rather present some of the main elements of the debate around them.

In this regard, we believe it is appropriate to begin our analysis by recalling one important aspect. That is, Barcelona has a special and unique legal regime that differs from other large cities in Spain due to its historical particularities, economic importance, and role as the capital of Catalonia.

However, Barcelona's special legal regime does not exempt it from fulfilling its general statutory duties,[13] which are regulated by two different legal norms. One is the Law of the Parliament of Catalonia 22/1998 of 30 December, which established the Barcelona Municipal Charter (*Carta Municipal de Barcelona).* The other is State Law 1/2006 of 13 March on the Special Regime of the Municipality of Barcelona (*Ley estatal del Régimen especial del municipio de Barcelona*/LREMB). It is the latter that actually empowers the Barcelona City Council to regulate different kinds of road use via the corresponding municipal by-laws. In any case, the aim of the LREMB is to promote compatibility in terms of road safety, traffic mobility and fluidity and environmental protection (Art. 18 LREMB).

To meet the sustainable mobility objectives of its different plants, the Barcelona City Council has not limited itself to merely using legal instruments that either promote actions or provide incentives. It has also adopted restrictive regulatory measures which have involved permanently reducing the places where motorized vehicles can circulate.

As noted above, the creation of superblocks does not completely prevent vehicle access in designated parts of the city. This circulation is maintained to some extent in order to allow other essential mobility functions (e.g. the movement of residents, including those with mobility limitations, or the loading and unloading of goods). From our point of view, this nuance is very important. Otherwise, we would need to question the constitutionality of the related measures.

In other words, the country;s constitutional system does not guarantee the citizens a right to mobility or circulating vehicles. Yet, citizens do have the Fundamental Right to freedom of movement, as recognized under Article 19 of the Spanish Constitution.[14] Therefore, if the Barcelona City Council had planned to absolutely restrict traffic in the areas involved, we might ask ourselves whether such a measure disproportionately restricted this Fundamental Right.

Having made this point, we can now turn to consider some of the legal debate surrounding the implementation of superblocks in Barcelona. We focus on two different issues: discussion over the degree of citizen participation

13 Tomàs Font i Llovet, 'El significat del règim especial de Barcelona i el seu impuls per a un nou dret de la ciutat', in Tomàs Font i Llovet (ed.): *La Carta Municipal de Barcelona i el dret de la ciutat* (Ajuntament de Barcelona 2022), 39.

14 Sofia Simou, *Derecho Local del Cambio Climático,* (Marcial Pons 2020) 465–466.

which has occurred in implementing the model and controversies that have arisen around the specific legal instruments used.

3.3.1 Citizen participation in the procedures creating superblocks

One of the most controversial issues has been, undoubtedly, the lack of participation by citizens in implementing the superblocks. This is not surprising given the importance of participation within the new urbanism (or social urbanism) movement, which highlights citizen involvement and the related issues of transparency and good administration and governance.[15]

In this sense, some of the main criticisms in creating the Poblenou Superblock in 2016 revolved around the project not being widely disseminated throughout the territory. Also, the speed of implementation made citizen participation in the initiative practically null.[16] As a result, the superblock initiative met with strong local protests that went so far as to call for a neighborhood hearing against the project. This hearing was held in May 2017 and attended by a total of 1,739 people, many of whom (87.2%) were largely against creating the superblock.

This period of initial criticism served as an apprenticeship one for the Barcelona City Council. They have subsequently tried to be more truly participatory in their procedures during successive superblock projects, even at the cost of delaying the implementation process. Their efforts have involved a wide range of actions (e.g. setting up working groups with representative associations, affected people and schools of architecture or holding public information sessions, etc.). The Barcelona City Council has also sought to better present this new model for organizing public space, better inform residents about the specific projects to be carried out and gather more information on problems and territorial needs.

A good example of the specific participatory actions carried out in implementing the new green axes in Ensanche can be seen in the Final Report on the participatory process of the Program on Superblocks in Barcelona in l'Eixample (*Informe Final sobre el proceso participativo del Programa Superilla Barcelona a l'Eixample*), prepared by the Barcelona City Council in December 2021. This report highlights the over 20 participatory actions conducted which involved more than 1,400 persons in the local neighbour.[17]

In our view, this kind of activity is legally relevant since the *Barcelona Municipal Charter* stipulates that the city council must guarantee "citizen participation, especially in matters that most directly affect the quality of life of

15 Jesús María Ramírez Sánchez, *Urbanismo para una nueva ciudad. El principio de desarrollo urbano sostenible* (Thomson Reuters – Aranzadi 2021), 546.

16 Beatriz Guijarro Turégano (n 8) 140.

17 Barcelona City Council (2021) *Procés participatiu Superilla Barcelona a l'Eixample. Final Report [09/12/2021]* 8.

citizens" (Art. 30.1). This *Charter* also effectively reinforces citizen rights on access to information and public participation with respect to the environmental aspects of Law 27/2006 of 18 July.

Article 22 of the Catalan Law 26/2010 of 3 August, on the Legal Regime and Procedure of the Public Administrations of Catalonia (*Ley catalana de Régimen Jurídico y Procedimiento de las Administraciones Públicas de Cataluña*/LRJPCat), similarly includes citizen participation as part of the right to good administration. This law states that:

> The public administrations in Catalonia must encourage citizen participation in relation to the administrative actions they are responsible for. This should be done in order to gather proposals, suggestions or initiatives from citizens through a prior process of information dissemination and debate.

However, these new participatory procedures have not been without their critics. The number of social actors invited for consultation has been seen as too limited. Also, there has been no real willingness on the part of the Barcelona City Council to discuss the implementation of the superblock model despite the hearings held.[18]

We are not able to enter into all these controversies in detail here. However, we believe that these criticisms are justified in some cases, for example, with regard to the implementation of the new green axes in the Ensanche district. There, the city council began vetting projects even while the initiative was still being presented to the public and when interested parties might still provide feedback on it.

In fact, the council's action was supported by municipal regulations, namely, the Mayoral Decree of 17 April 2012, which sets out procedures for preparing and processing projects and executing municipal works. Article 11.2 of this decree does allow public works to be tendered before their definitive approval. This may occur provided that the project has been initially approved and that joint processing of final approval alongside project activity is ensured. In this case, we do not see citizen participation strictly as a required process that has to occur before the city council makes a decision. Rather, we see the council's soliciting of citizen participation as a necessary step during the project approval and public tendering process. In our opinion, it would have been better for the tendering procedures to have been initiated once the steps of informing and involving the public had been entirely completed. This is also the case partly because the Ombudsman (*Síndic de Greuges*) of the city of Barcelona had warned in a May 2022 report that doing otherwise would counteract the possibility of public participation. This, in turn, might further increase the

18 Barcelona City Council (n 17) 26–34.

feeling that the project was being externally imposed. In fact, this was precisely one of the criticisms made by people in the involved neighbourhood.[19]

3.3.2 The legal aspects of the superblock model

The issues that have certainly raised most doubts from a legal point of view, however, are the regulatory instruments that have been used to implement the superblocks. In particular, there has been a debate on the type of urban planning action taken to carry out the reforms.

As in the previous case, this issue has raised strong opposition among some residents. It has even led to different neighborhood associations filing various complaints and lawsuits against the Mayor of Barcelona, Ada Colau. These have been based on the fact that implementing the Barcelona Superblock Program has potentially infringed on land use planning. However, the Public Prosecutor's Office decided to stop these proceedings in January 2023 on the grounds there was insufficient evidence of such an offense.

Problems in this area, though, have arisen because the Barcelona City Council believed they did not need to approve any new urban development plans to provide regulatory coverage for the superblock project or to create the green axes such as in Ensanche. On the contrary, they believed introducing superblocks did not affect the legal nature of the involved land or its functionality since the targeted streets were still considered urban roads. As such, they assumed what was involved was not an urban development project, but merely the execution of ordinary works.

The practical consequences of classifying certain actions under one legal category or another are relevant here. The Legislative Decree 1/2010 of 3 August approved the Revised Text of the Catalan Urban Planning Law (*Ley de urbanismo de Catalunya*/TRLUCat). This decree specifies that in the event of an urban development project, the involved urban planning entity needs to establish the basic principles for such activity at the start (Art. 72 TRLUCat). Therefore, introducing superblocks would have obliged the Barcelona City Council to modify the existing and affected urban plans or to make a new special or urban improvement plan covering the superblocks (Art. 67.1 and 70 TRLUCat).

On the other hand, executing ordinary works is much quicker. Two statutes are relevant here. One is the Legislative Decree 2/2003 of 28 April, which approves the revised text of the Municipal and Local Regime Law of Catalonia (*Ley Municipal y de Régimen Local de Catalunya*/TRLMRLC). Also relevant is the Catalan Decree 179/1995 of 13 June which approves the Regulation of any works, activities and services done by local entities (*Reglamento de obras, actividades y servicios de las entidades locales*/ROAS). Both these measures

19 Available at: https://www.sindicaturabarcelona.cat/wp-content/uploads/2022/05/05_Resolucio-Nous-Eixos-Verds.pdf [Last accessed 27 February 2023].

indicate that works projects require only prior approval to proceed (Arts. 234–235 TRLMRLC and Arts. 8–54 ROAS).

Moreover, the mayor can approve works projects in Barcelona without having to go through a government commission or before a plenary session of the city council (Art. 69.2, Barcelona Municipal Charter). In fact, the authority to approve ordinary works projects has been delegated to various municipal bodies. These include the Government Commission (for works of more than €500,000.00 and less than €15,025,302.61) or the plenary of the Municipal Council (works involving more than 20% of regular budget resources). This is the case in accordance with the Protocol for processing projects and monitoring ordinary infrastructure and/or urban development, conservation and improvement works and urban development projects carried out by different municipal operators in Barcelona (*Butlletí Oficial de la Província de Barcelona/* BOP of 31 July 2017).

As if this were not enough, there have also been legal challenges to the restriction of certain economic activities as a result of the program. In some cases, the Barcelona City Council has done this by introducing urban planning regulations into the new superblocks.[20] A good example of this is what occurred in the Sant Antoni superblock neighborhood. A superblock was created there in 2018 and was immediately followed up by the approval of a new "Special Plan for public establishments and other activities in the Sant Antoni neighborhood" (BOP of 15 October 2018). This special plan was meant to introduce several restrictions on carrying out certain recreational economic activities in the area. The aim was to make these activities more compatible with resident needs. These restrictive measures were quickly challenged in the courts by some of the affected residents and traders. They felt the planned restrictions infringed on their constitutionally guaranteed right to freedom of enterprise. They also asserted the measures did not meet the requirements of being of overriding general interest, proportional, and non-discriminatory pursuant to Article 9.8 of the TRLUCat.

Judgment No. 3.308/2021 of 6 June (ECLI:ES:TSJCAT:2021:7052) of the High Court of Catalonia (*Tribunal Superior de Justicia de Catalunya*) dismissed this challenge, however, on several grounds. With reference to constitutional jurisprudence, the judgement stated that freedom of enterprise does not include an unconditional right to freely set up of any commercial establishment in any space and without complying with any requirements or conditions. As noted above, the related plan sought to balance residential,

20 These limitations have also been a source of political tension between the different political parties that currently make up Barcelona's city government. They had difficulties in reaching an agreement on the new Use Plan relating to the green axes in Ensanche, which almost led to the disbanding of the city government. However, the related "Special plan for the regulation of public activities, food shops and other activities in the Ensanche district" (BOP of 22 February 2023) was finally approved in the end.

commercial and tertiary uses, while considering impacts on the urban space and landscape. Therefore, the judgement noted that the plan did align, in fact, with the overriding general interest. As such, applying restrictions to certain activities was allowable. In the opinion of the High Court, the measures adopted were thus sufficiently justified, proportionate to the objectives pursued and documented in the memorandum on the contested regulation.

3.4 Toward a conclusion

We have now come to the end of our discussion and might ask ourselves in concluding, "What ideas merit highlighting in the Barcelona superblocks model?". First, the overall general importance of this initiative should be emphasized in our opinion. Going beyond the initial doubts and reticence by affected residents, as well as the legal questions arising, the fact is that we are facing a major urban transformation in the city of Barcelona, probably the most significant one since the 1992 Olympic Games.

Above all, we believe this project stands out because of its objectives. That is, it is committed to creating a more sustainable urban mobility system for Barcelona. This will make it possible to claim back the city's public spaces, neighborhoods and streets for its inhabitants. It will also reduce noise, pollution and the other externalities generated by motor vehicles.

It is certainly too early to assess whether the Barcelona superblocks model will really achieve these goals. There are some reports that implementing the Barcelona Superblock Program will lead to more congestion on main transport routes, given that 80% of drivers come to the center from outside the city.[21] On the other hand, superblocks may lead to a growing fragmentation of the urban area.[22] Others point out that creating superblocks has already brought measurable environmental and health benefits. They urge even more rapid and comprehensive implementation of them throughout Barcelona.[23]

The above discussion also raises extra-legal issues. Be that as it may, I would like to end my presentation by referring to one last idea. That is, the need to make measures compatible with the undeniably metropolitan nature of public mobility policies. The Barcelona City Council has made efforts to promote measures aimed at improving traffic and air quality in the city. Despite this, environmental and mobility policies clearly have a supra-municipal or metropolitan dimension. These kinds of measures extend beyond the strict administrative limits of the municipality of Barcelona into neighboring municipalities.

21 RACC (2021) *Report. Impacto en la movilidad del proyecto de Superilla Barcelona en el Eixample.*

22 Lluís Frago Clols, 'Fragmentación urbana y comercio de proximidad: Un ensayo sobre el proyecto Superilla en Barcelona' (2022) 8 *Tlalli. Revista de Investigación en Geografía* 132–133.

23 Barcelona Institute for Global Health ISGLOBAL (2022) *Scientific Report – L'Impacte sobre la Salut de les Superilles de Barcelona* 45–46.

In our opinion, this is why responding to the problems that arise should not be tackled in a merely isolated way. Rather, it must involve using legal-organizational tools that allow a coordinated joint response by the different municipalities affected.

This is precisely where the Metropolitan Area of Barcelona (*Área Metropolitana de Barcelona*), created by the Law of the Parliament of Catalonia 31/2010 of 3 August (known as LAMB), can play a relevant role. This law involves 36 municipalities, including the city of Barcelona and a total population of approximately 3,400,000 inhabitants. It sees the Metropolitan Area of Barcelona as a new level of territorial government with a multi-functional sphere of action. In this way, it may assume an important role in establishing metropolitan public mobility policies.

This Law regulating the Metropolitan Area of Barcelona attributes important powers over public transport (the metro and buses) and taxis [Art. 14 B) LAMB]. Despite this, the Metropolitan Area has had only a limited impact on the circulation of other motor vehicle traffic as yet. Its responsibilities in this area are mainly focused on coordinating and planning functions and approving the Metropolitan Plan for Urban Mobility [Art. 14 B) LAMB]. However, the Metropolitan Area is not directly empowered to regulate the use of urban roads within its territory (which is a municipal responsibility). We believe this limiting of power undermines effective metropolitan action as we have pointed out elsewhere.[24] For example, it makes municipal action necessary whenever mobility policies are to be implemented and this means seeking approval under the corresponding municipal ordinances or urban planning regulations involved.

In short, we believe that in large urban areas and mobility-enhancing municipal projects, we need to contemplate introducing a metropolitan dimension and designing this into certain public policies. The superblock program in Barcelona is a good example of one such policy. Doing this will allow us to have a more comprehensive vision of the *real city*. This, in turn, may highlight problems that are sometimes more difficult to detect at the municipal level.

Bibliography

Ayuntamiento de Barcelona (2021) *Encuesta de movilidad en un día laborable*. Available at: https://ajuntament.barcelona.cat/estadistica/catala/Estadistiques_per_temes/Transport_i_mobilitat/Mobilitat/Enquesta_mobilitat_dia_feiner/index.htm.

Ayuntamiento de Barcelona (2015) *Pla de Mobilitat Urbana de Barcelona. PMU 2013–2018*. Available at: https://ajuntament.barcelona.cat/ecologiaurbana/sites/default/files/PMU-BCN-2013-2018_Introduccio_i_diagnosi.pdf

24 Marc Vilalta Reixach, 'Las áreas metropolitanas en España. Propuestas para una reforma', in Tomàs Font i Llovet (ed.), *Repensant el Govern Local: cap a la fi de la uniformitat* (Institut d'Estudis de l'Autogovern 2023), pp. 95–99.

Ayuntamiento de Barcelona (2015) *Compromís ciutadà per la sostenibilitat.* Available at: https://ajuntament.barcelona.cat/ecologiaurbana/sites/default/files/CompromisCiutadaSostenibilitat.pdf

Ayuntamiento de Barcelona (2016) *Omplim de vida els carrers. La implantació de les Superilles a Barcelona.* Available at: https://bcnroc.ajuntament.barcelona.cat/jspui/bitstream/11703/97356/1/mesuradegovernomplimdevidaelscarrerslaimplantacidelessuperi-160518111846.pdf

Ayuntamiento de Barcelona (2020) *Declaración de emergencia climática.* Available at: https://www.barcelona.cat/emergenciaclimatica/es

Ayuntamiento de Barcelona (2021) *Medida de gobierno. Superilla Barcelona para regenerar Barcelona y sus barrios.* Available at: https://bcnroc.ajuntament.barcelona.cat/jspui/bitstream/11703/126249/1/Llibret_SUPERILLA_MdG_A4_ES_web%20%282%29.pdf

Ayuntamiento de Barcelona (2021) *Procés participatiu Superilla Barcelona a l'Eixample. Informe final [09/12/2021].* Available at: https://ajuntament.barcelona.cat/superilles/sites/default/files/20220329_Informe_participacio_versiofinal.pdf

Ayuntamiento de Barcelona (2022) *Supermanzanas crece en el Eixample.* Available at: https://ajuntament.barcelona.cat/superilles/es/superilla/eixample#

Barcelona Institute for Global Health ISGLOBAL (2022) *Informe Científic – L'Impacte sobre la Salut de les Superilles de Barcelona.*

Boix Palop, A., 'Los desafíos internacionales de la regulación de la movilidad urbana y la nueva agenda urbana', en Fortes Martín, A. (ed.) *Movilidad urbana sostenible y acción administrativa* (Thomson Reuters – Aranzadi 2019).

Comisión de Ecología, Urbanismo y Movilidad, *Omplim de vida els carrers. La implantació de les Superilles a Barcelona* (Ayuntamiento de Barcelona 2016). Available at: https://bcnroc.ajuntament.barcelona.cat/jspui/bitstream/11703/97356/1/mesuradegovernomplimdevidaelscarrerslaimplantacidelessuperi-160518111846.pdf

Font i Llovet, T., 'El significat del règim especial de Barcelona i el seu impuls per a un nou dret de la ciutat', en Tomás Font i Llovet, T. (ed.) *La Carta Municipal de Barcelona i el dret de la ciutat* (Ajuntament de Barcelona 2022) 25.

Frago Clols, L.l., 'Fragmentación urbana y comercio de proximidad: Un ensayo sobre el proyecto Superilla en Barcelona' (2022) 8 *Tlalli. Revista de Investigación en Geografía* 116.

Guijarro Turégano, B., *Repensar los cruces: la implementación del modelo Superilles: el caso de la Superilla del Poblenou de Barcelona (2016–2021)* (Universitat de Barcelona 2022).

Ministerio de Transportes, Movilidad y Agenda Urbana (2022) *Áreas urbanas en España 2022.*

RACC , *Informe. Impacto en la movilidad del proyecto de Superilla Barcelona en el Eixample* (2021).

Ramírez Sánchez, J.M., *Urbanismo para una nueva ciudad. El principio de desarrollo urbano sostenible* (Thomson Reuters – Aranzadi 2021).

Rueda Palenzuela, S., 'Les superilles per al disseny de noves ciutats i la renovació de les existents. El cas de Barcelona' (2017) 59 *Papers. Regió Metropolitana de Barcelona* 78.

Simou, S., *Derecho Local del Cambio Climático* (Marcial Pons 2020).

Vilalta Reixach, M., 'Las áreas metropolitanas en España. Propuestas para una reforma', in Tomás Font i Llovet (ed.): *Repensant el Govern Local: cap a la fi de la uniformitat* (Institut d'Estudis de l'Autogovern 2023) 65.

4 València selected European Green City 2024

Clàudia Gimeno Fernández

4.1 Introduction: The European Green Capital Awards as soft policy instruments of the European Union regarding green urban planning

Policy and regulatory decisions play a critical role in guiding and accelerating the transition towards more sustainable urban models, as they effectively address blockages and entrenched misconceptions.[1] These decisions can be categorized into three main types of instruments: regulatory, financial or economic, and soft law.[2] Regulatory instruments encompass laws, standards, plans, technical requirements, environmental certificates, and other mechanisms that establish a set of rules to be followed. Financial instruments provide economic incentives or disincentives, such as subsidies, grants, financial aid, and tradable permits. On the other hand, soft instruments are informative, incentive-based, and voluntary in nature. They include policies aimed at improving education and information dissemination, establishing knowledge and innovation platforms, and promoting competition for prizes.[3]

For this reason, amid the various instruments that the European Union provides for the development and exercise of its environmental competences (Articles 11 and 191 to 193 of the Treaty on the Functioning of the European Union), a series of actions is also contemplated through soft law instruments. These instruments include various actions. Among them, in addition to promoting the adoption of agreements and the dissemination of information among municipalities through the Green City Accord,[4] the European Green

1 Alexander van der Jagt, Laura Tozer, Helen Toxopeus and Hens Runhaar, 'Policy mixes for mainstreaming urban nature-based solutions: An analysis of six European countries and the European Union' (2023) 139 *Environmental Science & Policy* 51.

2 Rüdiger K.W. Wurzel, Anthony R. Zito and Andrew J. Jordan, *Environmental Governance in Europe. A Comparative Analysis of New Environmental Policy Instruments* (Edward Elgar Publishing 2014).

3 Pieter J. Beers and Florentien Geerling-Eiff, 'Networks as policy instruments for innovation' (2014) 20(4) *The Journal of Agricultural Education and Extension* 36.

4 The Green City Accord is a movement of European mayors committed to making cities cleaner and healthier. It aims to improve the quality of life for all Europeans and accelerate the

DOI: 10.4324/9781032665184-14

Capital Award and the European Green Leaf Award, competitions opened by the EU to reward state-of-the-art practice by cities, stand out.

The concept of a European Green Capital originated during a meeting held in Tallinn, Estonia, in May 2006. This prestigious accolade is the outcome of a collaborative effort by 15 European cities (Tallinn, Helsinki, Riga, Vilnius, Berlin, Warsaw, Madrid, Ljubljana, Prague, Vienna, Kiel, Kotka, Dartford, Tartu, and Glasgow) and the Association of Estonian cities. Together, they presented the Tallinn Memorandum to the European Commission, proposing the establishment of an award that recognizes cities at the forefront of environmentally conscious urban living. In May 2008, the European Commission officially launched this initiative, and since 2010 each year a European city is chosen to be honored as the European Green Capital.

These awards acknowledge cities as key catalysts for driving change and implementing the European Green Deal.[5] Through them, the European Commission recognizes and rewards local efforts to improve the environment, and thereby the economy and the quality of life in cities.

The awards are an integral part of the the financial instrument for the environment or L'Instrument Financier pour l'Environnement (LIFE) Program, which provides for the financing of activities implemented by the Commission (such as the awarding of prizes) in support of the preparation, implementation, and integration of EU environmental and climate legislation and policies.[6] Consequently, the responsibility for managing these awards lies with the European Commission, specifically the Directorate General for Environment (DG ENV), in accordance with the Multiannual Work Program LIFE.

The existence of two awards (the European Green Capital Award and the European Green Leaf Award) responds to the different scale of the participating cities. The first one involves a financial award of €600,000 to the winning city and the second one of €200,000 per winning city.[7] The guidelines for granting

implementation of relevant EU environmental laws. By signing the accord, cities commit to addressing five areas of environmental management: air, water, nature and biodiversity, circular economy and waste, and noise. As of December 2022, 102 mayors have signed the agreement thanks to the support of the European Commission and have committed to take more measures in terms of air and water quality and management, waste/circular economy, nature/biodiversity, and noise to make their cities cleaner, greener, and healthier by 2030.

5 European Commission, 'How can your city become… the next European Green Capital?' (2020) https://environment.ec.europa.eu/topics/urban-environment/european-green-capital-award/about-awards/toolkits/green-capital-toolkit_en#how-can-your-city-become-the-next-european-green-capital.

6 Articles 5 and 6 of the Regulation (EU) 2021/783 of the European Parliament and of the Council, of 29 April 2021, establishing a Program for the Environment and Climate Action (LIFE), and repealing Regulation (EU) No 1293/2013.

7 After witnessing the achievements of the European Green Capital Award, numerous smaller cities expressed their desire for EU acknowledgment of their endeavors and dedication to sustainability and the environment. In response, the European Commission introduced the European Green Leaf Award initiative in 2015. This initiative focuses on cities with populations ranging from 20,000 to 100,000, acknowledging their commitment to achieving improved environ-

these prizes are outlined in the annual document "Call for Applications – Rules of Contest European Green Capital & Leaf Award".[8] This document specifies a limited number of criteria that cities must fulfill in order to be eligible for the award. Some of these requirements include the following:

Cities must be associated with the LIFE program at the time of the closing date of the call. It should be noted, in this regard, that it is not necessary for them to be cities in the European Union, and that cities in the European Economic Area countries (as well as EU candidate countries) can also participate in the call and win the award as long as they are associated with the LIFE program.

To be eligible for the European Green Capital, cities must have more than 100,000 inhabitants and, for the European Green Leaf, between 20,000 and 100,000 inhabitants. In countries where there is no city with more than 100,000 inhabitants, the largest city is eligible to apply.

In any given year, cities can apply for either the European Green Capital Award or the European Green Leaf Award, but not both at the same time.

Previous winners of the European Green Capital Award or European Green Leaf Award titles are not eligible to apply again.

In addition, the city applying must prove that it has a consistent record of achieving high environmental standards; is committed to ongoing and ambitious goals for further environmental improvement and sustainable development, and can act as a role model to inspire other cities and promote best practices to all other European cities.

The evaluation process consists of two steps. First, a technical assessment is carried out by a panel of seven international and independent experts. This technical assessment considers, in addition to the candidature submitted by the city, whether the city is affected by infringements in the field of EU environmental legislation (or equivalent important procedures in cities outside the EU). Secondly, a final assessment is made by the jury appointed by the European Commission,[9] taking into account the technical opinion of the experts and the factors presented by the Commission. On the basis of the jury's assessment, the Commission, as the awarding body, decides on the award of the prize. Entries are assessed on the basis of 7 indicators: air quality; water; biodiversity, green areas and sustainable land use; waste and circular economy; noise; climate change mitigation; and climate change adaptation.

---

mental outcomes, with a special emphasis on initiatives that foster green growth and create new employment opportunities.

8 European Commission, 'EGCA-EGLA 2025 – Rules of Contest with Annexes' (2023).

9 The jury is composed of members from 1) the European Commission's Directorate General for the Environment (Chair); 2) the European Parliament; 3) the European Committee of the Regions and/or the European Economic and Social Committee; 4) the European Environment Agency; and 5) city organizations and environmental non-governmental organizations.

Central to the process is the city's overall strategy, vision, and commitment to sustainability and its implementation in practice. The city's communication strategy and actions for its role as European Green Capital or Leaf are also taken into account. Of particular relevance are the actions planned in terms of communication, involvement, and driving changes in citizen behavior and the city's ability to showcase its sustainability vision and plans at the local and regional levels and to inspire other European cities. In this sense, concrete initiatives and measures should be proposed that exemplify the capacity of local planning to achieve the objectives of the European Green Deal, in particular those specified in the Zero Pollution Action Plan, the Biodiversity Strategy and Circular Economy Action Plan, and the Fit for 55 Package.

To support the winning cities in this effort, the European Commission condenses a list of activities to be carried out during the European Green Capital year into a non-binding agreement, called a "Letter of Intent", between DG ENV of the European Commission and the winning city. This Charter is complemented by the elaboration of concrete monitoring guidelines, an evaluation of the impact of the Green Capital/European Leaf title, as well as a communication toolbox.

Launched in 2008 and awarded for the first time in 2010 to Stockholm, the city of València has been selected as the European Green Capital for 2024 by the European Commission on the basis of a very comprehensive project that seeks to combine the potential of the city itself with the use of European recovery and resilience funds to advance towards the goal of meeting the United Nations Sustainable Development Goals and making the city carbon neutral by 2030.[10] The following sections of this chapter analyze the strategy implemented by the city, its planning instruments and key milestones, as well as the reasons why València should be understood as an example of the path to be followed by European cities in order to make progress. It will focus on the different legal and planning instruments developed in the city. Specifically, section 10.3 "València's Green and Biodiversity Plan" analyses in depth the Green and Biodiversity Plan of the city of València (2023), the key instrument of València's municipality's candidacy.

4.2 València's candidacy for the European Green Capital Awards: Key milestones

València's achievement in winning the European Green Capital Awards can be attributed to the conjunction of multiple factors. Firstly, the city benefits from a rich and diverse array of green spaces and biodiversity as part of its existing

10 València follows in the wake of Vitoria-Gasteiz, the first Spanish city to receive this award. Maite Uriarte Ricorte, 'Planificar la infraestructura verde urbana' (2014) 99–100 *Revista Vasca de Administración Pública* 2873, analyzes the strengths of the environmental policy that justified the selection of Vitoria-Gasteiz as the first European Green Capital.

heritage. Secondly, significant efforts have been made in recent years to implement numerous actions and policies aimed at enhancing, expanding, and making these green spaces more climate-neutral and environmentally sustainable while also respecting biodiversity. And lastly, València has recently developed a range of instruments at both the local and regional levels to safeguard, plan, and effectively manage this infrastructure for long-term sustainability.

As regards the first factor, the municipality of València boasts a well-developed system of green spaces. Notably, the Turia river, l'Albufera, and l'Horta de València contribute to preserving valuable environmental and cultural resources. These areas hold a deep-rooted heritage associated with water usage, featuring architectural and ethnological elements of high historical value, all connected through an intricate irrigation network. The presence of these spaces directly enhances the city's well-being and quality of life for its residents. Situated on the outskirts of the urban landscape, they serve as a buffer between the city and its rural or coastal surroundings. These spaces are complemented by a consolidated network of parks, gardens, and green areas – including certain spaces of great value for the city's biodiversity and which provide numerous ecosystemic and social services, such as the Turia and the Cabecera parks. These areas hold significant biodiversity value and offer various ecosystemic and social benefits.[11]

Regarding recent actions, we can highlight several notable initiatives. Firstly, there has been significant progress in pedestrianization, particularly in the historic center of the city. This measure not only contributes to the reduction of pollution levels but also enables the implementation of soil permeabilization measures and the introduction of plant species in areas previously occupied by roads.

Another noteworthy development is the establishment of a low-pressure water network for secondary uses. This system simulates the natural water cycle by returning the water extracted for irrigation of green areas back to the aquifer through infiltration. This approach, implemented by the València City Council in 2021, promotes sustainability and efficient water management. In addition, the València City Council has published documents like the Basic Guide for the Design of Sustainable Urban Drainage Systems. This guide provides valuable insights for incorporating environmentally friendly drainage systems into urban infrastructure.

The city council has also taken initiatives to naturalize urban spaces and promote biodiversity. This shift towards a more holistic approach to gardening

11 Ajuntament de València, 'Pla Verd i de la Biodiversitat de València' (2023), points out that in the specific case of large city parks and gardens, where the ecosystem services offered by green areas are found in greater abundance, about 82% of the census population in València has one within a distance of 1 km. Likewise, about 90% of the population has a large city park or a neighborhood park within 250 meters of their home. As a result, the available green area per inhabitant in València, while not uniformly distributed throughout the city, exceeds 10 square meters in 24 neighborhoods.

and ecological balance is evident through the development of naturalized meadows and urban orchards. Additionally, the installation of shelters for birds and bats, the introduction of beneficial fauna, the utilization of solar energy, and the increased presence of native vegetation and tree species all contribute to the enhancement of urban biodiversity. These combined efforts reflect a growing commitment to sustainable practices and a desire to create a greener and more environmentally conscious city in València.

Lastly, several planning instruments have been implemented in recent years to guide sustainable development. These include the Sustainable Urban Mobility Plan, the València 2030 Urban Strategy, and the Sustainable Energy and Climate Action Plan. These plans are designed to address various aspects of urban sustainability, including transportation, land use, energy efficiency, and climate change mitigation. Furthermore, the city has also adopted the Green and Biodiversity Plan, which will be discussed further in the following section.

A sustainable urban mobility plan is a tool used to help cities change their mobility model and show the way towards more sustainable and efficient mobility patterns. A mobility plan analyses the existing situation and problems, and proposes various mobility strategies, which include guidelines for the development of policies, actions, and transport infrastructures in the city. These guidelines must be translated into a set of coherent and coordinated proposals that encourage a change in habits, and make sustainable mobility more attractive. The València City Council approved an urban mobility plan in December 2013. The Sustainable Urban Mobility Plan of València carries out a comprehensive analysis of the forms of mobility in the city, in accordance with the criteria and objectives of Law 6/2011 of April 1, on Mobility in the Valèncian Community. Within this plan, green areas are recognized as appealing spaces for the community. Additionally, it emphasizes the promotion of public transportation with the aim of transforming roads into environmentally friendly routes, such as greenways, bicycle lanes, pedestrian paths, and boulevards. The plan asserts that the presence of green areas and recreational spaces plays a vital role in encouraging walking as a preferred mode of transportation. Recognizing this, the plan seeks to enhance the availability and accessibility of such areas to further motivate people to choose walking as a means of travel.

For its part, the València 2030 Urban Strategy develops, at the municipal level, a set of strategic priorities and specific objectives that position the city in alignment with the innovation and urban policies advocated by the European Union.[12] These strategies are developed in response to global challenges such

12 Although the European Union does not have explicit competences in relation to the regulation of territory or urban planning, it does have a determining power in planning through different sectoral competences and promotion policies, such as environmental or cohesion policy. On the other hand, the European Union has played a leading role in spatial and urban

as climate change and post-COVID-19 recovery, reflecting their local implications. The strategy serves as a guiding framework for the necessary transformations aimed at ensuring a dignified, healthy, and sustainable quality of life for future generations. Within the realm of green planning, the strategy incorporates the principles of Healthy City and Sustainable City approaches, which aim to improve the environment by fostering healthier lifestyles and defining the relationship between people and their surroundings. Additionally, the strategy emphasizes the values of territorial respect, biodiversity conservation, and the integration of urban green spaces. Of particular importance is Strategic Line 1: Climate resilience, territory, and renaturation of the city. This strategic line focuses on enhancing the city's connectivity with its surrounding territory through the integration of green infrastructure. It also addresses the imperative need for climate change adaptation, considering the city's coastal location. By embracing these principles and objectives, the València 2030 Urban Strategy sets a comprehensive framework for sustainable urban development, encompassing both environmental and societal considerations.

The Urban Agriculture Plan of València, passed in 2021, is the roadmap that programs the necessary actions to promote urban agriculture in the city of València. Among its objectives are the recovery of the links with l'Horta (the orchard that surrounds the city) and the promotion of the agro-ecological model, the recognition of the environmental services provided by urban agriculture, the definition of the criteria for its implementation or development and the lift of its social benefits. In this sense, it foresees the incorporation of urban agriculture in public spaces, municipal facilities and educational institutions, as well as in the domestic, community and social spheres, and also plans the development of demonstrative and informative forms of urban agriculture.[13]

---

planning through intergovernmental dialogue, albeit within the framework of what is understood as soft law, as they are generally agreements without binding effects. Nevertheless, these instruments [including the Urban Agenda for the EU (2016) or the Territorial Agenda 2030 (2020)] have helped to develop and introduce urban policies in many member statesthat did not have them, in addition to promoting the convergence of spatial planning systems in the Member States. In this sense, Dallhammer Erich, Gaugitsch Roland, Neugebauer Wolfgang, and Böhme Kai, 'Spatial planning and governance within EU policies and legislation and their relevance to the New Urban Agenda' (Publications Office of the European Union 2018) and David Evers and Joost Tennekes, 'Europe exposed: Mapping the impacts of EU policies on spatial planning in the Netherlands' (2015) 24(10) *European Planning Studies*, 1747.

13 The Urban Agriculture Plan outlines several key action areas aimed at promoting and enhancing urban agriculture within the city. These actions include the incorporation of agricultural practices into urban spaces, such as rooftops, parks, and vacant lots, to create sustainable and productive green areas; the promotion of biodiversity in urban agriculture spaces, the improvement of the coordination of initiatives in this area at the city level, the reconnection of the orchard with the city, and the visibility and support for urban agriculture initiatives. By implementing these actions, the Urban Agriculture Plan aims to create a more sustainable, resilient, and interconnected urban landscape that embraces the benefits of urban agriculture while enhancing the quality of life for its residents.

Finally, the Climate and Sustainable Energy Action Plan, ratified in April 2019 in accordance with the Covenant of Mayors for Climate and Energy, presents a forward-looking vision to address the imperative of attaining sustainable energy and effectively adapting the city to climate change challenges. This action plan centers around two core priorities: climate justice and energy democracy, aiming to guarantee equitable distribution of social, environmental, energy, and economic benefits. The Climate and Sustainable Energy Action Plan for the city of València is structured around two documents: the Baseline Emissions Inventory and the Climate Risk and Vulnerability Assessment. These documents serve as the foundation for developing strategies and initiatives that target emission reductions, climate risk management, and resilience building.

In addition to these local planning instruments, it should be noted that the Valèncian proposal is backed by a highly developed (by Spanish standards) regional planning.[14] In this regard, the Territorial Strategy of the Valèncian Community, passed in 2011 and whose functions include the definition of appropriate strategies for the planning and management of green infrastructure and for the management of the Valèncian territory, stands out. Other relevant regional plans develop its principles, such as the Territorial Action Plan for the Coastal Green Infrastructure, and the Territorial Action Plan for the Management and Revitalization of the l'Horta de València, which protects the green infrastructure and the agricultural lands that form it. It also specifically protects, in the municipality of València, around 2.375 hectares of productive orchard, granting the highest degree of protection to more than 60% of this area, and outlines possible corridors for linking these high-value agricultural pockets with each other and with the Albufera and Turia natural parks.

4.3 València's Green and Biodiversity Plan (2023)

After a two-year drafting period led by a technical team hired by the city council, the Green and Biodiversity Plan of València (*Pla Verd i de la Biodiversitat de València*) was officially adopted on April 27, 2023, during a city council plenary session. In the following analysis, we will inquire into the plan's most noteworthy aspects from the political and regulatory perspectives, including its regulatory nature, the public participation process, and its objectives and key elements. Prior to delving into this analysis, it is important to examine the 1994 Green Plan, a pioneering initiative for green planning in València.

14 Spain has frequently been criticized by experts for its lagging behind other EU Member States in environment protection and territorial planning. In this sense, Elin Slätmo, Kjell Nilsson, and Eeva Turunen, 'Implementing green infrastructure in spatial planning in Europe' (2019) 8(4) *Land 62*.

Although this pilot project was never officially approved, it has played a pivotal role in shaping the development of the Green and Biodiversity Plan of 2023.

4.3.1 A strong precedent for València's Green and Biodiversity Plan: The 1994 València's Green Plan

The pilot project of the Special Green Plan for the city of València was an ambitious, pioneer, and innovative project presented in a report to the European Commission in February 1997. It was a project elaborated during the years 1992 –1997 by the València City Council thanks to the sponsorship of the LIFE Program of the European Commission and the Man and the Biosphere Program of UNESCO. The Green Plan intended to develop measures that made it possible for citizens, both in urban and peri-urban areas of their city, to aspire to a better quality of life with an environment without aggression, compensated and with a reality of urban and peri-urban sustainability.

València's 1994 Green Plan was never approved nor executed. From the regulatory point of view, the Green Plan was articulated as a special plan (an urban development planning instrument in accordance with the Spanish Land Law of 1992) and provided for the approval of different binding regulatory instruments (to control and regulate uses and activities and situations affecting the urban landscape). The plan also provided for the revision of different municipal ordinances.

In a scenario that is certainly different from that of that time, in which concepts such as sustainability or climate change were just beginning to be heard, the 2023 Green and Biodiversity Plan builds on the work carried out for the development of that 1994 pilot project. Thus, in its elaboration, the 1994 plan is taken as a precedent or essential basis, and its approaches are updated according to current concerns and situation.

4.3.2 The regulatory nature of València's Green and Biodiversity Plan in the context of Spanish green infrastructure planning

Spanish environmental regulations at both state and regional levels do not regulate or foresee the possibility of approving regulatory plans for municipal green infrastructure. As a result, when deciding on the models and characteristics of a green infrastructure plan, two main alternatives can be considered. The first alternative involves conceiving a green plan as a strategic document that lacks binding legal force. This approach relies on soft law techniques, which offer guidelines and recommendations rather than mandatory requirements. The second alternative entails establishing an urban planning-type plan with legally binding effects, aligning with what is commonly referred to as hard law.

While the first option remains discretionary, it does find support in the Spanish Strategy for Green Infrastructure and Ecological Connectivity and

Restoration, approved by Order PCM/735/2021, of July 9, in accordance with art. 15 of Law 42/2007, of December 13, 2007, on Natural Heritage and Biodiversity.[15] The primary aim of the National Strategy is to provide guidelines for identifying and conserving the components of green infrastructure in Spain, including both terrestrial and marine elements. It seeks to ensure that territorial and sectoral planning undertaken by public administrations facilitates and guarantees ecological connectivity, functional ecosystems, climate change mitigation and adaptation, the restoration of degraded ecosystems, and the de-fragmentation of strategic areas for connectivity. In line with this objective, the strategy promotes the establishment of local planning and management initiatives for green infrastructure. It emphasizes the importance of undertaking actions at multiple scales to effectively address the challenges and opportunities in this domain.

The definition of a green plan as a strategic document implies, therefore, understanding this instrument as a non-urban planning technique for the natural, ecological, environmental, and landscape resources and values of the city. This means developing an instrument without clear requirements regarding its potential content, scope, or depth and whose proposals will not have normative effectiveness. Instead, they serve as a political or executive guideline, complemented by potential proposals for reforming local ordinances.

Cities like Barcelona and Madrid have adopted the approach of a strategic and non-binding green plan. Their proposals do not possess legal enforceability but rather establish guidelines and methodologies for their development. Essentially, they represent a soft technique for non-urban planning, focusing on the conservation and management of natural, ecological, environmental, and landscape resources within the city.

For instance, in Barcelona, following the adoption of the Green and Biodiversity Plan 2011–2020 (*Pla del verd i de la biodiversitat 2011–2020*) the Nature Plan Barcelona 2021–2030 (*Pla Natura Barcelona 2030*) was passed in 2021. Like its predecessor, the Nature Plan is a strategic instrument that serves three main purposes: (1) defining the challenges, strategies, and commitments of the municipal government in relation to the preservation of green areas and biological diversity; (2) conducting a situational analysis, assessing the current state of green spaces within the city, and establishing a vision along with quantitative objectives; and (3) outlining an action

15 The regulatory framework protecting most of the environmental elements addressed by the National Strategy for Green Infrastructure and Ecological Connectivity and Restoration is contained in Law 42/2007. Among the instruments provided for in the law, mention should be made of the Natural Resources Management Plans, as they are the specific instrument for the delimitation, classification, and integration into a network of the systems that make up the natural heritage and resources of a given spatial area and for the determination of their relationship with the rest of the territory. The law also establishes the regime for the cataloging, conservation, and restoration of habitats and natural heritage areas, which includes the most important elements of the Green Infrastructure and some of the protection measures.

plan that comprises 20 actions and 100 specific projects organized into three key axes ("expanding green spaces and enhancing biodiversity", "conserving and improving green areas and biodiversity", and "engaging citizens in ecological infrastructure enhancement"). The Madrid Green Infrastructure and Biodiversity Plan passed in 2018 (*Plan de Infraestructura Verde y Biodiversidad*) conducts an assessment of the city's natural heritage and its management, establishing a set of strategic objectives, lines of action, and measures that outline guidelines for conserving, improving, and enhancing the city's green heritage. The plan incorporates provisions for monitoring and evaluation, defining aspects related to implementation and effectiveness. Additionally, it lays the groundwork for the development of a new ordinance concerning the protection and promotion of urban green infrastructure and biodiversity.

On the other hand, cities like Salamanca have adopted the second approach, considering green infrastructure planning as a binding urban planning instrument. That is why in Salamanca, the Special Plan for the Protection of Green Infrastructure and Biodiversity passed in 2019 (*Plan Especial de Protección de Infraestructura Verde y Biodiversidad*) is formulated in accordance with Law 5/99, of April 8, 1999, on Urban Planning of Castilla y León. The plan aims to safeguard natural values and promote ecosystem services in the municipality of Salamanca. It seeks to foster a new, greener, and more sustainable urban model that aligns with other strategic plans such as Tormes+ EDUSI, the Old City Management Plan, and the Sustainable Urban Mobility Plan.

In summary, while some cities opt for a strategic and non-binding approach to green infrastructure planning, exemplified by Barcelona and Madrid, others, such as Salamanca, choose a binding urban planning instrument to ensure the protection and enhancement of green infrastructure and biodiversity. These divergent approaches reflect the varying regulatory frameworks and local contexts within which cities operate.

València's Green and Biodiversity Plan is conceived as a strategic document without regulatory authority, following the approach adopted by plans in cities like Madrid and Barcelona. As a strategic document, its purpose is to integrate and coordinate the future green infrastructure of València with other relevant instruments for the city.

Although the Green and Biodiversity Plan does not possess immediate regulatory effectiveness, it does lay the foundations for potential future legal establishment through specific proposals. Its practicality and usefulness are emphasized all over the plan, ensuring that its outcomes can serve as a foundation for the creation or modification of municipal regulations related to the management, implementation, conservation, use, enjoyment, and remodeling of the city's green infrastructure in a broad sense. For instance, the plan encourages the revision of municipal ordinances governing park and garden management, as well as urban planning regulations. By incorporating these proposals, the plan aims to provide a framework that can be legally implemented, should the decision be made to do so.

4.3.3 Main objectives of the plan

The Green and Biodiversity Plan of València is a strategic document that establishes the basis for taking advantage of the natural cycles within the city, understanding this territory as a great space of coexistence, more sustainable and resilient. The plan is structured and aimed at achieving six key objectives.

The first of these objectives refers to the necessary action in the area of climate emergency, and calls for adaptation and mitigation of its effects from the municipal level. This objective involves the proposal of measures to mitigate the special position of vulnerability in which València finds itself, due to its geographical location, in the face of a possible worsening of the adverse effects caused by the climate emergency. Its location in the alluvial area of the Turia river, its proximity to the coast, and the high level of impermeability of its soils make the metropolitan area a vulnerable area in the face of an uncertain context of exceptional meteorological episodes that could significantly alter the natural balances and the quality of life of its inhabitants. Thus, the first objective of the plan is to adapt València to the effects that this climatic emergency is already having on the city (by increasing the vegetation cover or optimizing the management of the integral water cycle) and to mitigate, from the local level, the sources that cause climate change, so that the city does not participate in the intensification of this phenomenon.

The second objective focuses on the protection of València's natural, social, and cultural heritage related to green and blue infrastructure. That is, the protection of the assets and values inherited from the city and that are part of the collective imagination of its citizens (its link to the agricultural landscape of the Horta, the Albufera, the Turia riverbed, its historic gardens, and unique trees, etc.). Yet the Green Plan goes beyond preserving existing heritage. It recognizes that urbanization processes have simplified the ecological dynamics of the urban ecosystem, resulting in increased reliance on external resources, heightened vulnerability to adversity, and a persistent state of imbalance. Therefore, as a third objective, the Green Plan seeks to restore complexity and biodiversity to the urban ecosystem. This entails creating a more resilient city that enhances the well-being and quality of life for its inhabitants. To achieve this, the plan emphasizes the restoration of lost biodiversity and the utilization of natural cycles within the city. Green areas will be transformed into more naturalistic, low-maintenance, and resilient spaces, embracing wilder and native species.

The fourth objective of the plan is to promote the connection between the city's green spaces and between these spaces and the regional green infrastructure. Thus, it contains proposals for the design of a multi-scale system that enhances this connection from the neighborhood level to the metropolitan area. This objective is intended to halt the fragmentation, degradation, and destruction of certain habitats of ecological and landscape interest in the city of València and its immediate surroundings. To this end, functional ecological connections are proposed in those places of opportunity that are strategic because of their location, such as the urban edges of contact between the city and the orchard, the coastline, or the Turia riverbeds.

Finally, objective 5 of the Green and Biodiversity Plan highlights the importance of dissemination and integration of the plan's principles. Its dissemination, from the perspective of generating in citizens ways of perceiving green infrastructure and urban biodiversity more in line with respect for natural cycles and the renaturalization of the urban environment. In addition, through the different mechanisms articulated through the public participation process and the resources generated in its drafting, the Green and Biodiversity Plan is committed to the construction of a new imaginary of València as a green city, resilient in ecological terms and adapted to the challenges posed by the climate emergency, which transcends the regional scale. A collective imaginary that should contribute, in turn, to the shared custody of a more complex and diverse urban landscape, product of the sum and synergy of both public and private initiatives.

This idea connects objective 5 with objective 6, which involves integrating criteria for the improvement of urban biodiversity into municipal policies, plans, and projects in a comprehensive manner. To this end, the plan offers a series of general guidelines to orient the elaboration of policies, plans, and projects of various kinds, aiming to create the conditions to increase the capacity of the urban environment to host biodiversity in a cross-cutting manner. Specifically, the Green and Biodiversity Plan proposes the adaptation of certain regulatory or procedural elements in its area of competence (for example, municipal ordinances or urbanization projects in public spaces) and suggests the creation of new ordinances or tools to introduce mechanisms to promote biodiversity in different areas of municipal management.

4.3.4 The process of public participation in its drafting

The development of the Green and Biodiversity Plan of València placed great importance on a collaborative public participation process. This process not only involved incorporating the knowledge of citizens and experts during the preparation of the plan but also aimed to communicate and disseminate it in order to engage citizens in its creation and subsequent implementation.

The participation process was not limited to a single step or phase of the plan. Instead, it followed more ambitious and deliberative models by incorporating participation throughout the entire drafting process. This approach ensured that participation was a structural element and took place in three fundamental phases.

The first phase involved presenting the plan and its timeline, during which the draft of the Public Participation Plan was prepared and the Plan's Driving Group was established. The Driving Group consisted of representatives from the local and regional administration, as well as experts from academia and the business sector, representing different social groups. The group met periodically to actively participate in the process and oversee the plan's progress. They also helped identify and propose new groups of experts.

In the phase dedicated to diagnosing the current state of the ecosystem and socio-environmental services of green infrastructure and urban biodiversity, a participatory approach was also adopted. This phase aimed to gather the perceptions of Valèncian citizens regarding the green and biodiversity of their city, as well as identify the problems, opportunities, and existing needs related to this infrastructure. Various participatory strategies were employed, including collaborative mapping involving both the general public and experts in the field, expert roundtables, discussion groups and debates, and experimental gardens to explore the benefits of biodiversity in València. Additionally, surveys and forms were conducted, targeting informal citizens, neighborhood associations, and organizations dedicated to environmental issues or those associated with green infrastructure in the city. Throughout this phase, ongoing meetings and collaborative work with the Plan's Driving Group were maintained. The Driving Group also reviewed and validated a second draft of the Public Participation Plan.

Lastly, citizen participation was also integrated into the phase of proposal development. This phase encompassed the information gathered from the diagnosis phase as well as a new participatory call for the collection of information and proposals from all citizens. To this end, the territorial variable of the city was divided into various scales (individual, neighborhood, district, and supra-neighborhood) and demographics (children, youth, adults, and seniors), and their opinions were incorporated using diverse information-gathering techniques. This phase of citizen participation concluded with the organization of a reflective and debate conference on the future green infrastructure of València, involving experts and specialists in the field. During this conference, the analysis results from both the drafting team and citizen participation were compared. The proposals generated from this phase were then reviewed and validated by the Driving Group, which also contributed its own suggestions to the plan.

In addition to these mechanisms, numerous training activities and semi-structured interviews with different expert profiles, forms and surveys, etc., have been carried out in order to collect both quantitative and qualitative information and data from the aforementioned perspectives throughout the entire plan elaboration process.

4.3.5 Key elements of València's Green and Biodiversity Plan

The fundamental elements of the plan are to be found in the analysis and global diagnosis of the current situation and in the planning proposals it incorporates, both from the point of view of green infrastructure and from the perspective of its monitoring, validity, revision, and of the communication of its results.

With regard to the diagnosis of the current system, the plan carries out an in-depth study of the regulatory framework in which it is located and goes on to analyze the city's current green infrastructure, the ecosystemic and socio-environmental services it offers, and other relevant elements such as existing water resources and the composition and nature of the soil. All these elements are systematized, as well as in different graphics and visual elements, in a strenghts, weaknesses, opportunities and threats analysis of the state of the green infrastructure, green areas, roadside trees and ecosystemic and socio-environmental services. The analysis confirms that, in the scenario of climatic emergency that particularly urban environments suffer, the opportunities for improvement in this regard are very broad. Besides, it reinforces the usefulness of the initiatives indicated in section 10.2, which confirm that the local administration has been working in recent years on strategies that, at the end of the day, are aimed at improving the quality of urban green areas and the socio-environmental services they offer to citizens.

As regards initiatives and propositional actions, the plan incorporates specific policy proposals aimed at the preparation or modification of planning instruments (urban planning, renaturalization of city elements, improvement of urban greenery and biodiversity, landscaping of different elements of the Horta and elements linked to urban infrastructures) and at the execution of specific actions that are articulated through seven strategic lines: 1) more and better greenery; 2) ecological gardening, naturalization and biodiversity; 3) connectivity; 4) socio-environmental services; 5) resilience; 6) participation and biophilia, and 7) implementation of support actions to strengthen the regulatory linkage of the plan and to concretize the previous strategic lines in the administrative and regulatory reality. Likewise, a series of action plans are developed for each of the strategic lines, which together make up the Green Infrastructure Master Plan.

From the regulatory point of view, the Green and Biodiversity Plan proposes a review of relevant municipal regulations and the development of a dedicated ordinance specifically addressing green infrastructure and biodiversity. Furthermore, the plan emphasizes the need for measures that incentivize private actions aligned with its objectives. This could involve establishing incentive policies, offering public aid or tax rebates, to encourage activities such as the restoration of unused or underutilized architectural spaces and infrastructure, the creation of temporary green spaces in vacant urban areas, or the promotion of agroecology in the peri-urban orchards.

To do so, the Green and Biodiversity Plan primarily focuses on the municipality of València. However, it also considers the broader metropolitan area and the key elements of the regional green infrastructure. This approach ensures a cohesive integration with the system of green spaces at the municipal level. The plan's reflection and planning intensity vary depending on the different scales of the green infrastructure within the territory. Thus, for areas that extend beyond the municipal scale, such as l'Horta or l'Albufera, where existing protection and planning instruments are already in place, the Green and Biodiversity Plan's role is to integrate and coordinate these provisions at the local level, ensuring their alignment with other elements of the local green infrastructure. On the other hand, within the consolidated city and its immediate surroundings, where urgent strategies to address the climate emergency are required and where local authorities have specific powers for planning, the Green and Biodiversity Plan undertakes more intensive work. It examines the elements that constitute the green infrastructure at a local and/or urban scale, aiming to integrate protected spaces or elements at the municipal level with other significant spaces that possess strategic positions or hold cultural, natural, or visual value.

Lastly, the plan includes a comprehensive communication strategy to disseminate its results effectively. It also incorporates a monitoring and follow-up plan to ensure the implementation of the proposed actions. This involves the establishment of specific monitoring indicators tied to each strategic line of the plan and recommendations for periodic assessments to track progress and make necessary adjustments.

4.3.6 Main threats to the implementation of the València's Green and Biodiversity Plan

The implementation gap poses a significant challenge when it comes to green infrastructure. This term refers to the situation where the city's chosen urban greening strategy fails to materialize and is not put into action for diverse reasons.[16] During the drafting process of the Green Plan, some weaknesses or threats were identified that may hinder its implementation. Among them is the lack of regulatory effectiveness of the Green and Biodiversity Plan of València. This is because its legal concreteness (and the correct implementation of many of the proposals and strategic lines indicated) depends on the impulse of the municipal ordinances that could be derived from it. However, while this could be seen only as a weakness, it was also considered a strength of the plan as it allows 1) for a more ambitious approach that is not limited by existing political consensus at the time of approval, 2) more flexibility in its approach to the changing reality of the city, and 3) to provide a strategy for the adaptation of local regulations to the plan in the short, medium, and long term.

Likewise, by its nature, the plan is dependent on and subordinate to local planning instruments, which, since they do have normative efficacy, take precedence over the Green and Biodiversity Plan in any case. However, the confirmation of the principle of non-regression of planning in relation to urban

16 Bettina Wilk, Andreas Vetter and Alice Schröder, 'Tackling the climate and biodiversity crises in Europe through urban greening plans: Recommendations for avoiding the implementation gap' (2021) *Scientific Opinion Paper German Environment Agency* analyze and propose recommendations for avoiding the implementation gap. Some of them include 1) translating the overarching Urban Greening Strategy into Urban Greening Plans as operational plans with clear targets, timelines, and responsibilities, 2) needing to include a participation strategy for all relevant actors, accompanied by a communication/narrative guideline to raise awareness about ecological and social benefits of urban greening plans, 3) prioritizing nature and biodiversity over competing land use in planning instruments and targets, 4) including measurable targets and requiring regular reporting, and (5) linking the plan to existing funding options as well as innovative, multi-stakeholder business, investment models, and financing mechanisms.

green land and environmental protection by the Spanish Supreme Court[17] implies a limitation (insofar as it requires a reinforced motivation) to planning innovations that negatively affect the qualification of green areas or the classification of specially protected land.

Furthermore, the plan is also subject to the influence of planning instruments and the execution of strategic infrastructures that are not within the jurisdiction of the municipal administration but rather the responsibility of the Generalitat Valènciana or the Spanish central government. These infrastructure projects considered of general interest already approved or projected, such as port expansions or road and rail access expansions, can significantly condition the fulfilling of the plan's objectives in not a minor way.

In addition, there are other relevant elements that may hinder the impact of the Green and Biodiversity Plan. In the first place, the existing divergence between the green spaces considered in the General Urban Development Plan of València in force and those actually implemented, which is very noticeable. In the second place, the identification of certain green spaces that have been completed but do not meet the minimum standards necessary to consider that they truly contribute to improving the resilience of the local green infrastructure and the urban ecosystem. And, in the third place, the fact that the possibilities of significantly expanding the existing green spaces are reduced, since the remaining space classified as a green area in the General Plan in force and that has not been implemented at present is slightly less than 80 hectares, although it is true that the margin for improvement through the redevelopment of what is considered as implemented is very relevant.

4.4 Conclusions: Last ideas on the future of València as the European Green City 2024

At the time of writing this chapter, it has been known the electoral defeat at local and regional level of the left-wing parties that governed both the València City Council and the regional government, and who had been responsible for drawing up the Green Plan (and many other relatively ambitious regional planning instruments that protect the green infrastructure, as indicated before). These governments will be replaced, in June and July 2023, by coalitions of conservative parties that, especially in the case of the far-right party VOX, have clearly shown themselves to be against environmental policies, the fight against climate change and the protection of green infraestructures and biodiversity -in this sense, they voted against the approval of the Green and Biodiversity Plan in the plenary session of the València City Council, while the Popular Party, the party that won the elections and will foreseeably govern in a minority in the

17 Among others, Judgment of September 30, 2011, appeal 1294/2008 and of October 14, 2014, appeal 3425/2012

city, abstained-. This political change may pose a threat to the implementation of the measures envisaged in the plan and the achievement of its objectives.

However, as elements that can counteract these weaknesses we find the existence of an important set of strategic plans and participatory bodies at the municipal level that work transversally in the field of green infrastructure and biodiversity, as indicated in 10.2 of this chapter: the València 2030 Strategy, the Consell de l'Horta and the Urban Agriculture Plan, in which there are different measures related to agroecology and environmental improvement of the València huerta. All these mechanisms underpin the principles, objectives and lines of action of the Green Plan, as do the various existing supra-municipal strategies on green infrastructure. In particular, the Territorial Strategy of the Valèncian Community, passed in 2011, and the regulatory framework of the state context, with the 2030 Agenda, the Spanish Urban Agenda and the National Strategy for Green Infrastructure and Biodiversity (2021) as a framework for improving green and blue infrastructures and linking them with the natural context. Also relevant at this point is the potential of civil society involvement in the design of the city's green strategy, which in the past led to successes such as the protection of the coastline and the Saler in the 1970s and the old riverbed in the 1980s, which have been milestones of urban transformation partly of popular origin.

Besides, the fact that València will be European Green Capital in 2024 will clearly reinforce and legitimize the implementation of the Green and Biodiversity Plan, and may be key to preventing it from ending up like the 1994 draft plan. Thus, the actions, activities and events to be developed in the framework of this capital, planned and agreed in the letter of intent formalized between the European Commission and the city of València, will be key to consolidating the project in a context that naturally would have been potentially unfriendly to these events. In this sense, the European Green Capital could be key for the momentum adopted by the last legislatures of the city council to continue and consolidate.

Bibliography

Ajuntament de València, 'Pla Verd i de la Biodiversitat de València' (2023) https://playerdvalencia.com/es/documentacion/.

Beers P. J. and Geerling-Eiff F., 'Networks as policy instruments for innovation' (2014) 20(4) *The Journal of Agricultural Education and Extension* 363.

Dallhammer E., Gaugitsch R., Neugebauer W., and Böhme K., 'Spatial planning and governance within EU policies and legislation and their relevance to the New Urban Agenda' (Publications Office of the European Union 2018).

European Commission, 'How can your city become… the next European green capital?' (2020) https://environment.ec.europa.eu/topics/urban-environment/european-green-capital-award/about-awards/toolkits/green-capital-toolkit_en#how-can-your-city-become-the-next-european-green-capital.

European Commission, 'EGCA-EGLA 2025 – Rules of contest with annexes' (2023).

Evers D. and Tennekes J., 'Europe exposed: Mapping the impacts of EU policies on spatial planning in the Netherlands' (2015) 24(10) *European Planning Studies* 1747.
Slätmo E., Nilsson K. and Turunen E., 'Implementing green infrastructure in spatial planning in Europe' (2019) 8(4) *Land 62*.
Uriarte Ricorte M., 'Planificar la infraestructura verde urbana' (2014) 99–100 *Revista Vasca de Administración Pública* 2873.
Van der Jagt A., Tozer L., Toxopeus H. and Runhaar H., 'Policy mixes for mainstreaming urban nature-based solutions: An analysis of six European countries and the European Union' (2023) 139 *Environmental Science & Policy* 51.
Wilk B., Vetter A. and Schröder A., 'Tackling the climate and biodiversity crises in Europe through urban greening plans: Recommendations for avoiding the implementation gap' (2021) *Scientific Opinion Paper German Environment Agency*.
Wurzel R.K.W., Zito Anthony R. and Jordan Andrew J., *Environmental Governance in Europe. A Comparative Analysis of New Environmental Policy Instruments* (Edward Elgar Publishing 2014).

5 Smart cities, landscape and urban regeneration: ranking methods

Giuseppe Franco Ferrari

5.1 The evolution of urban planning: From the origins to smart cities

Land use law has been a matter of major attention and repeated in-depth studies that have sought to map out the evolution of the concept, or rather its various conceptual manifestations over time.[1] In legal philosophical terms, the concept at issue here could now be defined as an "ethically contested" concept.[2]

Any attempt to provide a full account of the concept in terms of its historical development that sought to identify a *fil rouge* operating at a level situated above mere empirical data within the formants of legislation and case law must take account of the transformation of urban planning during the contemporary era. Throughout the history of humanity, the city and its building types have constantly represented the *topos* of a civilisation and its era. Although the relationship of continuity and juxtaposition between urban and extra-urban spaces has frequently changed – in some cases radically – over the centuries, the model of urban planning has always remained emblematic of its own specific epoch.[3]

During the last two centuries in particular, the way in which land regulation is understood has developed in line with industrial society. Initially, during the first stages of industrial society local power brokers and lawmakers responded by adopting mandatory rules on hygiene in homes as well as the healthy condition and fitness of buildings in order to deal with health problems associated with urban living. Later, during a second phase, protection of health and

1 Cf. Melvin Richter, *The History of Political and Social Concepts: A Critical Introduction* (Oxford University Press 1995).
2 This now commonplace terminology was first used by Walter B. Gallie, 'Essentially Contested Concepts' (1955–56) 56 *Proceedings of the Aristotelian Society* 167 ff.
3 See Giuseppe F. Ferrari, 'L'idea di smart city' in Giuseppe F. Ferrari (ed.), *La prossima città* (Mimesis 2017) 15 ff; the paper written by Louis Wirth, 'Urbanism as a Way of Life' (1938) 44 (1) *The American Journal of Sociology* 1–24, Italian translation *L'urbanesimo come modo dì vita*, Rome 1998 is still extremely useful.

DOI: 10.4324/9781032665184-15

hygiene was supplemented by, or incorporated into, a more holistic planning approach to the construction of buildings within urban settings. A third phase involved the extension of planning rules to all available land, including non-urban land, coupled with the need to build homes at a sustainable cost for the less wealthy, normally workers. The fourth phase of contemporary urban planning involved the relaxation to some degree of the public monopoly on planning, with the growing prevalence of agreements with private operators and urban planning consultation.

The final stage involves the search for intelligent models of land use: the notion of a "smart city" has emerged on a global level, taking on from the outset an extremely broad scope to include all aspects of land regulation: from building regulations to town planning law, and from networks through public services to the use of IT and participatory arrangements. This schematic breakdown into different phases is obviously rough and approximate and is liable to result in overlaps and inconsistencies (as is the case for any periodical classification). Moreover, it can be falsified as regards its minor details, as it is always the case for the practical application of any logical-inductive procedure. Nonetheless, it provides a useful interpretative framework with this issue, standing above the disparate and often asynchronous evolving formants.

Even a superficial glance at the European legal systems which are most similar to Italian law points to the existence of some common or at least similar trends operating in line with the evolution of urban planning, as a consequence of economic factors that can be identified within the various phases of development.

The aforesaid proto-industrial phase was characterised by the exclusive relevance of public interests such as hygiene, health, decorum, safety and security, which are only indirectly related to land use.[4]

This was usually followed by a second phase, generally engaged with according to old-school liberal instruments, whereby homes started to be subject to building and urban planning regulations (especially, although not necessarily, following the first wave of industrialisation). The aim in doing so was to regulate the structural fabric of buildings, as well as in some sense their expansion. This phase was characterised by absolute respect for private law ownership, other than perhaps the imposition of boundary distance requirements. Planning instruments that applied to a particular territory as a whole were only adopted under exceptional circumstances, and in some cases were enacted within legislation precisely due to their unique nature. In many cases, it was also considered necessary to complete special building projects for the working classes, with the primary goal of securing social cohesion, rather than rationalising post-industrial homes.

4 In the case of Italy this was, as is known, the approach taken by Annex F to the Law on Administrative Unification (Articles 55–76). Cf. on this issue, see Aldo M. Sandulli (ed.), *I lavori pubblici. Atti del Congresso celebrativo delle leggi amministrative di unificazione* (Neri Pozza 1967).

Later, a third phase saw the extension to the entire territory of urban planning, although the countryside outside built-up areas was ordinarily regarded as land designated for the expansion of towns and cities rather than as a green area to be preserved. During this era, also as a consequence of the dominant ideology, plans were conceptualised as hierarchically superior instruments, irrespective of the relationship between core and periphery that dominated within the various legal systems. This meant that central control, exercised through centralised planning procedures, was normally strong. However, other public interests soon emerged alongside, and indeed even within, the logic of plans focussing on strictly urban planning parameters. And while these interests were formally speaking external to plans, they increasingly needed to be interlinked, coordinated, and integrated with plans. A few of these public interests already existed, such as health and hygiene interests, which were considered to have been absorbed into or satisfied by land use regulations. On the other hand, previously overlooked public or collective interests proliferated, such as those relating to the environment, landscapes, energy and territorial security (with reference, for instance to water and earthquake risks). Their emergence was fuelled by further waves of industrialisation or development as well as the dissemination of new values, often at a constitutional level. Although other interests – such as those relating to infrastructure or the protection of state property – were also relevant, they were initially fulfilled automatically through the exercise of a variety of powers, which largely fell under the competence of state authorities. These powers were distinct from and yet prevailed over powers exercised locally, as the latter were in any case subject to central control. Urban planning law forcefully exerted its control above all over interests relating to business activities and the location of such activities, which had previously been considered to be entirely irrelevant for land use law in line with the precepts of the liberal mindset. As a result of this, the logic of separation was rejected, with urban planning law expressing its vocation to establish a global regulatory reach, even though this was not easy to achieve using the instruments available at that time. Moreover, this stretched to the limit the compatibility of urban planning with the political culture that had in the meantime become dominant, which was less inclined to accept the wide-scale recourse to planning.

The interplay, overlap and not infrequently tension between urban planning interests in a strict sense and external interests, which were soon defined as "differentiated",[5] was the main, if not the only factor in bringing about the shift to the next phase, which is still ongoing. Due to the variegated and heterogeneous nature of the interests now at stake, it is not possible to order them into a stable hierarchy. There is a constant need for balancing operations of the

5 See on all points the summary by Paola Chirulli, 'I rapporti tra urbanistica e discipline differenziate' in Franco G. Scoca, Paolo Stella Richter, Paolo Urbani (eds), *Trattato di diritto del territorio. Vol. I* (Giappichelli 2018) 20 ff.

kind typically used to weigh up constitutional values and principles during the era of neo-constitutionalism, which is carried out by the legislature, subject to review by constitutional courts. However, a different process of engagement and harmonisation is ongoing on the administrative level, and hence between different levels of territorial authority. During this phase, many legal systems with a fixed, written constitution have embraced the new previously unknown complexity of and interplay between interests and underlying values, formally abandoning the very concept of urban planning law as a formal discipline and shifting towards broader, all-inclusive categories such as land regulation (referred to in Italian as "territorial government") under Article 117 of the Italian Constitution, as amended in 2001, and before it the "*ordenación del territorio*" under Article 148.3 of the Spanish Constitution or the "environment and quality of life" under Article 66 of the Greek Constitution. A different choice – albeit one inspired by the same set of underlying issues – was made by the Constituent Assembly, as well as under the Portuguese Constitution, which chose to list together all of the various public interests within a non-hierarchical list, which pertains in general terms to land planning and management.[6] In any case, it is clear that, although urban planning as an area of the law has indeed expanded over time, it no longer embodies on its own the various rules applicable to land governance. Indeed, if it is not to be increased to an unnatural size, it will have to be classified under broader categories that are capable of operating as integrated (if not unitary) vehicles for different interests that need to be mediated and reconciled. A second reason for the shift towards a new conceptual formula – which is no less important though perhaps less apparent at first glance – has been the increase in the powers of regional or federal bodies in many western legal systems. This has meant that the constitutional provisions applicable to the transition generally fall under the provisions applicable to the division of powers between the state and sub-state bodies, which may precipitate wide-ranging disputes as to where those powers are vested. This approach normally involves broad constitutional disputes over interpretations concerning the extent and allocation of functions in this area of the law, as has occurred in Italy and Spain. Moreover, even within legal systems that, for various reasons, are not accustomed to constitutional disputes over the allocation of powers (such as France and the UK), there is still uncertainty as to whether land regulation should remain vested at the regional level, or whether it should be brought back under central control, in order to better regulate the inevitable balancing of interests, which, as has been seen, is an ever-present consideration.

The new model of urban planning enriched by interpenetration with variegated public interests, having been transformed into a larger vehicle, also reflects this contradiction: on the one hand, the mediation between expectations that are not rigidly ordained or at least only partially harmonised calls for,

6 Article 103.

and indeed demands, a centripetal approach; on the other hand, this requires the maintenance of, and in fact the increasing search for, some measure of local consensus, as is demonstrated in particular by experience in the UK. Here in 2011, the instrument of the local referendum, which had previously played no part at all in the colourful history of local government in the country, was placed on a formal footing.

5.2 Ratings and smart cities

The concept of "smart city" never ceases to hold its allure. It could in fact be said that it has attracted a growing fascination in recent years, despite some sporadic marginal criticisms relating to its usage.[7]

The success of the idea is apparent first and foremost in the increasingly large-scale recourse to ratings in order to measure the performance of urban areas with reference to the most disparate parameters, whether technological, administrative, social or cultural. The wide variety of approaches is mirrored by a high level of differentiation between monitoring parameters and the assessment of different factors, as well as the identification of benchmarks. The number of indicators has increased, as also has the underlying information that is fed into them, and similarly their relative weight is extremely variable. Often each parameter for evaluation is broken down into segments or components. In this way, comparison starts to mushroom and the concept takes on a totalising significance, or rather its interdisciplinary nature becomes so broad as to result in a suggestive yet fleeting all-inclusive status, under which modelling (whether explanatory, predictive or even prescriptive) ends up losing all sense. The application of algorithms with the support of classification bodies certainly does not enhance the transparency of evaluation procedures. Moreover, the major technological input into census and classification methods can not only arouse utopian expectations of semi-perfect cities (which do not exist in reality), but also risks triggering reductionist mechanisms, excluding the relevance of cultural and social considerations. Leaving aside the questionable definitional rigour and the debatable nature of the paradigms used, one must still consider the legitimation of assessment bodies: although they are largely private this does not prevent enormous investments from being de facto controlled by whether they award positive or negative ratings. These ratings are

7 Cf. in particular the reflections by Silvia Bolognini, *Dalla "Smart City" alla "Human Smart City" e oltre* (Giuffrè 2017), in particular 133 ff., who points to the democratic deficit and the risk of significant violations of individual rights within hyper-technologised citizen environments that are not sufficiently balanced out by the activation of administrative mechanisms to ensure participatory governance. Cf. also more recently, within the literature that is less wedded to scientific canons, Alessandro Barile, Luca Raffini, Luca Alteri, *Il tramonto della città. La metropoli globale tra nuovi modelli produttivi e crisi della cittadinanza* (DeriveApprodi 2019); Sarah Gainsforth, *Airbnb città merce. Storie di resistenza alla gentrificazione digitale* (DeriveApprodi 2019).

presented as being neutral, apparently premised on "data-driven" logics and as such considered to have scientific rigour.

As such, the urban dimension has now perhaps irreversibly embarked upon a classificatory pathway that has gradually become more technological in nature, in accordance moreover with the genesis of the idea of "smartness".[8] It is not and it will not be easy to moderate this holistic, "scientificating" claim, because concepts drawn from traditional sociology and political sciences (such as human and/or social capital, community initiatives, and democratic processes within governance and administration) must confront with the consensual self-legitimisation of technology, which offers an image of rationalisation that probably exceeds its very own capacities. Studies and research into terminology used in relation to urban "smartness"[9] appear to confirm, through textual analysis, frequent resort to words with technological connotations. This obviously explains the emergence, within the English-speaking literature first and in European continental literature later, of concerns about participatory initiatives, of the valorisation of civic empowerment and, in perhaps more conflictual terms, of qualms regarding the protection of political, civil and social rights within the new citizen arena.[10] On the broader politology level, concepts such as "human smart city" or "smart community" are becoming increasingly widespread, which it is assumed will be able to incorporate "smartness" instruments that can contain abstract, "technologised" power into technological platforms based on smartness. These should enable the consolidation of local democracy, whilst facilitating the emergence of forms of dissent and focussing urban smartness on reinvigorated welfare perspectives.[11] These aspects do not in effect appear to have been adequately taken into account within the most widespread and authoritative rankings that have become established over the last few years. The positions occupied by urban agglomerations such as Beijing, Shanghai, Dubai, Singapore, Kuala Lumpur, Jakarta, Bangalore and Suzhou suggest that factors that are not strictly technological have not been adequately taken into account.

5.3 Some types of international classification

Some rankings concern specifically, if not exclusively, competitive aspects in industrial terms or business in general.

8 See Giuseppe F. Ferrari (n. 3) 9 ff.

9 Such as, for example Simon Joss et al., *The Smart City as Global Discourse: Storylines and Critical Junctures across 27 Countries* (2019) 26 (1) *The Journal. of Urban Technology* 3–34.

10 Within the Italian legal literature, cf. on all points Francesco Gaspari, *Smart City. Agenda Urbana multilivello e nuova cittadinanza amministrativa* (Editoriale scientifica 2018).

11 Cf. the literature referred to by Silvia Bolognini (n. 7), Cfhapters 2 and 3. On this issue see also Aldo Bonomi, Roberto Masiero, *Dalla smart city alla smart land* (Marsilio 2019).

This is the case, first and foremost, for the *Global Cities Report* published by ATKearney.[12] The 27 indices used give priority to the presence of large bodies of wealth, top global service companies and capital markets. However, at the same time they do not overlook factors such as schooling, freedom of expression (with a particular focus on the most advanced technologies), the arts and sport, politics and diplomatic representation. Moreover, China is expressly called on to focus more directly on citizens,[13] almost as if to moderate the overestimation of the "urban success" of Chinese cities in the 2018 report.[14] The same approach is taken by *Global Outlook Global Cities of the Future*, originally created in Costa Rica but built up with the assistance of the Financial Times,[15] which uses no fewer than 84 data points, 21 of which are econometric in nature and 16 of which focus on support for business. This ranking classifies the cities assessed into three categories: large, medium and small. The *Global Financial Centres Index 25* has an even stronger focus on finance and the economy.[16] Similar considerations apply to the influential *Global Competitiveness Report* of the World Economic Forum,[17] which presents the opinions of the business community regarding what has been branded as the "fourth industrial revolution". It is comprised of 12 pillars, which focus on macroeconomic stability, the financial system, goods market efficiency, labour market efficiency, business dynamism and innovation.

The Japanese *Global Power City Index* is more balanced.[18] It has been in operation since 2008 and currently uses 6 general criteria – economy, research and development, cultural interaction, liveability, environment, and accessibility – this time adding sub-criteria, such as the objective criterion of the number of start-ups and the rather more subjective criterion of working lifestyles. The econometric criteria are in actual fact the most elaborate, ranging from market size and attractiveness to economic vitality, human capital, the business environment and the ease of starting up new businesses: it is clear that, in this area too, it is difficult to regard some assessment standards as being

12 *A Question of Talent: How Human Capital Will Determine the Next Global Leaders* (ATKearney 2019).
13 Ibid., 8 ff.
14 *Learning from the East – Insights from China's Urban Success* (ATKearney 2018). On the other hand, the previous year's report focused on innovation: *Global Cities 2017: Leaders in a World of Disruptive Innovation* (ATKearney 2017). The latest report has been released in 2022 and explores the challenges and uncertainties facing many of the world's most connected and influential urban centres following the coronavirus pandemic and the Ukrainian conflict.
15 CINDE (Costa Rica Investment Promotion Agency) 2019.
16 March 2019, published by the China Development Institute, which has been in operation since 2007, and the think-tank Zyen in London.
17 Geneva, 2018.
18 The Mori Memorial Foundation, Institute for Urban Strategies, 2022.

objective, and even the aspects focussing on livability also have a partial economic relevance.[19]

On the other hand, the group of ratings that are less tied to economic figures includes the *Economist's index* (which in fact is a leader in this category).[20] It draws on the work of analysts specialising in the individual countries as well as local correspondents. The parameters used are stability (10%), which covers the prevalence of acts of violence of various types, healthcare (20%), culture and environment (25%), education (10%) and infrastructure (20%), almost disregarding direct economic factors. This family also includes the *Mercer Quality of Living Ranking*,[21] which privileges European cities with reference to 10 analytical parameters, only one of which refers to the economic environment, considered in terms of currency exchange regulations and banking services. The Mercer method involves establishing direct contacts with municipalities with a view to providing advice and guidance. It aims to operate in the same way as the *Smart City Strategy Index*,[22] which focusses on dynamic projection towards the rationalisation of existing urban models. A total of 12 indices are used, 6 of which ("action fields") focus on the search for tangible remedies to effective needs, whereas the others reflect factors that facilitate the operation of an intelligent city ("enablers"). There are 31 sub-criteria, which are weighted according to a sliding scale of qualitative importance. In this regard, for example, the factor "government", which includes digital security and services, has a weight of 8.3%, whereas participation and acceptance of the model (defined as "stakeholders") has a weight of 7.5%. The annual report is accompanied by a series of detailed thematic and geographical monographs.[23]

This ambition of achieving global pervasiveness is also apparent within the now historic annual report of the University of Navarra,[24] which uses a total of 97 indicators: 10 refer to human capital, 16 to social cohesion, 13 to the economy, 12 to governance, 11 to the environment, 10 to mobility and transportation, 13 to technology (which has become much more significant over the last year), 6 to urban planning and 6 to international outreach. An idea of just how fleeting classification criteria of this type can be is apparent from the fact that the "international outreach" indicators include not only suitable airports and hotels, visitor numbers and other similar factors, but also the number of McDonald's restaurants.

19 The 2022 report used the same rating criteria, although with quite different results. Many of these reports have a certain degree of fluidity from year to year.

20 The Economist Intelligence Unit, *The Global Liveability Index 2023. A Free Overview*, 2023.

21 London, March 23 2019.

22 The most recent edition of the Report is *The Smart City Breakaway* (Roland Berger 2019).

23 Entitled *Think: Act*; one of the most recent focusses on French cities, and the first was entitled *Smart City, Smart Strategy*.

24 *Cities in Motion* (IESE 2019).

Some indices adopt an exclusively technological focus. The McKinsey index is emblematic of this family of reports,[25] applying the practically exclusive metric of digitalisation to the eight parameters used.

Another cluster of assessments focusses exclusively on the environmental dimension, such as for instance the *Green City Index*:[26] here the data used focus on water, air, waste and recycling, CO_2 emissions, transport, energy, building quality and environmental governance. This classificatory family also appears to include the *Grosvenor Research Report* on "Resilient Cities":[27] starting from resilience as the interaction between vulnerability and adaptive capacity, it ends up analysing liveability, considered also in terms of affordable housing. The concept of resilience is interpreted dynamically, taking account of both the historical and the technological evolution of locations chosen in previous times due to anthropization needs that are not always readily understood or explainable.

Finally, a small group of indices seeks to focus on the citizen's perspective, with a preference for the proper operation of political processes. One index that followed this approach is the Arcadis report, which is published by a Dutch group operating in the real estate sector:[28] a third of the parameters used considers social aspects, a third focusses on the environment and the relationship with the health of the planet, whereas the final third inevitably looks at the economy, although giving significance also to tourism and connectivity. The approach taken by the *Top 50 Smart City Government*[29] report is not too different, although it is focused more specifically on the quality of local government. It takes account of around ten factors, including the centrality of the human factor, vision, leadership, openness to innovation, innovative ecosystems and financial incentives.

The focus of the *Flash Eurobarometer*, which is linked to the European Commission, is even more strongly centred on wellbeing in a broad sense.[30] It essentially presents a survey, carried out through telephone interviews, of perceptions of European citizens as well as their level of satisfaction with the quality of life in their respective cities. The survey considers healthcare, sporting facilities, cultural and recreational activities, transport, trade, building, security, the environment, administration and employment. However, in actual fact, it seeks to gauge European citizens' satisfaction with local institutions, and indirectly with European institutions.

25 *Smart Cities, Digital Solutions for a More Livable Future* (McKinsey & Company 2018).
26 Drawn up by another research unit at the Economist, sponsored by Siemens.
27 Created in 2014 and published in the UK.
28 *Citizen Centric Cities, The sustainable cities index* 2022 (Arcadis 2022).
29 Produced by the Eden Strategy Institute, owned by ONG & ONG Pte Ltd., founded in China in 1972.
30 *Report on the Quality of Life in European Cities* (Publications Office of the European Union 2020), published every three years since 2004 by the Directorate-General for Regional and Urban Policy.

On the other hand, the World Bank's *World Development Report* is entirely *sui generis* in nature. It aspires to provide a real "x-ray" image of the various economic systems considered, which are analysed each year from various perspectives, providing insights into the future of urban areas, where a growing percentage of the world's population lives. For example, the 2019 report focusses on work.[31]

Bibliography

Barile A., Raffini L., *Il tramonto della città. La metropoli globale tra nuovi modelli produttivi e crisi della cittadinanza* (DeriveApprodi 2019)
Bolognini S., *Dalla "Smart City" alla "Human Smart City" e oltre* (Giuffrè 2017)
Bonomi A., Masiero S., *Dalla smart city alla smart land* (Marsilio 2019)
Ferrari G.F., 'L'idea di smart city', in G.F. Ferrari (ed.), *La prossima città* (Mimesis 2017)
Chirulli P., 'I rapporti tra urbanistica e discipline differenziate', in F.G. Scoca, P. Stella Richter, P. Urbani (eds), *Trattato di diritto del territorio. Vol. I* (Giappichelli 2018)
Gainsforth S., *Airbnb città merce. Storie di resistenza alla gentrificazione digitale* (DeriveApprodi 2019)
Gallie W.B., 'Essentially Contested Concepts' (1955–56) 56 *Proceedings of the Aristotelian Society* 167
Gasparri F., *Smart City. Agenda Urbana multilivello e nuova cittadinanza amministrativa* (Editoriale scientifica 2018)
Joss S. et al., 'The Smart City as Global Discourse: Storylines and Critical Junctures across 27 Countries' (2019) 26 (1) *The Journal of Urban Technology*. 3
Richter M., *The History of Political and Social Concepts: A Critical Introduction* (Oxford University Press 1995)
Sandulli A.M. (ed.), *I lavori pubblici. Atti del Congresso celebrativo delle leggi amministrative di unificazione* (Neri Pozza 1967)
Wirth L., 'Urbanism as a Way of Life' (1938) 44 (1) *The American Journal of Sociology* 1

31 *The Changing Nature of Work* (World Bank 2019). The previous year's report focused on Climate Protection and Development.

Index

Note: Page locators followed by 'n' refer to notes.

For Product Safety Concerns and Information please contact our EU representative GPSR@taylorandfrancis.com
Taylor & Francis Verlag GmbH, Kaufingerstraße 24, 80331 München, Germany

www.ingramcontent.com/pod-product-compliance
Ingram Content Group UK Ltd.
Pitfield, Milton Keynes, MK11 3LW, UK
UKHW020008200926
475702UK00015B/2542
9781032665160